Lincolnshire
The Way We Were

Lincolnshire Echo
GROUP NEWSPAPERS

Lincolnshire
The Way We Were

Peter and Pat
Washbourn

breedon **books**
PUBLISHING

First published in Great Britain in 2001 by
The Breedon Books Publishing Company Limited
Breedon House, 3 The Parker Centre, Derby, DE21 4SZ.

ISBN 1 85983 239 3

Printed and bound by Butler & Tanner, Frome, Somerset, England.
Jacket printing by GreenShires, Leicester, England.

Contents

Contributions

PETER BROWN is the longest-serving member of the *Echo*'s editorial department. Starting in journalism in 1962, he joined the *Echo* as a senior reporter in 1966 and later became deputy news editor and leisure and entertainments editor. He has been the writer of the six-days-a-week Gossiper column for more than a decade and has been heavily involved with *The Way We Were* since it started in September 1999.

Born in Lincoln and educated at local schools, Peter has a great love for the city and county. He is a regular contributor to BBC Radio Lincolnshire, an after-dinner speaker and travels extensively around the county giving talks on his work to organisations.

In his spare time, family man Peter appears all over the country as Pedro the Clown and for 20 years helped organise the Caenby Corner Steam Rally and Lincolnshire Steam Spectacular.

BETTE VICKERS was born in Yorkshire, but considers herself a good sample of a second-hand Yellowbelly, having lived in Lincolnshire for more than 61 years. Born in Bridlington, Bette was educated at St Joseph's Convent and then at Handel House Boarding School, Gainsborough. She has always had an affinity with children and became a nursery teacher. Her first post was at St Cuthbert's Nursery School, in Lincoln and then at Sheffield Manor, Market Rasen.

Her early married life was spent in the Fens and farming, but when she moved to Lincoln, she started and ran a very successful nursery school in the old Eastgate School, on Langworthgate. In 1971, Bette sent in a short piece to the *Lincolnshire Chronicle* and from there started her journalistic career. She wrote a page called City Life and was involved with the first free-sheet, *Lincoln Choice*.

Some 20 years ago, Bette started work for the *Lincolnshire Echo* and enjoyed a very good relationship. Bette writes the obituaries, Churchlines, Bette's Bygones, in *The Way We Were* and *Vickers in a Twist*. This has led to talks and becoming involved with various associations.

She has written Ladybird books and five faction (fiction based on fact) novels about her mother's family – all of which were serialised on Radio Humberside. Her latest book is *Bread'n'if'it*, published by the *Lincolnshire Echo* and consisting of recipes and country stories. Bette's life is very busy – she loves writing and perhaps most of all being a grand and great-grandmother.

PETER WASHBOURN started working at the *Echo* in 1956, as a photographic printer before becoming a photographer in 1960. Retiring, as he thought, in 1996, as the *Echo*'s longest-serving photographer, he soon found another niche in life, as a columnist for *The Way We Were* and jointly, with his wife Pat, compiling stories for *Lincolnshire in the News*, every Saturday evening.

In 1999, Peter was invited to produce a book of photographs, *Memory Lane – Lincoln and Lincolnshire*, for the *Echo* and this current book is the fourth which he and Pat have compiled.

His interests include local history, music and by necessity, gardening. When he has any spare time, he gives slide shows on local history and talks to many local organisations. He is also vice-president of the Lincoln Beevor Band and the Lincoln Asthma Swimming Group.

Introduction

NOSTALGIA seems to be the 'in' thing at the moment and fortunately, there is a wealth of newspaper stories and photographs to fuel this. In September 1999, the *Lincolnshire Echo* commenced publishing a weekly supplement, *The Way We Were*, which quickly became a favourite with the readers.

There were three main contributors for the early issues; Peter Brown, with The Gossiper column, which appears every evening in the *Echo*; Bette Vickers, who provides Bette's Bygones, with many tales from the county and Peter Washbourn, who, in his Lincolnian's Diary, blends a mixture of history, personal memories and recalls events and stories from the pages of the *Lincolnshire Echo*, brought up to date with suitable comments.

With such a diversity of subjects, it has not been easy to divide the stories into chapters. Each section is illustrated, as far as possible, with the original photographs, but where these are no longer available, substitutes have been made and are still relevant to the story. Included in the chapters are full page pictures which have appeared on the front page of *The Way We Were* and pairs of pictures from the 'Then and Now' series.

Readers soon became occasional, but regular, contributors and their stories provide a wealth of memories. The popularity of *The Way We Were* is reflected in the number of letters the contributors receive, often with further information about the stories.

We would like to acknowledge these reader contributions and also thank Russell Kirk and Martin Finney, of the *Lincolnshire Echo* for their help in the preparation of this volume.

Peter and Pat Washbourn
Autumn, 2001

Tales from the City

Silver Anniversary For Brass Band

IN 1975, a brass band was formed in Lincoln, with one major aim – to give youngsters the opportunity to lean to play music. Alf and Peggy Chandler formed the Beevor Youth Band with the intention of enabling any young person who wanted to learn to play a brass instrument just that opportunity. Now, 25 years later, the organisation is still going strong and has grown to two bands.

Alf and Peggy left the band after a few years and formed another at Bracebridge Heath and for a short time, the band came under the leadership of Harry Whitwell. He then handed over to Geoff Moralee, who had been in brass banding for many years and had formed other bands in the county.

The band took its name from Beevor Street, where their practice room was situated in premises owned by Ruston-Bucyrus. There was also a Ruston-Bucyrus Band, which a few years ago, became the band of the Lincolnshire Fire Brigade. Ruston-Bucyrus became R-B (International) Ltd and the company still provide practice facilities for the Beevor Bands. Two years later, the then Beevor Youth Band entered the McDonalds Child of Achievement Music in the Community Competition. After winning the regional final at Birmingham, they went on to win the national final, at Cardiff, beating musical groups from all parts of the United Kingdom. Part of their prize for winning was to play at the Child of Achievement presentation ceremony, in London, in the presence of the then Prime Minister, John Major.

So popular did the band become after this that it was necessary to split the band into two parts and these were named the Beevor Youth Band and the Lincoln Beevor Band. They entered the competition once again in 1993 and reached the finals in London and also had several successes in music festivals and competitions and raised thousands of pound for charities, including over £1,000 for the Skegness Lifeboat Appeal.

The musical direction of the Beevor Youth Band was taken over by Jane Parker, with Geoff Moralee at the helm of the Lincoln Beevor Band. A few years ago, Geoff was honoured with the award of the MBE and also a Lincoln Civic Award commendation and the Mayor of Lincoln's medal.

Lincolnian's Diary. March 21, 2000.

Learning: The Beevor Youth Band celebrate winning the Music in the Community Competition heat at Birmingham, in 1991.

Anniversary For New Political Era

A NEW era started in Lincoln politics 25 years ago this week when Margaret Jackson became the first woman MP in the city's history. And it marked the end for Dick Taverne – the man who successfully fought more Parliamentary elections than any other Lincoln MP this century. But it was a near thing. A majority of just 984 was sufficient to carry Margaret into the Commons and Harold Wilson went back into number 10 to carry on the job, but with a paper-thin majority in Parliament.

In Lincoln, everyone knew the result was going to be a near thing, almost from the moment the election was called. Socialist rebel Dick Taverne had managed to hold on to Lincoln the previous February, retaining the seat for his Democratic Labour Association. But there was no denying his 1,293 majority made him

very vulnerable. And when the result was announced in a noisy Broadgate Drill Hall on the stroke of midnight, many of his supporters wept openly. But after 12½ years as the city MP, Dick told me at the time 'I don't regret a minute of it.'

His farewell message to the electorate was 'I hope you give as much support to your new MP as you have given me. I was proud to represent you.' Dick never did return to the political scene in Lincoln, but he is still an active politician and as Lord Taverne, he still sits in the House of Lords.

An *Echo* colleague noted on election night how Margaret Jackson was visibly nervous throughout the count. But after the result was declared she predicted 'I think Lincoln is going to live again. We have been through a trying time. There has been too much bitterness but I think that time has come to an end.'

In those days, Margaret was a political adviser to Judith Hart, then Minister for Overseas Development. In later years, Margaret was to

marry Leo Beckett and her political career went from strength to strength. She eventually lost the Lincoln seat to Kenneth Carlisle, but for a long time she was one of the best-known faces in the Labour Government.

The third candidate in the Lincoln line-up a quarter-of-a-century ago this week, was Horncastle solicitor Peter Moran, Conservative, who finished in third place.
The Gossiper. October 12, 1999.

Steam days: The Oliver Cromwell *locomotive at Lincoln Central Station.*

Cromwell's Unsung Appearance

IT'S A LONG time since steam trains ran regularly through Lincoln Central Station but I well remember the last time that British Rail ran the last 'official' steam locomotive through the city. It was in August 1968, that British Rail ran a steam locomotive on a round trip from Liverpool to Carlisle. Late that night, I had a telephone call from a friend who was a signalman in Lincoln. He 'tipped me off' that the locomotive would be passing through Lincoln early the following morning, on route to a railway preservation museum, at Diss, Norfolk.

Up with the birds next morning, I waited at the station and soon after six o'clock, the BR Standard

Class Pacific 70013 *Oliver Cromwell* pulled into the station. There were only a handful of people around to see what was a moment of railway history in Lincoln. After a few minutes pause, the locomotive pulled away in a cloud of steam, passed under Pelham Bridge and out of sight.

British Rail had taken no chances with the locomotive. The nameplates carried on the smoke deflectors had been removed, as a precaution against souvenir hunters and the name was painted directly on to the deflector.

It's passing was certainly a moment of nostalgia for the rail enthusiasts gathered there and although there have been steam locomotives through Lincoln since then, on special excursions, to me *Oliver Cromwell* will always be the 'last steam in Lincoln'.
Lincolnian's Diary. April 18, 2000.

Elected: Dick Taverne is carried shoulder high by supporters after his first election win in 1962.

Busy times: Lincoln's Drill Hall was home to a variety of events. This picture was taken at a motorcycle show. (Echo Ref. 1084-25A)

Hall Closure Will Come As A Blow

It may not be the most attractive building in Lincoln and it may not be the best decorated, the cosiest or the most comfortable place you can think of... But, like it or not, the Broadgate Drill Hall has been an important part of the lives of Lincoln people for generations.

Its closure, until further notice, because of electrical problems, will come as a blow to many. And it does drive home, once again, how painfully short Lincoln is of multi-purpose buildings capable of seating 700 or 800 people.

For all its shortcomings, the Drill Hall fills a gap in Lincoln's social needs and events organisers will be anxiously waiting for the hall to reopen. Many of us will never forget those Saturday nights in the swinging '60s when some of the top groups of the day appeared on the Drill Hall stage.

The Tornadoes played Telstar there, on the week their record went top of the America charts. The now late Screaming Lord Sutch started a fire on stage, and dangled his long hair through the flames. When Alvin Stardust was known as Shane Fenton he was a regular visitor and even the Rolling Stones played there one New Year's Eve.

There were other times when the men would don evening suits and their partners would be attired in long, flowing gowns for a ball. Many people have spent New Year's Eve making merry at FFN wine tastings in the hall. There have been concerts where we sat on uncomfortable plastic chairs in row upon row. Beauty competitions have been held there.

Countless thousands have been raised for charities and good causes through bazaars. One of the most recent, before the hall's closure, was a Christmas Fair for the Cats' Protection League. It's been the home of Lincoln Motorcycle Show and Model railway shows. Wrestling, bingo, exhibitions and even a Christmas circus have been staged there. And until recent times, it was the place where the votes were counted at Parliamentary and local government elections.

Who will ever forget those scenes in the 1970s when the eyes of the nation were turned to Lincoln for its historic by-election when Dick Taverne won the seat for his Democratic Labour Association. The Drill Hall count that night was one of the most dramatic in the city's history.

Let's hope it won't be too long before the repair work can be put in hand and the Drill Hall re-opened.
The Gossiper. December 28, 1999.

The Great Northern: A Hotel To Remember

THE famous... The unknown... Glittering social gatherings with distinguished speakers... Modest family celebrations... The Great Northern Hotel had known them all. For decades it had been an important part of Lincoln's commercial and social scene. Many couldn't have imagined a time when it wouldn't be a city landmark. But in the mid-1960s, the winds of change were fairly howling through the city streets and were sweeping away things which many of us had come to regard as Lincoln institutions.

Among the casualties was the Great Northern Hotel, which stood immediately to the south of the central level crossing in High Street. It was one of Lincoln's biggest hotels and had been since the days long before the road outside its front door had become choc-a-block with traffic. But its days were numbered. National supermarket chain, Tesco, was anxious to come to Lincoln. The company looked around the city centre and its eyes settled on the site. During the winter of 1965-6, they pulled the final pint in the bar, served the last banquet in the function room and waved farewell to the last guest. Thirty-four years ago this week, the demolition workers began tearing down the property.

And today, apart from a few tell-tale pieces of stone on what used to be an adjoining building, you would hardly know that the hotel had ever been there. Tesco's occupation of the site was comparatively short-lived. The store needed to expand and offer its customers a large car park. So it moved to the new trading and industrial estate which was set-up just off Canwick Road.

Did you use to work at the Great Northern Hotel? Do you remember when the guest list used to include stars like Cliff Richard? Or do you have happy memories of a special event or occasion that took place there?

The Gossiper. February 8, 2000.

Entertainer's Impact On An Election

HE WAS one of the most colourful figures on the political scene in the 1950s. And although he may never have been a serious contender to the main party figures, Michael Roy certainly did his bit to enliven the municipal election of 1950. Entertainer Michael, who also had a shop in Canwick Road, contested the Park Ward seat on the City Council, as a progressive independent. And an *Echo* report of his first election meeting, 50 years ago this week, indicates that he was no ordinary candidate.

There were whistles, shouts and a man with a motor horn, who did their best to interrupt the business when Michael held his campaign meeting in a classroom at St Peter-at-Gowts Junior Boys School. By any standard, the meeting was well attended. And it wasn't on the short side, either.

After the first hour, the meeting was held up for a few minutes to allow another 60 people to come in and it was getting on for 10 o'clock before things came to an end.

Among the questions Michael was asked was what he would do to brighten up the entertainment world. To which he replied that for the young people who walked High Street on Sunday evenings, they could open a few church halls and let them dance from 9pm to 11.30pm. Just before the end of the meeting, Michael was told – in no uncertain terms – by a member of the audience 'Withdraw your candidature, I can tell you won't get any votes.' But he didn't, and he did.

At the election a couple of weeks later, Michael Roy duly squared up against Labour's representative in Park Ward, A. Mundin and independent sitting member, R. Hollingworth. Labour won the seat with 1,569 votes. the independent member came second with 1,459 votes and Michael finished in third place – with 144. But the number of votes he received could well have swung the election one way or the other, because the Labour candidate won with a majority of just 110.

The Gossiper. April 25, 2000.

Demolished: In January 1966, Lincoln said goodbye to the old Great Northern Hotel, in the High Street. (Echo Ref. RI-2518)

No Price War But Gossip Was Free At Corner Shops

I WAS reading through an *Echo* article recently which compared shop prices in 1930 following a slump in wholesale prices of raw materials. It has to be remembered that in those days, there were no supermarkets staging 'wars' and the largest grocery shops in town were probably John Scott & Co., in the High Street, Robert Seely & Son., in Bailgate and numerous branches of the Lincoln Co-operative Society.

Prices in general had gone down and the prices in those days would make your mouth water today, if you will excuse the pun. Bacon was down from 1s 8d a pound to 1s 3d. Sugar had been reduced by a halfpenny a pound to 2¼ pence. Butter had dropped by 3d a pound, the cheapest being 1s 4d. Eggs, cheese, tinned fruits and jam were all reported as being down in price since the previous year and the same applied to many articles of clothing.

As I said, there were no really large grocery shops and in many areas of Lincoln, there were 'shopping communities', where you could buy just about all of your needs. I lived in the Burton Road area of the city and even up to the 1960s, you could find most of the shops you needed. Many street corners had small grocery shops, several including a 'Beer Off Licence', where you could buy not only bottled beer, but also take along a jug and buy draught beer and stout (no lager in those days) by the pint.

There were the bakers (we even had a bakery on Burton

Off the boards: The diving boards were for the more competent swimmers. (Echo Ref. RI-2231)

Road), greengrocers, butchers, fishmongers, hairdressers and, of course, the local 'chippy', although it only opened a few times each week. Then there was the ironmongers, which always smelled of paraffin and a garage where you could get your radio accumulator recharged, if you didn't have the luxury of a mains electricity set. Those accumulators seemed to weight a ton, being made of glass and filled with lead plates and sulphuric acid.

Along came the supermarkets and put an end to much of this. While no doubt, it meant a reduction of prices, with their bulk buying, there was one thing missing.

The corner shop was the hive of local gossip. You didn't need to buy the *Echo* to find out what was happening. Ten minutes in one of these shops and you learnt enough to keep you talking for a couple of days!

Of course, there were some larger shops in town. Mawer and Colingham's, Bainbridges and the big Co-op department store in Silver Street were the big names, together with the High Street chain stores of Woolworth's, Marks and Spencer's and British Home Stores (previously known as Hills and Steele).

Lincolnian's Diary. November 7, 2000.

The Cold Waters Of Boultham

YOU never forgot your first visit to Boultham Baths. The water looked inviting. There were the shrills and shrieks of countless youngsters having the times of their lives. But the second you took a deep breath and plunged in, it was the moment of truth. You had probably never been as cold in your life. Yet for all its shortcomings, Boultham

Baths will always hold special memories for countless county people.

You had to be pretty hardy if you wanted to go swimming in Lincoln those years not long before and after the Second World War. If you were an accomplished swimmer and you were prepared to keep a lookout for the passing barge or two, then you stripped off on the river bank and plunged into the murky waters of the Witham, the Fossdyke, or Brayford Pool. If you were less accomplished then there were the public swimming pools.

At the end of Carholme Road was an outdoor pool where sessions were generally divided so that ladies were spared the embarrassment of having to share a swimming pool with members of the opposite sex. And those were the days when the most revealing bathing costumes still had sleeves and stretched all the way down to the knee. Wickham Baths, under the shadow of the Westgate Water

Busy at Boultham: Youngsters crowd the water at Boultham Baths in a rare warm and sunny day. (Echo Ref. RI-1306B)

Tower, was another place where many a Lincoln person learned to swim. Pupils of South Park Girls High School were lucky. Their school was possibly the first in Lincoln to boast its own pool – and an indoor one at that.

And then there was Boultham Baths. If ever they had a competition to find the coldest water in the swimming pools of the entire northern hemisphere, the chances are that Boultham Baths would have been right up there with the leading contenders! Even on the warmest of English summer days, Boultham Baths had the ability to keep the water at a bitterly cold temperature. One reader told me that he blamed Boultham Baths for the fact that he never learned to swim.

When his school had taken him for lessons there, back in the 1950s, he had rushed straight out of the changing rooms and jumped eagerly into the shallow end. And it was so cold, he thought he was going to die. 'I think I had been expecting something like the bath water we had at home. Instead, the coldness of the water took my breath away. I managed to get out again, but almost 50 years later I

have never forgotten the experience. I have been in other pools since then, but somehow I never did learn to swim.'

But many others did learn to swim at Boultham Baths and there will be happy memories of queuing up to go down the slide into the water; or of climbing to the top of the diving board and plunging into the deep end; or of paddling in the fountain. Boultham Baths was an open-air pool and could only ever open from May until the early autumn. In fact, back in the summer of 1937, it was hardly able to open at all because essential maintenance work had to be done and it took longer than originally planned because of a shortage of materials. Its days were numbered when the new sports centres started to appear in and around Lincoln. And they all boasted indoor heated pools which could open all the year round.

First came the North Kesteven Sports Centre at North Hykeham, followed by the City Sports Centre in Skellingthorpe Road and the Yarborough Leisure Centre uphill. Although Wickham Baths was eventually covered over and was a popular venue

for a time, it had a prolonged closure because of fire safety checks to its roofing material. And when it did reopen, it had lost much of its appeal and never regained its old

popularity. Although some were glad to see the back of Boultham Baths, I suspect there were others who regretted its passing.
The Gossiper. May 9, 2000.

Days At The Hospital Club Are Re-lived

It was one of the most successful clubs in the Lincoln area. The sort of place where members would gather to enjoy activities ranging from chess to rugby and from archery to whist. But since the closure of St John's Hospital at Bracebridge Heath, its staff social club has been lost as well, under a wealth of house building.

But memories of those days when the club played an important role in the lives of hospital staff and their families are revived in a publication lent to me by Jack and Sue Humphries. The publication was produced in 1986 to mark the 21st anniversary of the club building. But it gave former secretary John King the opportunity to look back before the days when the building was opened.

'The major objective of the club was to raise enough funds to build a clubhouse,' he wrote. 'This was achieved by holding monthly dances in the ballroom. These dances were extremely popular and 400 tickets would be sold and everybody attended in full evening dress and danced to an eight-piece band. The highlight of the dances was when Joe Loss played, at a fee of £1,500.

'When we thought we had sufficient funds, negotiations started with the Hospital

Management Committee for a plot of land and anything else they could give us. Some people thought the clubhouse would be a white elephant but I believe that its success has been achieved by the many hard-working officers.'

Another club stalwart, Sid Edenbrow, took up the story. 'Work started on the foundations of the club early in 1965 by the hospital bricklayers. When they had erected the shell, the artisan staff completed the electrics, plumbing, joinery and painting. Shortly after the clubhouse was open, a billiard hall behind the Norwich Union Chambers closed down and offered its tables to anybody who could remove them.

'So one Saturday morning we borrowed a laundry van and I got out my biggest screwdriver and set about the job. As luck would have it, we didn't damage the table or ourselves and the table was erected in the centre of the dance floor. Of course, everybody had to dance around it.'

The 21st anniversary of the building also marked the 40th anniversary of the club. But although the members could look back on the past with pride, they couldn't look forward to the future with the same confidence. Secretary Michael McHale wrote: 'The future life of our present club can only be guaranteed until 1989 when a great deal of the site will have been decommissioned. The chance of buying or leasing some of the site from the authority seems remote at this stage.'
The Gossiper. April 18, 2000.

Making a splash: Fun on the slide at Boultham Baths. (Echo Ref. RI-1829)

Prime minister speaks: Clement Attlee addresses an open-air rally in Lincoln back in 1951. (Echo Ref. RI-654)

Crowds Gathered In Election Fever

LINCOLN has had comparatively few visits from Prime Ministers throughout the decades, so when they do arrive they tend to draw a big crowd. Back in October 1951, election fever gripped the city and Lincoln had a visit from the then Prime Minister and from a future one as well.

First into the political ring came Clement Attlee, the Labour Prime Minister, who addressed a massive open-air meeting in the city centre.

He spoke from the balcony of the old Thornbridge Hotel and looked down on a crowd of around 2,000 shoppers and office and factory workers, who crammed the car park below and lined both banks of the Witham. He was speaking in support of the city's Labour Member of Parliament, Geoffrey de Freitas, who had been Secretary of State for Home Affairs in the previous Labour Government. Someone draped a Union Jack from the wall of the balcony and the Prime Minister spoke into a microphone which carried his message through loudspeakers and out into the crowd. And he was in a sombre mood, talking about the nation's ongoing problems with Egypt.

The Prime Minister wasn't the only big gun to be fired in Lincoln during the General Election campaign. Harold Macmillan – later to become Prime Minister with the nickname 'SuperMac' – was in the city as well. And that was hardly surprising because his son Maurice was the Conservative candidate. The future Prime Minister addressed a crowd of 1,600 people who packed into the New Central Market Hall, in the days when it used to be possible to clear the stalls away at night to create a large open space. When polling day came, the Lincoln electors found themselves with a straight fight between Labour and Conservative candidates. De Freitas held his seat with 23,400 votes, while Macmillan had to be content with second place and 19,840 votes. It was a majority of 3,560.

And no one could complain about the turnout. Almost 88 per cent of the people who could vote, did turn out on that October day, 49 years ago.

The Gossiper. May 16, 2000.

Rush hour: Lincoln Corporation and Lincolnshire RoadCar buses leaving St Mark's Street.

The Rules Of The Buses

REMEMBER those days when you could be standing in a shop doorway in the pouring rain in Lincoln, waiting for the next bus to take you home. And then, when it came along, it couldn't stop because it was the wrong colour. It regularly happened in the years when Lincoln Corporation and the Lincolnshire RoadCar were the city's two main transport concerns.

The Corporation had a monopoly of Lincoln routes. It could pick up and drop passengers anywhere inside the city boundary. But with the odd exception, it didn't run beyond the city boundary. The Lincolnshire RoadCar, on the other hand, was totally different. It's buses, on their way to destinations all over the county, could pick up people anywhere in Lincoln, but it couldn't let them get off again until they were beyond the city boundary. It was a simple enough, understood by everyone.

Then Birchwood was developed. There was a vast new estate in the city boundary, but it was served by RoadCar buses instead of Corporation ones. There were other anomalies in the rapidly-expanding Brant Road area as well. The Corporation Transport Department looked on enviously at the lucrative business it was missing. And the RoadCar looked at the business it was missing in other parts of Lincoln.

It was a situation which couldn't continue and 25 years ago this week, a proposal – which, in those days, was revolutionary – was announced by the City Council. To give residents a better bus service, the council – owners of the Corporation Transport Department – came up with a scheme which would give public transport in the city, its biggest shake-up for years. The City Council decided to seek permission from the Traffic Commissioners to operate its buses to all parts of the city – including Birchwood.

It was a move which could lead to joint services between the two companies all over the city. And at a time when the Corporation Transport Department was working hard to make ends meet, it seemed a good idea in the eyes of many councillors. But few would have expected that, in the not-too-many years ahead, the RoadCar Company would take over the Corporation Transport Department and its fleet of buses.

The Gossiper. June 6, 2000.

Turbulent Past Of City

IN THE years before the First World War, Lincoln was a turbulent place with frequent full-scale riots and incidents of disorder. Citizens acted in a shameful way and were probably responsible for the death of a fireman who died trying to protect a mob who hindered his work.

Alfred Clay (38) was with the City Fire Brigade when he was called to the scene of a blaze in Princess Street in the early hours of August 24, 1911. From the moment he arrived, there was a great crowd looking on from across the river. Many people hooted at the hardworking brigade and cheered when a shortage of water compelled the fire engine to slow down. What was infinitely worse was that half bricks and stones were flung at a police constable who was struggling in three feet of water to get the hose deeper into the Witham. The flames at the scene of the blaze at Messrs Osbourne's Motor Works were consuming everything within the four-storey building.

The street was one of the oldest and narrowest in Lincoln and police constables quickly drew a cordon across the top of Salthouse Lane, which opens on to Princess Street. The difficulty of getting to put the flames out continued and was made worse when the nearby standpipe broke. But once the hose was connected to another source on High Street the flames were controlled. It was after the fire was well damped down that Clay was killed. At his inquest it was said that he tried in vain to keep surging members of the public away from a collapsing wall when the whole of it fell and entombed him and a tradesman, Mr T.H. Starmer. They were pulled from the wreckage and Clay was carried into a house on Princess Street but he died immediately after being attended by a doctor.

Described in press reports of the time as a policeman as well as a fireman, he was also a caretaker at the Sessions House. The City's Chief Constable was also head of the Fire Brigade so it would seem his constables also doubled up as well. Clay came to the city as a farm labourer and joined the force on June 1, 1892. But did he ever receive a commendation for this act of bravery and are there any generations of his family still surviving in Lincoln who can tell us more about him and what happened to his children?

One of his sons joined the brigade after his death but there is little else known about him.

The Gossiper. July 25, 2000.

Moving?: Lincoln Stonebow, could it have become the entrance to a new museum's grounds. (Echo Ref. RI-45)

Century Of Debate For Museum Site

MAKE Newport Arch the main entrance to a new Lincoln museum. And move the Stonebow uphill, to become the entrance to the museum grounds. Those were some of the suggestions made in the 19th century when – as now – there was controversy over where the new museum ought to be. And although all kinds of possibilities were put forward as the most ideal spot this time, none of the suggestions were as outrageous as the 19th century ones.

My thanks to local historian Cliff Buttery who tells me that towards the end of the 19th century, a book was published called *Lin-*

colnshire Notes and Queries. One section began 'A museum for Lincoln; A want.' It went on 'Every few years some energetic person or society tries to stir up Lincoln to its great intellectual want, that of a museum. After the great success of the Lincolnshire Exhibition of 1897, an attempt was made by the Lincoln Science Club to induce the county magistrates to approve a scheme for converting a portion of the unused county jail into a museum. It is a disgrace that no Lincolnshire Museum exists and there can be no doubt whatever that its proper place is in Lincoln, the county town.'

Towards the end of the 20th century, all this sounds a familiar story. And so does the next section. 'It has been proposed and with a good deal of reason that in the case of a building being erected for a free library, one storey could be reserved to be used as a museum. And if a library is to

come into existence, either on the vacant piece of land at the corner of Broadgate and Silver Street, or at the late Central National Schools, either would be an exceedingly good place for a museum.'

Newport Arch: Suggested entrance to a new Lincoln museum.

The first site mentioned would be the one now occupied by the old Constitutional Club, which is up for sale and was mentioned several times as a potential site for the 21st-century museum. With remarkable foresight, the book went on to mention the possibility of the new museum being sited in the castle grounds – another idea we heard quite a lot about earlier this year! And the argument against the castle idea, is also very familiar.

The book went on 'The one objection to the castle site is that it might not be very available for the mass of the population living below the hill.' Later on in the publication, came the sort of idea we never heard of this time. The suggestion was made that the north end of Bailgate should be diverted to the right, immediately after Bailgate Methodist Church. 'This would set Newport Arch at liberty for the principal entrance to the county museum. A more suitable entrance in an archaeological point of view can scarcely be imagined. Part of the present road and a large space of ground to the west of this, on which are very few buildings, would give a fine site.

The plan would also include the removal of the Stonebow from the High Street and its re-erection as an entrance from Church Lane to the museum. The removal of the Stonebow from High Street will someday become a necessity – but this part of the scheme could wait.'

Strangely enough, in those days, no one thought about building a museum on a multi-storey car park site in Danesgate!
The Gossiper. September 14, 1999.

Evenings At The Co-op Ballroom

WE WILL never forget those glorious evenings at the old Co-op Ballroom and Restaurant in Free School Lane, Lincoln. That's the message from many readers after my recent items about the building. Dances, dinners, fund-raising events, meetings, even a darts exhibition were among the many different kinds of events held there. And as readers walk by and see the boarded-up windows, they are thinking back to the building's happier times.

Ray Grimmer, of Doddington Park, Lincoln, has memories dating back to the late 1930s when Frank Marshall used to hold dancing classes there on Fridays from 7pm to 8pm. 'During the 1940s, we would dance there on Saturday nights, alternating with the dances at the Broadgate Drill Hall and at other venues. In the 1950s, Friday night dances were very popular and they were run by various organisations to raise money. In my case, they were run for the Lincoln Wellington Athletic Club. I had to book these a year in advance to avoid losing them and they were a good source of income for the club. Dancing was from 8pm to 1am and tickets were 3s (15p). There was no admission after 10pm because that was when the pubs closed. A small bar in the room at the right-hand side of the stage, was run by outside caterers. For our evenings, it was run by Jack Hartshorne, of the Hop Pole. Committee members would man the box office and the cloakroom at the top of the stairs.

Difficult picture: The funeral of Bishop Hugh in the Dean's Eye Window in Lincoln Cathedral.

Photograph Was Not So Easy To Take

I WAS walking around Lincoln Cathedral the other day and couldn't help but notice the progress of restoration work on the Dean's Eye Window, in the North Transept. It made me think of an incident more than 10 years ago, when I was asked if I would take a photograph of one of the window's panels, depicting the funeral of Bishop (later Saint) Hugh. It was needed for an exhibition at the Bodleian Library, Oxford, to commemorate the eighth centenary of his consecration.

This panel was some 40 feet from the ground, but I was told that I would be able to get up to that level to take the picture. Armed with camera and tripod, I arrived to find a tall tower of scaffolding, mounted on castors and 'secured' with ropes to various parts of masonry inside the transept. There was also an almost vertical ladder, up which I had to climb! Having got up the ladder, I discovered that every little move I made caused the tower to shake, only slightly, but enough to create camera-shake and blur the picture. It was only by sitting very still on the platform and using a delayed-action timer on the camera that I could get a steady picture.

The exhibition print was duly printed and two days before the exhibition, I had a phone call. Someone had told me the wrong stained glass panel and I would have to retake the picture. They would put the scaffolding back in place. No thanks, I said, I will manage it with a telephoto lens from the ground. It's not that I haven't got a head for heights, it was just easier to take from ground level.
Lincolnian's Diary. March 28, 2000.

'We had no need for bouncers in those days because the police hovered not far away to see that nobody gained admission without a ticket. Lincoln Wellington AC also held its annual dinner there and in 1950 Councillor Les Priestley and in 1959 Alderman Fred Todd, both Mayors of Lincoln at the time attended as guests. Ruston and Hornsby Foremens' Association held its dinner dances both in the upstairs and downstairs halls. Midweek during this period, many darts finals and dances were held in the ballroom and around 1980, John Lowe gave a darts exhibition there. They were happy days.'
The Gossiper. March 14, 2000.

The Savoy Cinema, later to become the ABC, then the Cannon, was nearing completion when the old picture was taken in the mid-1930s. To the right of the cinema was the old A1 Fish Shop, which over the years had seen many other uses, including being the first home of Lincoln Liberal Club from 1874 to 1890. One of the many barges which passed along the River Witham to and from Brayford Pool can be seen in the foreground.

Today, only the old fish shop building remains, having been restored in 1979 and converted into The Witch and The Wardrobe public house. The cinema and all of the buildings along Waterside North, up to High Bridge were demolished some 10 years ago to make way for the Waterside Centre, which was officially opened by Princess Diana in 1992.

A Jigsaw Puzzle of Newport Arch

NEWS that vandals have attacked the centuries-old Newport Arch, has revived memories of that night in 1964 when the arch came up against much stiffer opposition. At the weekend, youths climbed onto the top of the Roman arch and hurled stones down on to the road beneath. And it prompted an outcry from police, councillors, archaeologists and people living in the area.

But back in May 1964, the arch suffered even more damage when it was attacked by a lorry carrying frozen fish. The driver, travelling down Newport towards the city centre, thought he was on the right road. But he wasn't. In the darkness of the night, there

Try sorting this one out: This is how Newport Arch looked in May 1964, after a lorry carrying frozen fish got stuck underneath it. (Echo Ref. RI-2032)

was a bang, a crunching of metal and the tall vehicle came to a halt with the arch resting on top. It gave the City Council a once-in-a-lifetime challenge to sort it all out again.

Obviously the arch had to be restored, but it was going to be a bit like doing a massive 3-D jigsaw puzzle. With the lorry still in place, all the stones were numbered and

gradually taken down. The offending lorry was eventually removed and instead of the arch we know, all that remained were two upright sections of ancient stone. Newport Arch was an arch no longer. But it was going to be put back together again.

A wooden frame was built between the uprights. The stones were carefully put back into their own positions and then the framework was removed. The result was an arch which, if you didn't know the full story, looked more or less as it had done for centuries. Since then, councillors have taken steps to ensure that no other drivers of tall vehicles can make the same mistake. And the arch is floodlit after dark. But it seems now as if closed circuit television cameras might soon have to be mounted in the area to prevent any further damage from the hands of mindless vandals.

The Gossiper. June 20, 2000.

A Fairy-tale Story About Pubs In Lincoln

Once upon a time, ADAM AND EVE were walking by the MONK'S ABBEY, when through a HOLE IN THE WALL, they noticed a HOP POLE. Stood by it was THE JOLLY BREWER, talking to the THE FARMER'S BOY, who had with him his GREYHOUND, which was a real GAY DOG. Up came the RECRUITING SERGEANT, a real NOSEY PARKER, who asked if they had seen the LINCOLNSHIRE POACHER, the real PRIDE OF LINCOLN.

In the corner of the garden, BESSY BEDLAM was

talking to THE SILENT WOMAN, who had brought along her BLACK GOATS. They thought of going down to THE BARGE, for a trip on the river, or even to the BOWLING GREEN, for a game, but suddenly, they heard a RING OF BELLS.

It was announcing the arrival of a load of very special guests, including the PRINCE OF WALES, the MARQUIS OF GRANBY, the DUKE OF CUMBERLAND, SIR ROBERT PEEL and LORD NELSON. They had come along for the entertainment, which included poetry by SHAKESPEARE and LORD TENNYSON and music by THE HOLLIES.

I know that this is a pure load of fantasy, but all of the names mentioned are, or were, licensed premises in

Lincoln. Colleague Peter Brown has had stories recently about some of the old public houses in Lincoln which have closed, but no one has mentioned the nicknames of some of Lincoln's pubs. My grandfather always used the name 'The Kicker', when he was referring to The White Horse, now the Tap and Spile. Another name he used was 'The Shekker', but how many regulars of the Shakespeare Inn know it by that name. 'The Brickies' was the name by which many knew the Brickmakers' Arms. And if you were going to 'The Wagon', then it was either the Waggon and Horses, on Newark Road, or on Burton Road.

Lincolnian's Diary. July 4, 2000.

The flags were out for the silver jubilee of King George V and Queen Mary in 1935 when this photograph was taken in Bailgate, Lincoln. Leachman's butchers shop is still a butchers today, but under different ownership. (Echo Ref. RI-165)

Landmark Rose From The Ashes

TOURISTS pause to have their pictures taken alongside it. And the locals gaze affectionately at the building which has been a part of the Lincoln hillside for longer than any of them can remember. The Ellis Mill is among the most prominent of city landmarks and after dark it's a floodlit monument which can be seen from several miles away. Yet, just like a phoenix, it really did rise from the ashes. And it could so easily have been swept away as part of a new development.

Twenty-five years ago this week, the future of Ellis Mill

Restored: Ellis Mill in Lincoln as it looked after the restoration.

hung in the balance. Years after the sails had turned for what everyone had thought as the last time, a public inquiry was taking place at City Hall to decide its future. The old mill had been acquired by a property company which originally had thoughts of incorporating the structure into a mews of a dozen flats. But the city council was unhappy about the plan and thought that 12 flats were just

too many for the site. Eight would be a better figure, said councillors, but the developers said it wouldn't be viable. It looked as if deadlock had been reached. Then, early in 1974, fate took a hand. The old mill was swept by fire. Damage was extensive and the cost of restoring the mill was just too great for the property developers.

The warning, 'Danger! Keep Clear! Unsafe!' was painted in large letters on the blacked wall. The building, which for so long had been an eye-catching landmark, had overnight become an eyesore. The property developers held an open day and issued a general invitation to people to go along and have a look at just how dangerous the mill had become. Only a handful of people accepted the invitation and the developers saw it as a mark of the lack of public interest in the building's restoration. But the city council could see a future for the mill and the public inquiry heard the then director of planning and architecture, John Anderson, predict that restoration could turn the mill into a tourist attraction.

There may have been some who disagreed, but he was quick to point out that the mill was the last of what used to be a series which ran along the edge of the hill. It was a piece of townscape sculpture with historic associations, giving character and identity to that part of Lincoln, he maintained. It was also unique because there wasn't an example of a complete mill of its kind in the county, he said. A Government inspector went along to take a look at the mill himself and it was saved.

The structure was later taken over by Lincoln Civic Trust, who masterminded the restoration as a project for the

Queen's silver jubilee of 1977. In 1998 it celebrated its 200th birthday and now, with sails turning once more and a steady stream of young and not-so-young visitors calling almost daily to see milling in the old fashioned way, the future of Ellis Mill is assured.
The Gossiper. July 4, 2000.

Dog Steals Show

A NEW chapter in the history of Lincolnshire Police began 25 years ago this week, when the Duchess of Kent officially opened the city's new £80,000 divisional police headquarters in West Parade. For the men and women of the division, it marked the end of years of working in cramped conditions at the Sessions House. People lined the streets for a glimpse of the royal visitor on her journey by car from RAF Scampton to the headquarters, where the Duchess – on her first official visit to Lincoln – unveiled a plaque in the main entrance foyer. She then joined guests in the gymnasium for the official opening ceremony, which followed a speech of welcome by county council chairman Councillor John Hedley Lewis.

Afterwards, the Duchess had an opportunity to see

Released: The little dog who dared to do what all dogs do, at the royal opening.

some of the many new and ultra-modern features of the building when she was taken on a private conducted tour. Meanwhile, visitors caught up on what they had missed in the entrance foyer, by watching a videotape recording of the unveiling ceremony – something of a novelty in those days.

But although the event is still fondly remembered by those of us who were there, the opening day of the new police station – quickly dubbed Ryvita House because of its outside appearance – is recalled for a very different reason. It was a little dog which stole the day. As the crowds were waiting in Beaumont Fee for the royal visitor to reappear from within, the dog trotted quietly across the red carpet and did what dogs normally do, up against the wall outside the foyer. Then, to the sound of laughter from the waiting crowd, the dog quietly trotted off again.

But that wasn't quite the end of the story. Moments later, the dog was back and looked set for a repeat performance. By now, the police had decided that enough was enough. An officer stooped down, picked up the dog and took him inside until the royal visitor had reappeared and had gone on her way. Only then was the dog released and told never to dampen their doorstep again.
The Gossiper. October 3, 2000.

Convenient wall: The dog makes its mark inches from the red carpet.

Brayford At The Heart Of City Life

Bedecked: Boats fly a variety of bunting for a boat rally on the Brayford.

IT'S THAT time of the year again when boats throughout a wide area gather in Brayford Pool and put up their bunting for the annual Water Carnival. It is an event that's rapidly becoming Lincoln's summer equivalent to the Christmas market. And it's a way of showing off what is generally regarded as one of Lincoln's brightest features.

But not so many years ago, Brayford was a very different place. Once described as Britain's nicest surprise, the undiscovered jewel in the historic city of Lincoln's crown, is its ancient waterway around Brayford Pool. The waterfront area has been a significant factor in the life of Lincolnians since prehistoric times when the River Witham turned to cut through the Lincoln edge and formed small pools. The largest of these, known as Bradeford, was a natural site for a settlement. The river provided communication and trade, while the hill overlooking the pool, offered the perfect defensive stronghold. This is where the Romans built one of the finest cities in their empire and where William the Conqueror ordered the building of the Cathedral and Castle which still dominate the city's magnificent skyline. In the 14th century, Brayford Pool was Britain's fourth busiest port, even though Lincoln is 40 miles from the sea.

Nowadays, the pool is a peaceful and relaxing haven for boaters, local people and many visitors who come to Lincoln for its heritage. shopping and special events. Three boat operators at present offer cruises along this historic stretch of waterway, giving passengers a chance to view city life from a completely different angle. Cathedral City Cruises oper-

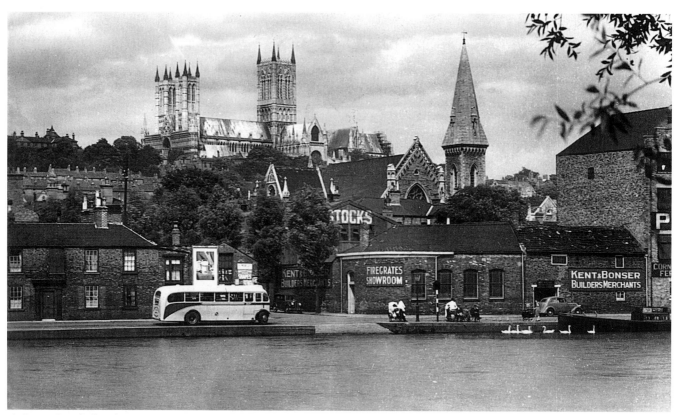

As it was: Brayford Pool 50 years ago.

Changed scene: Brayford Pool, half a century ago presented a very different scene than today.

ator Ian Smith, who has captained a popular trip on the pool since 1985, says: 'The Romans realised the potential of the Brayford when they came to Lincoln in the 1st century. They built a fortress with fine public buildings, constructed roads like the Fosseway and Ermine Street and excavated Brayford Pool as an inland harbour to transport goods to what was then the most northerly point of the Roman Empire. They also drained the Fens for agriculture and fortunately, for Lincoln's boating future, cut the Fossdyke Canal to connect Lincoln to the Trent. Lincoln became one of the finest cities in Europe and a major centre for culture and trade.'

Paul Owen is another familiar figure on Brayford. He captains the Brayford Belle which moors on Waterside North alongside the Waterside Shopping Centre. The *Belle* was built in 1922 and is a former Dunkirk veteran. It was one of the flotilla of little ships which helped rescue Allied troops stranded on the Normandy beaches during the Second World War. Says Paul 'The Brayford's finest days came in the 18th and 19th centuries when its wharves bustled with large sailing barges bringing grain, seed and other products to the mills, warehouses and breweries. The waterfront also hosted Lincoln's industrial revolution, as engineering foundries were developed along the river by local entrepreneurs such as Ruston and Hornsby, Ruston and Proctor and Smith Clayton Forge. The successors of many of these firms still survive in Lincoln today and continue to generate employment and wealth for the growing city.'

In the early 1900s, the once-proud area of Brayford and its adjacent waterways, fell into decline as the factories closed and many of the vessels around its wharves were allowed to deteriorate. Such was the state of the area's dereliction at the time that there were discussions in the 1960s about filling in the pool with concrete to create a car park. With this threat hanging over it, a committee was established to revitalise the Brayford. The untidy wrecks were cleared and the City Council, local businesses and other interested parties, set up the Brayford Trust which now looks after the interests of the area and the boat owners.

In the 1990s, Brayford was selected as the location for Lincoln's new university – a £30 million development which has triggered significant investment in new amenities around the waterfront area. A new marina has been built, together with new centres for the canoe club and the Sea Cadets. New pubs and restaurants have sprung up around Brayford and a multi-screen cinema is under construction as one ingredient in plans to turn Brayford into Lincoln's cultural quarter. Once again, the area is set to become the life blood at the heart of city life.

The Gossiper. July 4, 2000.

Daredevil: A lone skater risks the ice on the frozen Brayford Pool in 1959. (Echo Ref. RI-1943)

Boats in Brayford Pool were being decorated with bunting ready for a water carnival in 1956 when our old picture was taken. Brayford Head bridge was still in use, causing delays to road traffic every time it was opened for a boat. The old buildings, which had been a familiar part of the scene for many decades, included a timber merchants, a fertiliser warehouse and a banana store.

   Today, the only building around this part of the pool still standing is the Royal William the Fourth public house. A block of residential dwellings replaces the old banana store and offices stand in place of the fertiliser warehouse. The bridge carrying Wigford Way replaces the old swing bridge.

Mysterious happenings: The old Green Dragon public house – was it haunted?

Strange Features Of A Public House

THERE was something strange on the landing in one of Lincoln's best-known public houses. Young Colin Hayes couldn't see it. He couldn't hear it. But he could feel it and so could his sister.

For months Colin quite literally rubbed shoulders with a ghost at his home. It was back in the early 1950s when he was a pupil at Rosemary Secondary Modern School, in Lincoln and his father, William, kept the Green Dragon. 'You could feel someone pulling your hair every time you went along the landing to the bedroom. My sister experienced it as well,' he tells me.

Legend has it that the pub was haunted by someone called Umbrella Mary who used to have an umbrella shop at the side of the pub. But at the time Colin never knew the ghost as a person, just a strange tug at his hair as he went to bed every night. That wasn't the only strange feature of the Green Dragon. It boasted what they used to describe as a bottomless well. 'My dad dropped a bottle down it once and we never heard a splash. He later boarded it over.' Another strange feature of the place was a room that they used to call the Snake Pit. It was a little room which he remembers as being full of boxes and cases of stuffed birds and reptiles which had probably been used to decorate the public rooms in days gone by.

Mention the Green Dragon to many Lincoln people and their thoughts usually turn to the difficult question of where exactly it is. It has featured in The Gossiper column from time to time when controversy has arisen over its address. There are three possibilities. Some people think of it as being in Broadgate. Others maintain it's in Melville Street and there's another body of opinion which says it's in Magpie or Magpies Square. Colin comes down on the side of Magpie Square, although he does remember mail arriving there with all the possible addresses. Colin comes from a family of publicans.

Over the years, his father was the first steward of the then new Railways Club, in Lincoln. He was later at the Golden Cross, in High Street before taking a shop at the bottom of King Street. Colin's uncle, Edward Hayes, was landlord of the Shakespeare and Steam Packet over the years. And Colin's grandfather once had the old City Arms, up The Strait.

The Gossiper. August 22, 2000.

Familiar sight: This corporation double decker heads south on its was to Hykeham Road, in the 1950s.

Memories Of The Old Buses

NEWS that the old Corporation bus garage and offices in St Mark Street could soon be destined for demolition has revived memories for many city people of the days before the company was taken over by Lincolnshire RoadCar. This article takes a look back at the days when city councillors used to control a major part of Lincoln's public transport.

It is beginning to look as if it will be only a matter of time before the final vehicle is moved out of the old Corporation bus garage in St Mark's. At around the same date, the last piece of office

equipment will be carried out of the adjoining offices and the building will close its doors for ever. Soon afterwards, demolition workers will move in and start knocking down the building which has been a city centre landmark for so long. It's been more than just a bus garage.

Over the decades, the buses have been moved out from time to time, so the building can host the occasional boxing tournament or mass meeting. But once the Lincolnshire RoadCar Company bus station across the road was closed and demolished, to be replaced by a new store, many people began to realise that sooner or later a similar fate would befall the Corporation bus garage. With the recent shopping expansion in and

around St Mark's railway station area, the site has become far too valuable for it to remain as a bus depot. Ambitious plans for retail, residential and leisure facilities are already being talked about for the site. But whatever happens, its certain that one of the most tangible reminders of the days of the old Corporation Transport Department will be lost forever. It was the Corporation which provided almost all the city's public transport services.

With the odd exception, the RoadCar was unable to move people from one part of the city to another. The Corporation had the right to do that and generally did it very well. A group of powerful councillors who made up the Transport Committee took the policy

decisions which kept the buses on the road and a transport general manager and his staff were responsible for the day-to-day running. It was the councillors who held the pursestrings. They kept a watchful eye on the weekly passenger figures and decided just when worn-out buses could be replaced by new ones. Any application to increase fares had to be presented to the traffic commissioners who would look at the evidence very carefully before saying yes or no.

The Corporation buses were a mixture of single and double deckers and – apart from the occasional private hire job or Sunday evening excursion into nearby villages – many spent the greater part of their working life labouring up and down

Helping hand: In March 1963, this Leyland double decker had to have a tow up Lindum Road. (Echo Ref. RI-2058)

Lindum Road and providing the services that linked the far flung estates with the city centre shops. There was also a time when all the passengers seemed to know all the bus crews and all the bus crews seemed to know all the passengers. The clippies – the men and women who took your fare and handed you a ticket – were among some of the best-known characters in the city. Many had the ability to stand in the gangway of a jolting bus, while operating the ticket machine, handing you your change, discussing the latest fortunes of Lincoln City FC and pinpointing passing places of interest for visitors. For many passengers, things were never quite the same again when the City Council decided to get rid of the conductors and conductresses and to convert to

one-man operation in the interests of economy.

At many periods in the life of the Corporation buses, there seemed to be a war going on with the RoadCar. There were anomalies between what each could do. The RoadCar, for instance, could run services to Birchwood, which was within the city boundary. And the Corporation had a toe-hold into North Hykeham with a service which terminated at Highfield Terrace. When the rules changed to allow the Corporation to run to Birchwood as well and to enable the RoadCar to pick up and drop passengers within the city it was obvious things were coming to a head. Eventually, after much speculation, the RoadCar took over the Corporation and gradually the name

began to disappear from the side of the surviving Corporation Transport vehicles. The city bus station became the principal departure and arrival point for all Lincoln services.

But, in the eyes of a generation of older city people at least, it still seems strange to see the RoadCar buses running through former Corporation bus route strongholds like the Ermine estate. There was a time when that would never have happened.

The Gossiper. August 29, 2000.

Pride of the fleet: Councillors and officials gather in the Corporation bus garage in November 1962 to welcome these new additions to the fleet. (Echo Ref. RI-877A)

Never contenders for the winter Olympics, but it was just as much fun for these youngsters back in 1935 when the boys, most of whom are wearing their school caps, found the snow covered slopes of the West Common just as good as any Cresta Run. In the background is Ellis' Mill. (Echo Ref. RI-211)

Tennis Heroes At The Bank

THERE'S been athletics... cricket... wrestling... even greyhound racing... But have they ever played tennis on the pitch of the Lincoln City Football Ground at Sincil Bank? If your first answer to that is 'no' then be prepared to think again. Because hardly had the Wimbledon championships of 1950 come to an end than the crowds were gathering at Sincil Bank to see two tennis legends in action.

Triple Wimbledon champion Fred Perry – by then a 40-year-old – was there with another of the sport's greats, Dan Maskell. Dan was later destined to find television commentary fame as BBC's voice of tennis. Fifty years ago this week, the pair were in Lincoln. And the *Echo* reported how 'Sincil Bank took on some of the glamour of Wimbledon's centre court. On a specially prepared piece of turf on Lincoln City's football pitch, Fred Perry and Dan Maskell exhibited their skill in the dual roles of player and coach.'

The two were on an extensive Focus on Lawn Tennis tour of provincial centres organised by the Central Council for Physical Recreation. Dan explained it was designed to further fundamentally the game of tennis players of all grades and to minimise their errors. Dan and Perry gave sideline comments as four well-known local players took part in a doubles match. They later took part in a single set exhibition singles match which Fred won 6-4.

An *Echo* reporter noted: 'Although Perry is not now so sprightly on his feet, he would often reveal flashes of that formidable technique and armoury of strokes that made him one of the outstanding tennis personalities of the pre-war years.' Spectators, who had paid up to 7s 6d to watch the evening of tennis, were delighted by it all. And it was a memorable evening for 21-year-old Keith Marriott. Keith, then a member of Londales Tennis Club in Lincoln, achieved a long-standing ambition when he played against Fred, while Dan told him what he was doing wrong. At the time, Keith lived in Riseholme Road and was tennis correspondent of the Cambridge University publication, Varsity. While serving with the RAF in Germany, he was sports correspondent of the British Forces Radio Network.

Am I wrong, or a decade or so later, did he find fame as a disc jockey and host of television's trendy *Ready, Steady, Go* programme, under the name of Keith Fordyce? *The Gossiper. July 11, 2000.*

Advertising Bus Didn't Have The Power

ANOTHER one along in a minute? Well, maybe there would have been, but on the roads and streets of Lincoln in the 1970s there was nothing quite like this bus. This was Lincoln's first example of an 'all-over advertising' bus. For years, buses had carried a host of adverts, but the idea of devoting the entire livery of a double decker to a single advert had never been seen in Lincoln before.

It was the Theatre Royal which was at the time going through a new era in its life, that hit on the idea of this spectacular advert. Under the skilful hands of the

Underpowered: Lincoln's advertising bus couldn't get up the hill.

painters, this Lincoln City Transport bus took on a new and eye-catching appearance.

But, as magnificent as the vehicle looked, it did have one shortcoming and it had nothing to do with its appearance. A colleague recalls: 'On one occasion it was used to take a party of visitors from Lincoln's German twin-town of Neustadt to an open day at RAF Waddington. 'But the load proved too great for the vehicle, which was underpowered and it ground to a halt on Cross o' Cliff Hill. It was only possible to get it started again when the hosts got off the bus to rejoin it at the top of the hill.'
The Gossiper. July 11, 2000.

Plans For Lincoln's Stations

EVER since the first rail tracks were laid across Lincoln High Street a century-and-half ago, people have been talking about ways of getting rid of them.

Schemes ranging from the possibly plausible to the laughingly ludicrous have been voiced many a time. And although one of the two High Street level crossings is no longer in use, the problem of trains vs traffic is still as bad as it ever was. But 30 years ago this week, there was fresh hope on the horizon.

You might have thought that any proposal by British Rail to rid Lincoln of either of its hated level crossings would have been welcomed with open arms. But back in the summer of 1970, an announcement by British Rail looked as if could lead to a clash with the City Council. In those days the city still had two railway stations – the Central and a couple of hundred yards down the High Street, St Mark's. And they both had a level crossing which ran right over the busy High Street. But the time was coming when it was becoming increasingly obvious that one or other of the two stations would have to go.

Over the years the pendulum swung in both

Full steam ahead: Holidaymakers leaving Lincoln Central Station in 1960. (Echo Ref. RI-3317)

Numbered days: St Mark's Station shortly before its closure and conversion to a shopping centre.

directions. There was a suggestion that the Central Station should be closed and all trains diverted through St Mark's. Then there was a suggestion that St Mark's should go and all the trains be diverted through the Central Station. Someone even put forward the idea that both existing stations ought to be closed and a new one constructed alongside the high level avoiding line further down the High Street. One by one the alternatives were considered and eliminated.

A new station was seen as costly and impracticable. Facilities at St Mark's were limited. To extend its life into the new Millennium would have been expensive and there didn't seem enough space for the future expansion of services. So eventually it was decreed that St Mark's would have to go and a new spur constructed to divert everything through the Central Station.

But in July 1970, several options were still open when the *Echo* revealed British Rail's latest multi-million pound plan. It would have meant closing the Central Station and the track from under Pelham Bridge, across the High Street and along the south bank of Brayford. You might have thought there was a lot of merit in the scheme, but the city council squared its shoulders and braced itself to do battle. Because the British Rail scheme had implications for a plan of its own. Once the Central, its car parks and large areas of rail track thought the heart of the city, became vacant, the land could be used for a new city centre complex. This was all very well, but it clashed head-on with the council's own scheme – also running into millions of pounds – to develop land in the Sincil Street area.

The *Echo* recalled how the council had put a high priority on solving the city's level crossing problem. And while the new plan could probably help to relieve the situation, it cut across the council's own ideas for developing the city centre. It was felt the city centre wasn't big enough to cope with two major schemes and one may have to go. If it was the council's scheme, it would lead to a big upheaval among the planners who had spent several months working on the scheme.

If it was the British Rail's proposal, the city would be left without any hope of solving its level crossing problem in the foreseeable future. In the end, the British Rail scheme came to nothing. If it had gone through, the centre of Lincoln today would have taken on a totally different appearance There would have been no magistrates court building in lower High Street and the St Mark's Shopping Centre would never have existed. On the credit side, both the Central Station level crossing on High Street and the one on nearby Brayford Wharf East, would now just have been an unpleasant memory in the minds of motorists and pedestrians alike.

It's probably easy to suppose many of the problems would have simply moved a couple of hundred yards down the High Street to St Mark's.

The Gossiper. July 11, 2000.

Diesel days: St Mark's Station could have become Lincoln's only railway station.

In 1932, the Brayford Pool in the centre of Lincoln was drained to help in the removal of weeds and mud which were making things difficult for boats. On the left of the picture are the railway sidings of Holmes Yard and in the distance can be seen some of the old buildings at the western end of the pool, where the Foss Dyke Navigation starts on its journey to Torksey. Old hulks of barges litter the pool and the whole area has a rather depressed look about it. It may not have been the sort of place where you would have felt inclined to stand and enjoy the view for any length of time.

But what a difference in the modern picture! Narrowboats line the edge of the pool and the campus of the University of Lincolnshire and Humberside stands where the former railway lines stood. On the right, modern buildings have replaced the old warehouses and a flour mill and in the distance is the bridge joining the Ropewalk with Carholme Road.

This was the scene looking down upper High Street in the early 1960s when work was about to start on the building of a new shop and office block. Traffic still used the street, with no hint that the area was eventually to become part of the pedestrian area. (Echo Ref. RI-2762)

Looking up the High Street, beyond the scaffolding is another site undergoing change. A new shopping mall was under construction. The tall building behind the traffic light is Boots the Chemists, which later moved to a new building below the Stonebow. (Echo Ref. RI-2762)

Childhood Memories

Bygone Toys For Xmas

YOUNGSTERS today expect Pokemon, Play Station and any manner of electronic toys for Christmas, but what was on offer in Lincoln's toyshops 90 years ago?

Dolls were popular with the girls and at one Lincoln shop, the favourite was the 'Character Baby', an 'almost uncannily realistic kiddie dressed', as the great Coquelin would have put it 'all naked'. Different facial expressions were available, from the angelic sweetness of a choirboy, to one with a scowl 'which tempted one to soundly smack the little screamer'. But of course, they didn't walk, talk or even wet their nappies like today's dolls do.

Mechanical toys were, of course, clockwork. Aeroplanes were not yet 10 years old, but toy versions were popular which, once wound up, flew around a stand 'soaring gradually higher and higher, with a spiral movement until planing down to earth as the clockwork runs down.' Another novelty was a monorail, which had two cars running on single wheels on a single circular line. An 'amusing toy' was called the 'Elephant family' who amble

Teachers Were Relied Upon

DISCIPLINE, manners and obedience were the order of the day when the village schoolmaster or mistress reigned supreme in line with the parson and the doctor. The three R's – Reading, Writing and Arithmetic were the main subjects taught. Very few village schools had uniforms – most of the children dressed for their lifestyle. Those who walked a long way – sometimes as much as five miles each way – wore Wellingtons and warm clothing in the winter. For the summer out came the sandshoes (plimsolls), cotton dresses and shorts.

The first village school I came in contact with was at Laughton, near Gainsborough. Miss Marsh was the headmistress and Miss Fillingham the assistant teacher. For some reason the children referred to Miss Marsh as Shush – very confusing. But she was a good teacher, Miss

Fillingham – who I believe was one of the old school who did not train at a college taught the little ones to read through phonetics and the numbers through times tables. They were both excellent teachers and true to the faith of the Church of England. When Miss Marsh left to go to another school the whole village gave her a farewell concert. It included items by the children – Home Guard and a lengthy song by the gamekeeper Mr McGlashen who had fortified himself with whisky.

On Ash Wednesday the children attended a service before having the rest of the day as holiday. The parson went in twice a week to teach Scripture and also the Catechism which they had to know off by heart.

Can anyone remember Mr Mawson of East Stockwith? That was a council school but I am sure he will go down in history as the one teacher who allowed his pupils to throw buckets of water down the playground on frosty nights so that they could have a good slide the next day. He was also an excellent teacher

who held the respect and friendship of his pupils. And then on to Wold Newton – a school of four children taught by Mrs Day whose husband was serving in the RAF. In spite of the small numbers she taught the whole curriculum as if the school was full.

Most children could read by the age of seven. And the day you graduated from pencil to pen and ink was a major step in life. Those who showed leadership were encouraged with positions such as milk monitor, ink monitor or blackboard monitor.

They were given responsibility and although it may seen trivial it was excellent training for life. Every Monday morning teacher collected 2½d (around one new pence) for the week's milk which was given out at playtime.

Teachers earned the respect of their pupils. They were held in awe but you knew if necessary they could be relied upon for advice and would practically help!
Bette's Bygones. October 5, 1999.

along with perfectly natural movements.

There were also trainsets, tramcars and cars. And there was one 'toy' on sale which is

still popular today. What would we do without our Teddy Bears? There was even a teddy in an animated display which when you put a

penny in the slot, came out of its cage and delivered a small present.
Lincolnian's Diary. December 19, 2000.

What Was It Like When You Went To School?

THEY always say that your schooldays are the happiest days of your life. A chance to combine youthful fun and enthusiasm with a capacity to acquire the sort of knowledge and skills which would stand you in good stead for your working life. But what do you recall most about your own days at school? Were they an era you will remember for ever? Or was it a period you would more rather forget?

If you were growing up in post-war Lincoln, then the chances are you shared a classroom with up to as many as 40 other pupils. Classes were large and you would sit in two-seater desks which contained just enough room for your exercise books, the odd sheet of blotting paper and your pen. And at the very top corner of your desk would be an inkwell where you would dip your pen nib before setting out to write an essay which you hoped your English teacher would recognise as a masterpiece. How many times did a shaky hand produce a large blot of ink, which used to fall from your pen nib, right in the very centre of the cover of your exercise book?

In the 1950s, as the nation got over the shortages of the Second World War, exercise books and text books were still in limited supply and we were urged to take the greatest possible care of them. At the start of most terms, you would be told to take your books home and provide a suitable cover for them. That normally meant finding some leftover pieces of wallpaper and making rough book covers out of them.

Although most pupils started their school careers in buildings designed for both boys and girls, by the time you had reached the age of seven, boys would be sent off to one school and girls would go to another. And never the two would meet again. If you were a pupil at Lincoln area schools in the 1950s, then comprehensive schools were still a generation or two away. Lincoln had four grammar schools in those days and to gain a coveted place at any of them, you had to take what was known as the dreaded 11-plus examination. That consisted of a lot of written examinations and then an interview at the school of your choice. If you were a boy, then your choice of grammar schools lay between the Lincoln School, on Wragby Road and the City School, which in those days was still in Monks Road. Girls had the option of going to either the High School, halfway up Lindum Hill, or South Park.

Uniforms were very much the thing in those days and most pupils were so proud of their schools that even during holidays and at weekends, you would find them walking around town in their blazers and caps. Right through the 1950s, if you went to the Lincoln School, then you actually had lessons on six days a week.

Classes took place every morning, but you did have Wednesday and Saturday afternoon off.

Spring Hill, St Giles, Rosemary and Sincil Bank were among the city's secondary modern schools. And from a child's point of view, perhaps the main differences were that grammar school pupils tended to have more homework than secondary modern school pupils. But, on the credit side, if you went to a grammar school, then you tended to have longer holidays during the summer.

The Gossiper. June 6, 2000.

Terrified By My First School Day

DO YOU remember your very first day at school? How you were suddenly taken from one world to another. How you had played in the street one morning and the next expected to sit still for hours on end behind a desk? And worse still, not say a word.

My first school was a convent and as the great oak doors opened I was absolutely terrified. I was almost in a coma as they banged shut behind me leaving me in a world I had never seen or heard of. I didn't know a soul. Didn't anybody realise the I'd never been anywhere on my own before? I was scared out of my wits. A nun came towards me dressed all in black.

She took me into a room where there were rows and rows of desks with gleaming brass inkwells. Another nun, with a big apron covering her dress, was trying to light the fire.

'Don't you look at the fire – you'll put it out.' The older nun said to me. I suppose it was meant to tease and be funny but I didn't understand and tears welled in my eyes. 'Don't be such a cry baby,' she said as I struggled to get my hanky from my knicker pocket. 'I'm not a cry baby!' I sniffed. 'Not what?' she said, 'When you speak to me you say, Sister,' her tone was very sharp. 'Your not my sister,' I replied. 'I'm an only one. Mam didn't want anymore when she saw me.'

She looked shocked but insisted I called her Sister Maria. It was all double dutch to me. Soon the room was filled with an assortment of children, some obviously used to school life and others, like me, very new. I tried to be friendly and offered a sweet to a girl sat next to me called Diana. She turned her nose up and looked away. 'We are not allowed sweets until break,' she said. I was mortified. What was 'break'?

Sister had noticed and said sweets were not allowed to be taken into school. 'Give them to me! We have our own tuck shop!' she said. But I got my own back a bit when we started lessons. I knew most of my basic numbers and alphabet and could write a lot of them down. 'That's quite good!' sister said. 'Well, you can read them so they must be alright,' I snapped.

I was getting fed up with sitting there all dressed up just to scribble. I didn't realise that you went to the toilet at break and by lunch time I was bursting. I asked three times to go to the toilet but she ignored me. Finally the bell went and as I ran I wet myself. I was mortified. Tears rolled down my cheeks and my sobs rang through the cloakroom. 'What's all this,' said a kindly voice. I told her what had happened. This kind lady hugged me, got me a clean pair of knickers, a sweet and told me not to worry. My opinion of school changed immediately through the kindness of Mother Superior.

Bette's Bygones. August 29, 2000.

Street games: A convenient lamppost makes an excellent set of stumps for a game of street cricket. (Echo Ref. RI-859)

Children's Games Made Memories

I WAS trying to amuse my grandchildren one wet afternoon and suggested we play 'hunt the thimble'. 'What's that?' they asked, which took me back to the games I played as a child. Does anyone remember 'hunt the thimble'? How one stayed in the room to hide the thimble and the other returned to try and find it. Shouts of 'hot', 'cold', 'warm' or 'freezing' filled the air as the searchers got closer or further away from the object.

Games of Ludo, Snakes and Ladders, Solitaire, Snap, Old Maid passed many an afternoon or evening. Young artists loved a box of paints and a painting book. Personally I wanted nothing better than an exercise book and pencil to write stories. Summer holidays passed in a haze of hop scotch, whip and top, marbles, tiggy or hide and seek. And the skipping rhymes of 'I am a girl guide dressed in blue, these are the actions I must do', or 'Nebuchadnezzar King of the Jews, bought his wife a pair of shoes, when the shoes began to wear Nebuchadnezzar began to swear.'

A row of kids backsides lining the streets as they leapfrogged over one another.

And if you won or had got a blood alley marble you were a king. Taking turns was done diplomatically with a rhyme and 'dip' such as 'Little pig walk out' or 'One, two three – one, two, three O'Leary – I saw my Aunty Mary sitting on her bum t'reary – out goes

he/she.' Three chalked lines and a solid rubber ball added up to a great game of cricket, often involving the Dads as well. Invariably once during the holidays there would be a smashed window or greenhouse and an empty street in seconds flat. And every street

Popular board game: The lid from a game of Ludo – c.1930 – even the dog was interested.

Upended: A wartime ring of sandbags around the lamppost at the junction of Moorland Avenue, Rookery Lane and Skellingthorpe Road, Lincoln, provides a playground for these youngsters.

had an old grump who scared us to death. And invariably the ball went in their garden and we 'dipped' to see who would go and ask for it or leg it over the fence when they weren't looking.

Winter nights meant reading or making inexpensive gifts from the instructions in the books for boys and girls. Jokes, riddles and puzzles were a vital part of our education. Holiday notebooks and other hobbies made us use our brains. The stories and poems were thrilling adventures and always had a moral.

Fresh air, games in the streets and homes, Sunday School events with games where everyone was involved – all good character building stuff.

Bette's Bygones. April 11, 2000.

How We Played The Dating Game

WHEN I was cutting my teenage teeth there was an art to dating. It usually started at a dance. **Do you remember the wonderful days of the Co-op in Free School Lane – or the Drill Hall in Broadgate? The lads would eye the girls – who always tried to look disinterested – and as the music started they would saunter over and deliver the opening line. 'May I have this dance?'**

After a couple of twirls around the hall he usually led in with: 'Do you come here often?' If the girl was interested they were away.

'Where do you come from? May I have the next dance? Would you like a cup of coffee?' If they clicked then they would dance together all night. And things could get really serious if he asked for the last waltz. They would glide, cheek to cheek, to that romantic oldie *Who's Taking You Home Tonight?*

Then the romantic moonlight walk to the bus or the gate – no fear of rape or any hanky panky. If he asked 'Can I see you again?' the next stage was the flicks (cinema). And what a choice Lincoln had! The Radion – now the home of BBC Radio Lincolnshire, The Grand at the top of High Street, The Savoy, Ritz, Regal and Exchange, all with a double bill or different films. The seats were 1s (5p), 1s 6d (7½p), 2s 3d (12p) and 3s 6d

(17½p). He usually pushed the boat out and went for the 3s 6d on the first date. As the lights went down he would ask, shyly, if he could hold your hand.

Those films had everything to encourage romance. Tear jerkers and horror stories – reasons to snuggle up close. All very innocent and very romantic – it was special. After a few regular dates you became a couple and tried to be at the front of the queue to secure two corner seats on the back row. (I'll leave the reason to your imagination!) Meeting parents – a rather terrifying experience – a proposal engagement and then marriage.

Oh yes! Those old haunts have a lot to answer for.
Bette's Bygones. October 3, 2000.

You might think that there has been a mistake in the choice of viewpoint for the modern picture compared with the old one, but no! The old picture shows a scene totally unfamiliar today, when shops etc. and properties on the west side of upper High Street ran continuously from St Martin's Lane to Park Street. This picture was taken in the 1890s, from what is now Clasketgate (then Butchery Street), before the properties were demolished to make was for Corporation Street. The Danish Butter Depot was open for business, as was the shop of A. Fisher. The butter depot shop was no doubt a 16th century half-timbered building under the later façade, as was possibly the Flying Horse Inn, just to the left of the centre. This was a notorious 'rough house' at the weekend and appears to have closed when the photograph was taken. At the top right can just be seen the sign for Boots' Cash Chemists. Today, the premises is Lincoln Job Centre. The shops in Corporation Street are modern replacements for the original shops built when the street was made.

September Brings Back School Memories

THE MONTH of September brings just one thought to many people. To mums, its a spot of relief; to children, its the dreaded Return to School. I found a photograph which brought back to me memories of the time when I left my junior school and went to the City School, Lincoln. It was in 1946 and at the tender age of 10, when I joined some 90 other new pupils at one of Lincoln's four Grammar Schools. The change from my days at Westgate Boys' School came as a bit of a shock to the system.

I had already visited the City School a few months earlier. To pass the exam to get to the school, you had to take a written test and then be interviewed by the head-

Reunion: Sponsoring Peer of The City School, Lincoln, Association, at the House of Lords, Lord Molloy (third from right), with, left to right Alec Wood, John Hudson, Frank Harris, John Lello and John Maddison (president).

master, in this case, Mr Arthur Sutcliffe, who later became Director of Education for Lincoln. The first person we met was our form master, Mr John Hudson and we soon learned that his nickname was 'Soapy'. We were issued with more books and equipment than we had ever seen before. We learned what a vocabulary was. Log tables were a complete mystery to use (no calculators in those days) and there were lessons in subjects we had never taken before. Chemistry, Physics, Technical Drawing, Woodworking.

Physical Education at junior school had consisted of simple movements. Now it took place in a fitted gymnasium and we were introduced into such sports as football, cricket and boxing. Then, there was the school orchestra. If you were inclined and not completely tone deaf, then there was the opportunity to learn to play an instrument. I chose the violin and later also played the viola. The love of music has stayed with me to this day, but I no longer play.

But perhaps one of the biggest changes came in our appearance. Now that we were at Grammar School, we had to wear school uniform. Blazer, with badge. Grey short trousers (in the early days at the school). Socks with the school colours incorporated and of course, the school cap. Woe betide you if you were caught without it. It became something you either loved or hated. All I can say is that I have never worn a cap since! I remained at the school, which was then on Monks Road, for the next six years and made many friends, some of whom I am pleased to say, I still see today.

The photograph which brought back these memories to me? It was taken in 1993 when I was invited by the City School, Lincoln, Association to attend their annual reunion to take photographs for the *Echo*. It took place at the Houses of Parliament and present were Mr Hudson, my first form teacher, who recently died, together with two of my other teachers, Mr Alec Wood and Mr Frank Harris.

Lincolnian's Diary. September 2, 1999.

Activities To Keep Boys Attention

THE BOYS BRIGADE was founded in October 1883 at North Woodside Mission Hall in Glasgow by William Alexander Smith (later Sir William) who started as a teacher in the Sabbath School held in the Mission Hall.

He found the older boys bored and suspicious of teachers who told them to sit still. In short typical teenagers. He had the idea of Drill and Discipline and set up a programme of games, discipline, gymnastics and sport as well as hymns and prayers. Their badge was an anchor

and the motto Sure and Steadfast. This new way of dealing with boys soon spread and by the end of the third year the movement numbered 2,000 and then filtered into England.

The Lincoln Burton Road Methodist Boys Brigade was founded in 1950. Carl Markham now their captain was one of those founder members and recalls the early days when the ranks were full. 'We had a full band in the '60s which won many awards and in the '70s a very successful drum and fife band. In those days there were not so many diversions and outside activities to take our interest. The cinema and church just about covered it all. But through the brigade we had some great times,' he said. The

activities covered sport and the company gave regular gymnastic displays to capacity audiences in the Lincoln Drill Hall. The band would parade at civic and other events.

In those days there were also other companies attached to various Methodist Chapels in the city but the Boys Brigade is totally undenominational. 'We welcome all young lads from six onwards. We still keep the standards set in 1883 but have more up to date activities in line with modern life,' said Captain Markham. In the beginning William Smith did not find it all plain-sailing. The lads often faced opposition and criticism. The uniform would attract scorn and in the worst cases drill parades were conducted under a barrage of stones.

Summer camps were organised which gave the lads a chance to relax. The summer camps, organised in conjunction with the Battalion, are still a highlight of the programme and this year the Burton Road Company are going to Burnham-on-Sea in Somerset. 'We really enjoy these breaks. We get to know the lads and it gives them a bit of independence,' said Captain Markham. 'Burton Road has commemorated this golden anniversary with reunions and services. It was a wonderful weekend recalling many memories. It's a method of gentle training and persuasion into a discipline way of life that brings it's own rewards. Nothing can change those aims.'

Bette's Bygones. April 18, 2000.

For many years, Sincil Drain had been a stream with grassy banks from which youngsters frequently fished. In the 1960s, it was all change when the drain, prone to flooding after heavy rain, was drained and a concrete lined waterway constructed. (Echo Ref. RI-4194)

Boxing Memories From The City School

ONE of my old school chums who regularly writes to me, Nev Needham, found an old school photograph and thought I might be interested in using it on this page. It is of the City School Boxing Champions and was taken in 1947, the background I recognise as 'The Huts', as the lower school classrooms were called, on account of them being just that, wooden classrooms. Nev, who was Light Heavyweight Champion, is on the right at the back, next to the Heavyweight Champion Roy? Esberger. Seated, in the centre of the picture, is Physical Education teacher Bob Summerson, known to some as 'Ginger' but to many as 'Tiger'.

I remember him trying to teach me the rudiments of the noble art of fisticuffs, but as I was mostly on the receiving end of everything, I soon took up the job of 'second' at the boxing tournament and got

quite adept at waving a towel as a fan during the intervals. For some reason, I have hated boxing ever since. Nev thinks I might recognise some of the others on the picture. I can pick out Frank Rylatt, on 'Tiger's' right, with, I think, Roy Fines, on his left. At the right hand end of the front row is Alan Campling and there are a couple of other faces I remember, but not the names. No doubt someone will.

The picture caused much interest and further information, with phone calls from two former fellow pupils who I had not spoken to for several years. The first call came from Richard Fines, who said that no doubt his brother Roy would be delighted that I had taken about five years off his age. I had confused Richard with Roy, my apologies. Richard and I went to school together even before the City School! Another call came from Barry Kinnersley, after someone told him that he had seen the picture in *The Way We Were*. Barry said he was the one with he skinny arms on the right of the middle row. He thinks it must be because the picture was taken just after the war and they hadn't been 'fattened-up' yet.

Fifties fighters: Boxers of The City School, Lincoln, in 1951-2.

As a result of these calls, I now have an almost complete list of names, although some first names might be wrong. Back row are John? Marvin, Roy Esberger and Nev Needham. On the centre row are Ray Hall, Frank Rylatt, Mr Bob Summerson, Richard Fines and Barry Kinnersley. The front row list is not quite complete, but could be ? Eccleshare, Ken Mason, the next person's name has eluded everyone (although they all remember him), and Alan Campling.

It now appears that the picture may have been taken a year later than originally thought, ie, in 1948 and I have just had a letter from Raymond Hopes, who now lives in Newmarket (just shows how far *The Way We Were* travels). Raymond says that the 'big lad' standing in the middle of the back row is John Thurgur and not Roy Esberger. He tells me that Roy played soccer for the school and then went on to play for London University. John was often called 'Henry' at school, says Raymond. It was bestowed on him by Canon Ozzie Jones, a teacher at the City School, for no better reason than that was John's brother's name. I can also remember we had a very talented pianist at school, A.P. Percival, who was always known as 'Appy'. Now I wouldn't mind betting that it

was Ozzie who gave him that name!

Then in came another picture. An old friend, David Wilson, who now lives in North Hykeham, sent it to me and he is on the front row, second from left. David remembers some of the names, Talbot, Bebbington, Hinch, Challis, Bob White, Billy Beevors and Mayer. I can recognise Bill Hird (back row, third from left), Jim Bebbington (back row, fifth from right), and Ken Wood (middle row, third from left). Ken was the same build and weight as myself, so we were usually paired up during boxing lessons. He always won! His school nickname was 'Timber' and by coincidence, he worked at one time for a Lincoln timber company. Sadly, Jim Bebbington and Ken Wood have died recently. The Physical Education teacher (centre of back row) was Mr Newman Lister. Unlike the other picture, which was taken in the school playground, this one was taken on the stage of the school hall.

Like David, there are a number of faces on the picture which I can recognise but can't put names to. I would like to bet that someone can!

Lincolnian's Diary. Various dates, December 2000 and January 2001.

Best boxers: The title holders pose for their picture at The City School in 1947.

In 1901, Saltergate was just a narrow lane which at one time, was called Prison Lane, with the city jail being situated in what is now part of Lincoln Guildhall. On the left are the premises of C. Pratt and Sons, a noted Lincoln wine and spirit merchant and beyond them is T.L. Lidgett's shop which sold mainly watches and clocks, but with other household commodities also on sale. Jacksons have been dyers and cleaners in the city since 1841, but their business dates back to 1791, with origins in Newark. On the right is the Falcon Hotel, the proprietor in those days being Frank Lobley. Now it is the Falcon Inn.

The present day scene shows a much wider street (it was reconstructed in 1904) and there is a reminder of Pratt's to be found in the sign of The Still, which was the name of their public bar in 1901 and now the name of a public house.

Home Made Fun And Games

I WAS watching children playing during their long summer holidays the other day and it set me thinking of my own schooldays half-a-century ago.

We didn't have videos to watch and electronic games so how did we amuse ourselves? Mechanical toys, if we had any, were usually clockwork and many of our playthings were home-made. In the summertime, two split canes and some strong paper or light cloth would make a kite, a long string tail with pieces of rolled-up newspaper helping to keep the balance and keep it stable. But we were not allowed to fly kites during the war years in case they got caught up in aeroplane propellers. Those planes would have to have been flying very low to get tangled up with our kites!

Cricket was usually played with a bat cut from a piece of wood – a piece of old gate or fence was ideal and the wicket was either chalked on a house wall, or a convenient lamppost was used. No hard ball, just a tennis ball or rubber ball. Mind you, if the local bobby came across us playing in the street, we were in for a good telling off. Football was also a street game, again with a lookout for the law and with a small ball instead of a proper football.

We used to make furnaces out of clay if we could get it from the old brick pits near to the West Common, in Lincoln. It would be fashioned into a hollowed-out rectangular block with a loose fitting lid and holes in the sides. Filled with material which would smoulder when lit, we would then run down the street holding the furnace in the air to leave a trail of smoke from the holes. Sometimes, the material burned too well and the furnace would become so hot, you burned your fingers. A tin can was a good substitute if you didn't have clay. This was carried with a string handle. We also used the clay for another game. We called it 'snobs', but in other places it was known as 'jacks' or 'five-stones'. Clay was shaped into cubes, about the size of a beefstock cube, dried and painted and then thrown up into the air to be caught on the back of the hand. If there was no clay available, we made them from Plaster of Paris.

Whip and top was another popular pastime and the tops had coloured patterns chalked on them so they would change colour when spinning. We also played cowboys and Indians, but without weapons. Our fingers and hands imitated these, though sometimes a piece of wood was shaped into the shape of a 'six-gun', but if you had this, then you were 'posh'. Games in which you took tuns to play usually heard the call of 'foggy', 'seggy', 'laggy'; these expressions indicating that you wanted to go first, second or last.

Picture cards found in cigarette packets (or 'fag-cards') as we called them, were used in a variety of games and if you couldn't get hold of these, then the round cardboard tops from milk bottles were a good substitute.

Lincolnian's Diary. August 10, 1999.

There is a clue in this old picture of Lincoln as to its location. The sign above the Black Swan Inn is still there today, locating the scene as being at the junction of the Cornhill with High Street. The old picture shows a cobbled High Street and on the left of the picture, the tall building was the first Lincoln Dispensary, dating from 1826. On the corner, the building with shuttered windows displays the name E. Robinson, a jeweller. This shop and Luddington's hosiery, boot and shoe warehouse was demolished in 1873 to make way for the erection of the Midland Banking Company's premises, which later became and still is, Barclay's Bank. The original bank building was demolished in the second half of the 20th century and replaced with a modern metal and glass construction, but the original inn and shops still retain their old character, except for modern frontages at street level.

A scene full of nostalgia for many and seldom seen today. Steam traction engines and threshing machines have been replaced with combined harvesters and pictures like this, taken at Grange-de-Lings in 1938, are just a memory. (Echo Ref. RI-390)

How many children can you get on to a tree in the park? These youngsters back in 1957 seemed to trying to provide an answer at Boultham Park fete and gala, held to raise money for the blind. (Echo Ref. RI-1376B)

In War and Peace

Historic Meeting Above The Clouds

MANY people fly when going on their holidays abroad, but not many are privileged to be able to fly over their 'home area' and see familiar sights from a 'bird's-eye view'. Over the years, I have done more flying over Lincolnshire than I have in airliners, in planes ranging from two-seaters up to a giant Hercules. My first flight was from RAF Hemswell with Lincoln Aero Club over Lincoln Cathedral and since that time, back in the 1960s, I have flown over the city many times to take pictures, including a flight in a helicopter, which provided a wonderful platform for taking pictures.

The flight in a Hercules was with members of the local Territorial Army Parachute Regiment, who were taking part in a parachute drop in Norfolk, as part of a training weekend. It is an aircraft which is huge inside and very noisy when the rear doors are opened to allow paratroopers or payloads to be dropped. I was

Spectacular view: The memorable occasion when a Vulcan and a Hastings carried out a rendezvous above the clouds.

allowed up on to the flight deck for the return journey to Coningsby and it was amazing to see how much space there was on the flight deck compared with the cramped conditions on most of the planes in which I had flown.

Gliding was another flying experience I have had and it is wonderful soaring up in the sky without noise. My first glider trip was on the day when American President John F. Kennedy flew into RAF Waddington on his way to a family grave in Derbyshire and I had to wait for take off until his plane had cleared the area.

But the most spectacular flight was with the Royal Air Force, in the 1970s, when

they realised that there were no pictures of a Vulcan flying with a Hastings. Two Hastings took off with

photographers aboard for a rendezvous with the Vulcan. It was a very misty day, so after take off, we never saw land again until touch-down. The door and windows had been taken out of the Hastings to give us better pictures and the three planes kept swapping positions to give everyone a chance for pictures. But the most spectacular sight was when the Vulcan, flying only a few feet away, peeled off, presenting us with a view of the giant plane from underneath. We also saw the shadow of our own plane on the clouds below us, circled by a complete rainbow.
Lincolnian's Diary. October 31, 2000.

When The Evacuees Came

WHEN the evacuees came we took in three. A brother and sister – Gladys and Albert Hogg and Sylvia Jennings. They came from Grimsby and at first were as wary as I had been of country life. When Dad lit the old oil lamp it cast eerie, dancing shadows on the walls. Sylvia looked apprehensive.

'Look' said mam, 'Let's make pictures on the wall' and cupping her hands she made images of butterflies, dogs and elephants dancing across the flowered wallpaper. It became a nightly game and then we would listen to programmes like *Monday Night at Eight* – try to guess the mystery guest and off to bed with a cup of cocoa made with water. Tucked up in a feather bed and blankets and an eiderdown on the top it was the thing that dreams were made of.
Bette's Bygones. September 14, 1999.

Celebration: Crowds gather at Lincoln Stonebow in May 1945, to celebrate Victory in Europe. (Echo Ref. RI-578A)

Proud Of The Home Front

THE evacuees were installed. Dunkirk was history and we had conquered the skies. Now the war turned to the civilians and the bombardment began. The Underground became the shelter – the bedroom of thousands of people. Others slept in the Andersons – corrugated arks sunk in the ground and covered with earth. Small paraffin heaters were the only warmth. Bunk beds were built – probably the forerunner of the modern day bunks for children. But the mattresses were made of straw and with condensation they became damp. But it was a haven against the bombs – the noise and the whining of the He's spiralling down.

Barrage balloons covered the skies in the hope of forcing attacking aircraft to heights at which accurate bombing became difficult. Balloons were made by girls at Littlewood's of Liverpool, the football pools firm. Thousands of people were killed during the air raids – many of them in London but the coastal and industrial towns also suffered. It has been said that people in the Laughton area of Lincolnshire could see flames from the Sheffield big raid lighting up the sky. And Hull got a pretty good hammering. And it is only this week, 60 years later that a memorial has been unveiled in their honour.

Civilians, especially women, faced every day life of home and hearth. Many had husbands in fighting zones and many had no idea where they were. Others were war widows or one of that twilight brigade with husbands posted 'missing'. But they had to carry on each night after a hard day's work, after planning the meals from meagre rations, seeing that the kids were alright. They faced the bombing not knowing if they would wake up again.

On April 12, 1941, that great orator Winston Churchill said: 'I see the damage done by the enemy attacks; but I also see, side by side with the devastation and amid the ruins, quiet, confident, bright smiling eyes, beaming with a consciousness of being associated with a cause far higher and wider than any other human personal issue. I can see the spirit of an unconquerable people.'

Graffiti slogans appeared on walls saying: 'We Can Take It', or 'Back as soon as we beat Hitler'. And a famous one outside a bomb damaged police station warned: 'Be good – we are still open.' The Air Raid Wardens and Auxiliary Fire Service were heroes. An Air Raid Warden tackled fire bombs, equipped his post with first aid supplies, found the injured against all the odds and always had a word of comfort – unless you did something daft like showing a light or trying to loot. Then you were in real trouble. Nurses, very often, young girls in their teens dealt with the injured and kept going night and day. Emergency facilities were set up for the homeless by the social services.

These very ordinary people were the unknown warriors who kept up morale not only for the people at home but also through letters and radio programmes for the forces. Home Front was something to be proud of!

Bette's Bygones. September 12, 2000.

Back in 1957, there was the rare sight of a Red Indian Chief, in full costume, riding his horse through the centre of Lincoln. It was all part of a publicity stunt for Chipperfield's Circus, which was appearing on the South Common, Lincoln. Big Chief Eagle Eye rode his horse, at the head of a covered wagon through the city centre to advertise the circus's visit. (Echo Picture Ref. RI-2425) In the background are buildings which have disappeared to make way for a road improvement. Gone are the Great Northern Hotel, St Mark's Church (it's spire can just be seen) and Whitton and Ashley's wine merchants, together with Whitton's Bar.

Today's picture shows the changes which have been made and in place of the buildings are shops and a multi-storey car park with the beginning of Wigford Way, linking High Street and Newland. This was originally planned to form part of an inner ring road for the city, but after Wigford Way was built, the remainder of the scheme was scrapped.

National Service Was Two Years Of Freedom

IN THE 1950s Lincoln was invaded with a sea of khaki and airforce blue – the uniform of the lads serving their two years National Service. In 1947 the war heroes had returned and were settling into civvy street. Those called up at the end of the war were ready for demob and Labour Prime Minister Clement Attlee needed a peace-keeping force. On January l, 1949 he bought in National Service calling lads of 18 and over to serve in the forces.

Injured: Arthur Mann reflects on his experience of the Korean War where he was seriously wounded by a hand grenade.

The Sobraon Barracks, Lincoln hosted thousands of young recruits for their square bashing basic training and Royal Air Force Swinderby was the training ground for the RAF. They were trained to a high degree of fitness and after a few weeks confined to camp or barracks they were raring to go – the lasses of Lincoln had a field day! Best-selling author Leslie Thomas made his name by including autobiographical fragments of his National Service days in his book *The Virgin Soldiers*. Later made into a film it told the story of recruits serving with the British army in Singapore. It was a ground breaker for the British film industry with below the belt tales of sex and prostitution.

English cricketer Freddie Trueman was stationed at RAF Hemswell and was often seen bowling his way through the main gates. It was at the start of his success and he was surrounded by both genders when he went to dances or for a drink in the Palm Court of the White Hotel, Gainsborough. He was admired not only for his cricket but for not backing out of his duty as many other famous people did.

As soon as he was 18 young Hermun Eaton of Waddington Heath, was called up to serve in the army. He first went to Oswestry in Shropshire and then for six weeks square bashing at Rhyl. 'It was a rude awakening but if you adopted the right attitude you got on OK and could even enjoy your service', he said. He was posted to 15 Medium Royal Artillery and served in Germany, the Far East and Hong Kong. But he did not bite the carrot Attlee offered of more pay for those who signed on for extra time. National servicemen feel that the service they gave in spheres such as Malaya, Kenya, Cyprus and Palestine has been shovelled into the ground. Many Lincoln lads served in these areas and were killed in uprisings that have never been recognised as wars.

Arthur Mann of Lincoln who describes himself as being a 'bit of a lad', trained national servicemen. 'I was a regular but trained and served with national servicemen who did an excellent job' he said. Whilst serving with the Royal Northumberland Fusiliers he was sent to Korea. 'On October 5, 1951, we were ordered to attack what became known as Hellbox Hill, as we reached the top of the hill we were fired on from three sides. A hand grenade exploded in my face and I sank to my knees. But not for one moment did I realise the extent of my wounds which had blown half my face away including the jawbones', he recalled. There followed many years of suffering, hospitalisation, bone and skin grafting. But Arthur has turned trouble into triumph. He is well known throughout the world for his evangelism and ministry and for the work he did as director co-ordinator of the Lincoln Nomad Trust.

A lot of the lads saw this era as two years of freedom – an opportunity to get away from home. And with every other building on Lincoln High Street a pub or hotel drink was a problem that often resulted in fights. Military and RAF Police were a familiar sight rounding up the lads for the wagons which took them back to camp after a night out. The Co-op

Policemen: Corporals Steven Vickers and John Avery in Royal Air Force Police uniforms, while at RAF Hemswell, near Lincoln.

Ballroom and the Drill Hall weekly dances were excellent mating grounds and many a romance started with a quickstep or modern waltz. When dances were held at local camps the girls were bussed in and the bus inspected before they were allowed through the gates. On one occasion at RAF Hemswell a girl put her hand through the bus window and knocked the sergeant's hat off – the buses were turned back and the dance cancelled. She was never allowed back on camp.

Short: Corporal Steven Vickers after three hair cuts all in one day.

The rock and roll era dawning – Teddy Boys with long hair took the scene – much to the consternation of the national service lads who still had short back and sides. And on between 30s (£1.50p) and 35s (£1.75p) a week they could not compete with civvy street earners. Cinema tickets ranged from a shilling (5p) to 3s 6d (17½p). If your date hit pay day you could manage the 2s 3d's (11½p) – otherwise – hard cheese.

This part of the era was very important and heralded new horizons that have gone on to change our lives in a way we never imagined. But it was a good time, the war was over and everyone was set to enjoy the peace.

Bette's Bygones. September 7, 1999.

Sombre Reflection On Quiet Beaches

WE MAY have re-treated but we were not defeated – we were not beaten – not by a long chalk! This was echoed and re-echoed throughout the weekend of May 30–June 3, 1980 when I was privileged to return to those beaches with a party of veterans from the 237/60th Field Regiment Royal Artillery Old Comrades Association, men from other regiments and friends from Lincoln. To look at the peaceful beaches and dunes it was hard to imagine the hell they had gone through after France had fallen.

'The order came through – all roads lead to Dunkirk – every man for himself. God Bless you all,' said Jack Bartlett. 'We were told to destroy all weapons and make our way to the port.' 'The noise, smoke and flames were horrendous,' said Mr Ben Owen who for many years was the proud standard bearer of the association. 'When we hit Bray Dunes at Le Panne we dug ourselves in with bare hands and mess tins.'

Bert Atkinson recalled the horrific scenes on the beaches and the scenes of great bravery. One member of the Royal Medical Corps found himself in a Le Panne hotel where the wounded lay in the basement. 'We were cleaning the wounds with spirits and wine – it was all we had. When the end came we drew lots to decide who was to get away. We left an officer, three non-commissioned officers and about 18 men. I never knew if they made it,' he recalled.

Remembering friends: Standards mustered for the annual parade through Dunkirk, in 1980.

When the Lincoln party first arrived they were laughing and joking among themselves and then one by one, they strolled along the beaches, picking up the sand

Scene of great bravery: Bray Dunes, at le Panne, where many of the survivors dug in before being evacuated.

and letting it sift through their fingers in moments of sombre reflection. 'The thing that amazed me most was that as we looked across the channel the water was as smooth as a mill pond. Otherwise I don't think the evacuation would have been possible,' said one veteran. But at the Le Panne parade they marched with pride through the town they had crawled from 40 years before.
Bette's Bygones. May 30, 2000.

Enemy Aircraft Became Trophy

IT WAS a warm summer evening in July 1942. And not far from Lincoln City football ground, a group of boys were playing. The horrors of the Second World War seemed a million miles away, as they clambered onto the roof of an air raid shelter at the bottom of St Andrew's Street. Suddenly all thoughts of play came to an abrupt halt as the drone of an aircraft could be heard. If they had known anything about enemy aircraft they would have spotted it was a Junkers 88. And they watched as it flew above nearby South Park and headed east.

Although it was too low for them to see, another Junkers 88 was flying parallel to it, above Scorer Street. The aircraft were on their way home after a bombing mission over Manchester which had left a 10-year-old girl dead and her brother seriously injured in New Mills and had killed a chapel caretaker. But the two aircraft were never to leave Lincolnshire.

Lincoln war historian and author, Fred Hurt, recalls the incident which happened 58 years ago yesterday. 'The two enemy aircraft were spotted by the Saxilby Observer Corps post. The RAF at Kirton Lindsey sent up four Spitfires and a Beaufighter to counter the threat. The Junkers continued so low along the River Witham that they made waves on the water as they passed Washing-borough. Four Spitfires were in hot pursuit as the planes swooped over Bardney bridge and the first one was shot down south of Baumber, crashing into a barn and bursting into flames. The second plane was chased across Horncastle before the same Polish Spitfire pilot scored hits on one of its engines causing it to crash land in a small field at As-wardby. The crew scrambled clear as the plane caught fire and they were arrested by the local Home Guard.' Fred adds: 'The tail plane of the second Junkers was cut off and taken as a victors' trophy to No 303 Polish Squadron headquarters at Kirton Lindsey.'
The Gossiper. July 4, 2000.

Scampton At Forefront Of Aviation Technology

RAF Scampton's illustrious history dates back to November 1916 when it came into being under the name of Brattleby.

Throughout its 80 year plus of history the station has been at the forefront of aviation technology. According to records of the RAF Scampton Historical Museum, who supplied our information, the first function of the station was that of a Searchlight Defence Unit. However, as the First World War progressed, the base became an Operational Training Unit using a variety of well-known aircraft of that day such as the Avro 504, Sopwith Camel, Pup and Dolphin. When the First World War ended in 1918 Scampton was slowly run down and in the 1920s the land was returned to the agricultural community.

When Hitler came into power during the 1930s and the threat of war hovered on the horizon the government decided that the armed forces needed strengthening and began a vast rebuilding programme on RAF stations. Scampton became a permanent establishment of the RAF. The base was reactivated in 1936 and four 'C' hangars and the Technical Site was built. By the outbreak of the Second World War, Scampton had the new Handley Page Hampden operated by 49 and 83 squadrons. In 1940 the base achieved acclaim through a double award of the Victoria Cross. Flight Lieutenant Rod Learoyd and Sergeant John Hannah won the award for their bravery during the attack on the Dortmund Em's Canal.

Bravery: Sergeant John Hannah who was awarded the Victoria Cross at the age of 19 for putting out flames when his aircraft caught fire.

In May 1943 the base again brought to the forefront of Bomber Command with the famous attack against the

Intelligence: Briefing before a raid at RAF Scampton. The basket of homing pigeons on the table were taken to use if the plane crashed.

Mohne and Eder Dams. The raid was led by Wing Commander Guy Gibson who earned the station its third and perhaps most famous Victoria Cross. Up to the end of the war Scampton was one of the most fully operational bases in Bomber Command. During the Berlin airlift in the late 1940s the base was used by the United States as a loading station with the mighty B-29 Super Fortress. It has had a chequered history.

In 1952 with the introduction of the English Electric Canberra, RAF Scampton entered the Jet Age. 1954 saw the station being used as a film set when the industry made the wartime classic of *The Dam Busters* starring Richard Todd as Guy Gibson and Michael Redgrave as Barnes Wallis the inventor of the bouncing bomb. The base was closed in 1956 for an expansion programme to cope with the mighty Vulcan bombers. In 1983 it changed from Strike Command to Support Command and for the following 10 years was also the home of the world famous Red Arrows aerobatic team.

When the drastic cuts were made in the defence budget the base was reduced to a care and maintenance unit but it's reputation and contribution to our history will live forever. *Bette's Bygones September 28, 1999.*

Preparations: A wartime photograph of Hampden aircraft in the process of being bombed up on the field of RAF Scampton ready for another operation.

City's War Effort Is Part Of History

THOUGHTS will be turning this month to that time, 60 years ago, when the Battle of Britain was raging in the skies above our country. But 86 years ago, on August 4, 1914, the First World War started. Some called it 'The Great War'. Why, I wonder? What is great about war, if it lasts six days, six weeks or six years?

However, there is no doubt that it changed the lives of many in Lincoln although thankfully, the city suffered much less than many through bomb damage. Perhaps the most important thing for Lincoln in the First World War was the invention of the tank, at the Lincoln factory of William Foster and Co. Ltd. For secrecy purposes, the project referred to these weapons as 'Water Carriers for Mesopotamia' a name soon changed by workers to tanks.

On September 15, 1916, they rolled into action across the Somme ridges. Only 48 of the new weapons went into

Important invention: A 'Matilda' tank leaving Ruston and Hornsby factory in 1941.

action. Had it been 10 times more, it might have resulted in a major victory, but whatever, it caught the enemy by surprise and may have been the turning point in the war. During the Second World War, tanks continued to be made in Lincoln, this time at Ruston and Hornsby's factory. They were Matildas and their name is still remembered today in the name of a road in Lincoln. The first Matilda tank to be sent to the Middle East was made by Rustons and by the time they had been superseded by heavier weapons, some 400 were used by both the British and Russian armies. As a weapon, it was slow and heavy. It's armour was three and a half inches thick and it weighed 26 tons, but it could take a lot of punishment. It's main armament was a 2 pounder gun.

It wasn't the only thing made in Lincoln for the war effort and Ruston engines powered equipment for all services. On the last day of the war, a map was found in a captured Luftwaffe headquarters. It was of one of bombing targets and was in fact, an aerial photograph of Lincoln, showing the Ruston factories. It was taken on September 3, 1939, the day war broke out. Thankfully, it seemed not to have been used a lot and no doubt some of that had to do with the skill of the RAF and defences around the city.

One of the great pleasures in writing stories for this diary comes from some of the unexpected sequels after the publication of the story. A few weeks ago, I wrote about tanks being produced in Lincoln and illustrated the article with a picture of a Matilda tank rolling out of the Ruston and Hornsby factory. Sat on the tank were a man and a woman, together with a teenage boy.

Last week, I had a phone call from London, with some very interesting information. On the front of the tank was the name Garfield Weston. My caller was Mr Guy Weston and the young boy on the tank was his father, Garry. The other people were Guy's uncle and aunt, Grainger and Miriam Weston. The name Garfield Weston was that of his grandfather, who was Member of Parliament for Macclesfield. He was also an entrepreneur in the world of bread and biscuit bakeries, taking over Burton's, a well known biscuit manufacturer. He paid for the tank and also a number of Spitfire's and Guy has just discovered that there is a model of a Spitfire on sale, bearing the name Garfield Weston.

During the Second World War, many individuals, companies and towns bought tanks and Spitfires to help the war effort. In Lincoln, a fund was set up to purchase a Spitfire. Garry Weston was the person who 'invented' the popular chocolate biscuit, Wagon Wheels and he retired earlier this year as chairman of Associated British Foods. Guy tells me that his father is still alive, as are the other eight children of the generation and he was thrilled to see the picture published in *The Way We Were.*
Lincolnian's Diary. August 15 & September 5, 2000.

Tank's birthplace: Tanks of the 'Mother' type under construction at Foster's factory, in Lincoln.

There was plenty of snow around in February 1955 when these two boys spent part of their half-term holiday building a snowman in the grounds of Lincoln Sessions House and then using it as a target for their snowballs. (Echo Ref. RI-2550)

Women Proved A Point

HAVING been one of the first women to be trained as a meteorologist, leading aircraftwoman Rose Bell and two of her companions were posted to RAF Waddington and found themselves the first girls in an office still staffed by civilian men. It was all very strange. Rose, the daughter of a Yorkshire farmer, had joined the Women's Auxiliary Air Force in rebellion against her father who had refused to allow her to take up her chosen career of teaching.

'We were between two worlds. The civilian one of the met office and the service one of the Women's Auxiliary Air Force. With low cunning we soon found that we could use the requirements of the office as an excuse to evade the more irksome service duties. We did shift work so had an excuse for absence from parades and inspections.' But they were caught out! 'For some weeks the "met" girls absented themselves from the weekly "free from infection" inspection. Then we got a notice that stated that we must attend the next FFI. We chose to ignore it. The next evening found us scrubbing out the "wafferie" as a punishment. Needless to say we did not default again,' she said. 'The inspection was for lice, scabies and venereal disease. At first the men thought it a joke to have women in the exclusively male meteorological office. We had to work hard to prove that were capable of doing the job. Any feminine foibles, such as fear of the dark had to be suppressed because we had to do weather observations every hour – day and night – and anyone who needed escorting outside in the dark to do her observations was not very popular.

'Occasionally they would walk us back to the "wafferie" if it was very dark and on one pitch black, foggy night I set off with two of the forecasters to get back to my billet. We walked and walked without getting to my destination. Finally I asked them if they knew where they were taking me. Amid guffaws of laughter they told me we had just walked three times around the biggest hanger and they had a bet to see how many times I would do it before I smelt a rat. After that I bought a torch and became independent.'

Rose was promoted to Corporal. She stayed in Lincolnshire and married a farmer – something she swore she would never do.
Bette's Bygones. July 18, 2000.

The Days Of War

THE PEOPLE of Lincoln have been thinking back to those dark days of the Second World War, for a project by the organisers of next year's Community Play. The stories have been published in a new book, *Memories of Lincoln,* which was so successful it sold out in under two weeks. Now a second edition is available. There's one memory that a wartime child living near Lincoln will never forget.

'During one night-time air raid, my dad fetched us out of the cellar and into the back yard which overlooked the whole of Lincoln and the Trent Valley. There were no lights, only searchlights from the aerodromes. Some bombers were coming back and there were tracer bullets flying all over the place. I think German fighters had followed them and there was a bit of a fight going on over Lincoln. I remember my dad saying, 'I'll show you this because you'll probably never see it again'.' The story is recounted in the Lincoln Community Play 2001 publication *Memories of Wartime Lincoln.*

It's packed with first-hand accounts taken from interviews with people who were around at the time. And the memories are neatly combined into sections dealing with the different stages and aspects of the hostilities. The only disappointment is that people recalling the events of the war, aren't named and you don't know their ages. So it isn't always clear whether the memory is that of a girl or boy, or a man or woman. But that aside, it's compelling reading and the memories come thick and fast. Air raid shelters in Sincil Bank are recalled by someone who was 11 at the time.

'The shelters were between the railway line and the school so if the school had suffered a direct hit we would all have been squashed. And there were no doors on the shelters. They were ever so cold, with just slatted seats down the side of brick walls running in water in winter. There we had to sit, with the wind blowing through like fury. It was a constant wind tunnel through these shelters. We used to sing and if the teacher was there we would recite tables. But we used to think it was better than being in the classroom.'

Another contributor to the book recalls, 'I remember very clearly the Battle of Arnhem, seeing the planes go over. We had been on Canwick Road and we looked up towards the cathedral and you could see them. It was like a traffic jam in the air. Nearly bumper to bumper the planes were going on, hour after hour.'

There are tales of narrow escapes. On the day the County Hospital was bombed, a woman was walking her dog down Canwick Road. 'One of the Germans shot at her near the railway bridge. When the bridge was taken down years later, you could see the bullet marks where they had cut the bricks. Fortunately, she wasn't hurt, because she stayed under the bridge.'

People worked long hours during the war and even routine jobs took on a dangerous side. A contributor recalls 'My dad was on the munitions trains and this time the sirens had gone. They used to have a knocker-up for the late shift, in case you didn't wake they got somebody round to knock you up. Mum and I were up because of the air raid and someone knocked on the passage door. They nearly frightened us to death. I grabbed the poker, mum grabbed the coal tongs and we went to see who was at the door. It was the knocker-up and he said 'I've come to remind Frank he should be at work.' Mum said, 'Well he hasn't come home yet from yesterday.'

And in those make and mend days, people learned to share even when times were at their hardest. Recalls a contributor, 'There was a wonderful air of camaraderie because you were all in it. If you got a parcel from overseas, or if you knew anyone in America or anywhere and they sent you a parcel, you shared it. After my husband went in the forces, I got a parcel from Denmark of bacon and butter and everyone in the street had a rasher.'
The Gossiper. April 11, 2000.

Reality Of War A Rude Awakening

IT TOOK two or three days for the declaration of the First World War to reach the villages. They held services, sang the National Anthem and waited. Then the recruiting campaign started. Volunteers and regulars in smart uniforms told of money in their pockets and women at their feet. 'You'll never regret it, lads,' said the Sergeant-Major. 'If enough men come in we shall polish them off by Christmas.'

The lads crowded to sign up. They marched out of the village to the sound of cheers and flag-waving children – they felt important for the first time in their lives. But it was a different story when they marched into the rat-ridden trenches – the singing turned to gunfire and they saw the price paid as they passed the field Red Cross stations with rows of wounded and dead. Many were shell-shocked, their nerves and minds shattered. There were no counsellors in those days – their reward was life in a military nursing home for the rest of their days. Many scared young lads were classed as cowards and shot.

Young Joe Vickers, wanting to get away from the

War veteran: Joe Vickers aged 20.

Lincolnshire Fens, volunteered when he was 18 and served with the Lincolnshire Regiment. 'It was a rude awakening! Before we went into battle we had a drumhead service, sang hymns and marched into hell!' he said. He was wounded three times in the shoulder, face and lungs, all gunshot wounds received in close combat. He served in several battles in France and then in Gallipoli where our troops withdrew in darkness. He lay wounded in a shell hole for 36 hours, playing his mouth organ to keep up the spirits of the others around him. When he was finally invalided out, he

went home – no bravery awards, no bands playing, just tossed back to where he came from. His pension was a pittance and Joe became an angry young man.

When he was fit enough, he got a job as a saddler. As soon as the pension board heard of it, they cut his award to 4s 6d (22½p). He welcomed the founding of the British Legion and became one of it s staunchest supporters. As a result he was made a Life President. His son visited the hill that had cost him so much – a mere mound in a field. As he got older he would bend and run – as if dodging machine gun fire. He

never forgot. One of his proudest duties was to lay the poppy wreath on the village memorial – and Joe always saluted as he did so. He rarely left the village again and spent his life on same road on which he was born. He'd seen enough of the world!
Bette's Bygones. August 1, 2000.

Medals: Memories of war pinned to his chest, Joe Vickers' war wounds earned him the right to wear the single blue and gold ribbon.

Digging Deep To Make Prototypes

IT IS SAD to hear that a Lincoln engineering company which once employed thousands is now reduced to a staff of about 40, with an uncertain future. Ruston-Bucyrus was a household name in the city and the present company is R.B. International Ltd. I remember is the 1960s going down to the factory in Beevor Street almost every week to take photographs and they produced a variety of excavators and cranes. Some of these are still in use today and only a few years ago, I saw one just outside Cologne, in Germany.

But it was during the Second World War that they might have produced a different product, indeed, they did produce prototypes. Winston Churchill, at the beginning of the war, was in the Admiralty, but as in the First World War, his thoughts were elsewhere at times. He

came up with the idea of a trench digging machine, to get our soldiers up to the Siegfried Line and surprise the Germans.

The idea was developed at Ruston-Bucyrus and a model made by the firm of Bassett-Lowke, a well-known name in model railway circles. It was taken from the secrecy of a Bath hotel to London, in a wooden box six feet long by two feet wide. When it was carried on to the railway platform at Bath, passengers bared their heads in respect and kept away from it in the first class carriage! After a few trials, the model worked so the order was sent to Lincoln to commence building the prototype. It was built in a bricked off section of the Lincoln factory and very few knew the real truth of what was happening.

Originally it was given the code name 'White Rabbit', but Churchill changed it to 'Cultivator No 6'. But the machine had been ordered by the Admiralty's Naval Land Equipment section, NLE, so the workers called it 'Nellie'. Unfortunately, the machine had been designed on a Rolls-Royce Merlin Aero Marine

engine and the Air Ministry requisitioned all of these engines for aeroplanes, so a different engine had to be found. Churchill came to see trials at Clumber Park and was delighted to see that it worked.

'Nellie' was a monster! More than 70 feet long, eight feet high and six-and-a-half feet wide. She weighed more than 120 tons. The trench she cut was five feet deep and the earth excavated piled up three feet on either side. Two hundred were ordered with 40 more of a larger type which could cut a trench large enough for a small tank to use. But 'Nellie' and what would have been a whole brood of 'White Rabbits' never came into action. The Germans had retreated from the Siegfried Line before the machines could be assembled, but the engines developed for 'Nellie' were put to use propelling tank landing craft in the Normandy invasion.

Who knows what might have been the fate of the Lincoln company had their skills been turned from making excavators and cranes into producing giant 'moles'?
Lincolnian's Diary. August 22, 2000.

When this bygone picture was taken in 1938, 'the policeman in the barrel' was a familiar sight at the bottom of Lindum Road controlling the traffic before the installation of traffic lights. He was there in all weathers, with only his cape for protection and had an impressive view of one of the city's busiest thoroughfares. On the right is the Constitutional Club and beyond it can be seen Broadgate Drill Hall. Further down Broadgate is Shipley & Co's ironmongers shop, on the corner of Unity Square (which at one time was called Jobber's Square). All of the buildings on the left, beyond Unity Square have now been demolished, with the exception of the public house on the corner of St Rumbold's Street.

The modern scene still has the Constitutional Club, but traffic lights have replaced the policeman and in the centre of Broadgate, there is now a barrier where cars once parked.

Waiting For War In The 1990s

IT WAS the sort of headline that *Echo* readers thought they would never see again. But 10 years ago today, the message was only too clear. 'Waiting for war' was how we announced the country was on an emergency footing as the Middle East situation deteriorated. And today we recall how the county was bracing itself for the worst.

Almost seven years had gone by since the last patient had left the old USAF hospital at Nocton Hall. It had served the community and the military authorities well for many years. But when the doors had slammed shut, it had been difficult to imagine any circumstances when the hospital might ever be pressed into service once again. Then, of course, we didn't know about the horrors of a Gulf War. By December 1990 it was on everbody's lips. And Nocton Hall was gearing itself up for an expected influx of casualties from a war in the Middle East.

The *Echo* reported how the hospital was ready to cater for up to 750 troops suffering from almost any kind of injury if fighting were to break out in the Gulf. The plan of action included flying American and British injured via RAF Waddington and then transporting the injured the last few miles by road, using a fleet of up to 16 ambulances. Commanders at the old American military hospital were even anticipating calling on people living in the area to help as volunteers if and when the going got really tough.

Colonel Dr Fred Fishburn, commander from Lakenheath Military Hospital, told one of my colleagues at the time 'We will need all the help we can get. I am certain the local villagers will help as they always have in times of war and national disaster. They can help serve meals, help with the home comforts and personal attention the patients will need.' He added 'They certainly won't need any medical experience to help as volunteers. We hope we won't have to put these plans into use. Nocton Hall is like a seat belt on a car – as long as the possibility exists, we have to be here.'

During the seven years when the hospital has been without patients, it was far from deserted. Cleaning, maintenance and keeping drugs and supplies up to date had kept a dozen US Air Force staff busy since 1983. But the prospect of a Gulf war meant the hospital could soon resume the role it had during the Second World War. The station commander at Nocton Hall back in 1990 was captain Steve Drinan. Until the crisis arose he had been expecting to move on, at the end of his three-year posting. But he was now destined to stay on until the situation had come to an end. He recalled at the time 'The hospital was built in 1943 by the US army as a contingency facility. We never stop fixing the buildings and getting in new supplies and drugs. It has been a dynamic process since 1983 and has always been a busy job – even more so since August when the Iraquis went into Kuwait.'

The *Echo* reported how there were $7.5 million in supplies and equipment at the hospital and the facilities were ready for use at the drop of a hat. A dozen staff had been keeping the 21 wards ready for action, but as the threat of war loomed, 50 more were drafted in to prepare for the worst.
The Gossiper. December 5, 2000.

Straight To Bed

TWO weeks ago, in *Lincolnshire in the News*, there was a story, from September 1940, about the alarm caused when church bells rang in Lincoln.

Lorna Nicholls has vivid memories of that night, when as a teenager, she lived with her parents on Canwick Road, only a few yards away from St Andrew's Church, which was one of the five churches in Lincoln, where the bells were rung in error. They should have only been rung if invasion was imminent. She says that they were fast asleep and were awakened by the ringing of the bells. They all got up, dressed and went into the street, as did their neighbours. They really expected that German troops had landed and after waiting for a short time, with nothing happening, they all went back to bed.

Next morning, they learnt that it had been a mistake and it was not until reading the article in the *Echo* that Lorna realised that there were only five churches in Lincoln which had rung the bells. Lorna, a retired schoolteacher, says that that she thinks it was the only time she was really afraid during the war years. The bombs which dropped on Lincoln in the following years were not so alarming as hearing the sound of those bells in the middle of the night. Later, from January 1943, Lorna did fire-watching duty and was on patrol every time the sirens went, but nothing was so frightening as that night in 1940.

More memories of wartime Lincoln have come from Joy Cooper, who now lives in Totnes, Devon. (It's amazing how *The Way We Were* gets around!) Joy recalls that her father had built an Anderson shelter at the bottom of their garden, but after several cold, damp and sleepless nights, she rebelled and decided that she would rather be killed in her own cosy bed and stayed in it every night until the enemy started bombing in real earnest a year or so later. At the start of the war, Joy worked in Boots shop, at the junction of Clasketgate and High Street and remembers the three floor shop, with a lift up to the restaurant at the top. The restaurant had an orchestra and palm trees, which was patronised by the elegant ladies of the city for morning coffee and afternoon tea.

Joy remembers being issued with gas masks which they had to carry around everywhere, but after a few months of this and deciding that wearing them made them look too hideous, they put them back in their boxes and pushed them into a cupboard and forgot about them. I also remember having to take my gas mask to school every day! Promotion in 1940 saw Joy in charge of the cosmetics and toiletries department at the Boots branch at St Marks, which she enjoyed to start with, but as supplies of cosmetics dwindled, Joy got bored with telling customers 'I am sorry – it's out of stock'. She volunteered to do something for the war effort and was sent to the offices of Ruston Bucyrus, which turned out to be even more boring!

Joy had many more memories and has even put these down in a little book called *My War*. I only wish more people would do this and save their memories for future generations.
Lincolnian's Diary. October 17, 2000.

Lancaster Still A Favourite

THE DRONE of four Merlin engines is heard overhead. In office blocks throughout the city, windows are flung open and workers stare upwards. People at home leap out of their armchairs and rush to their front doors. Everyone wants to see the RAF's last-flying Lancaster bomber go by. And even after a quarter-of-a-century the old aircraft hasn't lost its appeal.

On the day which also marked the 30th anniversary of the end of the Second World War, VIPs and guests gathered on the runway at RAF Waddington to watch a unique occasion. The aircraft which had been a familiar sight above Lincolnshire for so long, was officially adopted by Lincoln. Some war veterans shed a tear as the Lancaster flew overhead, escorted by a Hurricane and a Spitfire. And although the Lancaster was about to move to a new home outside the county at RAF Coltishall, in Norfolk, we were promised 'It will still be a familiar sight above Lincolnshire for some years to come. It will pay flying visits to the city on its way to and from air displays in many

Favourite: The City of Lincoln Lancaster, still seen over the city. (Echo Ref. 3-3-B)

parts of the country.' And the promise is still being kept today, although we perhaps don't see as much of the 55-year-old aircraft as we used to.

On that day at Waddington, the then Mayor of Lincoln, Councillor Tom Ward, was there to do the honours, accompanied by the City Sheriff, Frank Wright. They inspected the guard, along with Air Marshal Sir Peter Horsley and the City Council's chief executive, Philip Watts. And watching intently were more than 100 former Australian aircrew and their wives.

The Gossiper. May 2, 2000.

Victory Street Party Went With A Bang

THE DAY war broke out... that was the catchphrase which comedian Rob Wolton always used to start his stage act or radio broadcast.

I have to say that I am too young to remember the start of the war. I was three-and-a-half, I can't remember anything about it. My earliest memory is while at Mount Street Primary School, Lincoln, where we had to have a rest, on a folding bed, every afternoon for one hour. When I went on to Westgate Junior School, I remember having to take my gas mask, in its cardboard carrying case, to school every day. They were horrible things to wear and thank goodness we never had to use them!

The first real 'war' memory came on August Bank Holiday Monday, in 1942, when I saw the planes which dropped the bombs causing damage to the County Hospital Nurses' Home and Coldbath House. Another memory from those days, which lasted until the end of the war, was the Morrison table shelter. A steel table, with steel mesh sides served a triple purpose. In the day, it was a table. At night, it was a bed – you slept under it and the mesh sides were fixed in place after you had got into bed. The whole structure then became a shelter in case your home was bombed, although I don't think it would have survived a direct hit.

A photograph in *Memory Lane – Lincoln and Lincolnshire*, also brought back another memory. It was War Effort week, in 1943 and in the grounds of the Usher Art Gallery, there was a fighter plane on display. Inside the gallery was a 4,000lb 'blockbuster' bomb. In those days, you could buy 6d and half a crown savings stamps, which you collected in a book until you had saved enough to buy a 15 shillings National Savings Certificate – a bit like Premium Bonds, but if you left it intact, you gained interest instead of a prize draw. In 1943, they had the idea that if you bought the stamps, you could stick them on the bomb case and the money would go to help fight the war. I remember going along, buying my 6d stamp and sticking it on the bomb.

I also have clear memories of the night when Victory in Europe was announced. My father was in the Fire Service,

War effort: A novel way of raising money was by sticking National Savings Stamps on a 4,000lb bomb on display at the Usher Gallery, Lincoln, in April 1943.

so was on duty, but my mother took me, with some neighbours, to Lincoln Cathedral, where there was a searchlight shining on to the central tower. I was lifted up to press the button and the morse code for the letter V (for victory), three dots and a dash, illuminated the tower.

After that, every street held its own street party and I remember at ours that the organisers had managed to get hold of some fireworks. These had been banned during the war, so a firework display was something special. Dad, being a fireman, was put in charge of the display and professionally kept them in a tin. But, somehow, someone managed to throw a lighted cigarette end into the tin. The result was brief, but spectacular, with fireworks going off in every direction. But best of all, perhaps was the words from the local bobby, who arrived too late to see the display. Really, I never thought policemen spoke like that!

Lincolnian's Diary. September 7, 1999.

One of the biggest building schemes in Lincoln for many years was the construction of Pelham Bridge, in the mid-1950s, to try and relieve the city of some of its level-crossing problems. All of the houses in the right and middle of the picture have now been demolished.

Looking southwards, Pelham Bridge was under construction in the mid-1950s and a variety of wagons and coaches stand on the railway lines. There was no smoke control in these days before the Clean Air Act. The church of St Andrew's can just be seen at top left of the picture.

World Left In Ruins After Plane Crashed

BRENDA Scrimshaw was just a few weeks away from her 12th birthday. She had gone to Skellingthorpe Road School as usual and when the bell rang, she had said cheerio to her friends and gone back home for tea. But it was a meal she would never eat. Before the end of the afternoon, the world she knew would disappear in ruins. The home she loved would be reduced to rubble. All her possessions – her clothes and all the toys she treasured – would be destroyed. The 11-year-old schoolfriend who lived nearby would be dead. And nothing would ever seem quite the same again.

It was June 1943. Britain was in the grip of a Second World War, and every day RAF bombers would roar overhead on their way to and from enemy occupied Europe. But at their home at 22 Highfield Avenue, Brenda, her younger sister Sheila, and their parents Fred and Winifred, were trying to put thoughts of war out of their mind. There was fish for tea, and Winifred was carrying a plate towards the table. In the kitchen were lodgers Harry and Esme Bishop. Above them, the crew of a Lancaster were fighting for survival. Their aircraft, which had taken off on a training flight from RAF Wigsley a few minutes earlier, was in trouble. They desperately searched for somewhere to land, but it was too late. The wing clipped a telegraph pole at the bottom of the Scrimshaws' garden and smashed into the house. In the kitchen, Esme just had time to cry out 'There's a plane coming. It's too low!'

Brenda recalls 'The front of the plane hit our house, then it went across the road onto the other houses.' Their homes collapsed about them. Flames lit up the scene. 'My father went out the front door to see what had happened. By then everything was on fire. Mum threw us out of the back door.'

By a miracle, Brenda, her sister and her mother were unhurt. Her father had to go to hospital with burns to his head and Harry and Esme were kept in hospital for a time. Six of the seven crew were killed. The only survivor was the rear gunner who was thrown clear but spent the rest of his days in hospital. Brenda and her sister were ushered away from the ruins, as firemen fought in vain to save their home. Five people on the ground, including Brenda's friend, 11-year-old Margaret Mott, were dead. The family had lost everything. 'Mum didn't even have a handkerchief to wipe away the tears,' recalls Brenda. 'She turned grey overnight.'

The family moved in with relatives until the council could re-house them, and Fred's fellow ARP wardens had a whip-round and raised more than £9 to help get them back on their feet again. 'My school work suffered a lot because of it. Right up to my late teens, if an aircraft came over on the low side, I used to have hysterics,' recalls Brenda. 'But it gradually eased. Later, I made myself go to air shows and go close to the aircraft.'

Then, in adult life, Brenda married, became Mrs Andrews, and met her fears head-on when she plucked up courage to fly to Canada. And since then she has flown to and from Canada on two other occasions to finally lay the ghosts of her childhood to rest.

The Gossiper. September 28, 1999.

Lights Out As The Drone Closed In

THE people of Lincolnshire were curious and scared as they had no defence from the enemy who flew high above their heads that January night in 1916. They could only watch and wait as the drone of the Zeppelin engines grew even nearer and then faded away into the distance. Now, memories of that night the lights went out all over south Lincolnshire, are revived in an article by Les Gostick, in the latest edition of Lincolnshire Past and Present – the magazine of the Society for Lincolnshire History and Archaeology.

'One of my earliest memories is of the sight of a German Zeppelin flying above Sleaford in 1916,' he writes. 'It looked really beautiful caught by the searchlights, like a huge silver cigar. It appeared perfectly harmless. We had no idea of the damage they were to inflict that night. There was no positive defence against them. The Navy guns were few and far between and in any case it was pure luck whether any shell from them could be set to explode near enough to damage the Zeppelins.'

A railway worker on duty at Sleaford that night, described how they were given news of the Zeppelin's approach. It came in a verbal message from Spalding, that hostile aircraft were heading their way. 'All lights except the signals were immediately put out, goods sheds closed, shunting stopped and all trains were held up at the nearest signal box,' noted the unnamed railwayman. 'All Sleaford was in absolute darkness. Motor cars and bicycles continued to run but were stopped by people who insisted on lights being extinguished. A period of anxious waiting commenced. There was no panic and scarcely any signs of fear. Curiosity seemed to be the predominant feeling. At 8pm we heard a noise approaching and growing every moment, more distinct. At 8.15pm the noise of motors was very distinct and on looking up I saw a Zeppelin right over our heads, at a height of about, as near as I could judge, one mile. It was travelling at great speed, due west.

'No bombs were dropped on Sleaford. But we heard a succession of dull muffled reports and Digby reported bombs dropped there and a barn on fire. No one was hurt. Several bombs were dropped in a fled at Bloxholme and great craters were made in the earth. We heard that bombs were dropped at Frodingham and at various places in the Midlands, considerable damage being done and a good many killed and injured. On the whole, Lincolnshire escaped very well.'

The Gossiper. May 2, 2000.

Only a few landmarks remain today from this scene of Brayford Wharf East, dating from the 1930s or '40s. C.S. Dickinson's flour mill has a very smoky chimney and there is no fence along the edge of the wharf to prevent pedestrians or vehicles from falling into the water. The floating crane is working near to the cut alongside the railway warehouse.

Today, the structure of the footbridge to the railway engine shed remains, although no longer in use and the mill has been replaced by a multi-storey office block. Railings now help prevent accidents and the old warehouse on the right of the old picture, with its sign for O.C.O. Cakes, Cubes and Meals, has been replaced by the Lincolnshire Echo offices and printing works, opened in 1984.

Those Special Times

Wine Tasting Society Had A Busy Month

NOT TOO many years ago, June was always a busy month for me. I was a member of the Lincoln Section of the Feucht Frohliche Neustadter, the wine appreciation society and our busiest time of the year fell in this month.

In 1972, the German FFN brought their wine house to Lincoln and repeated the visit in 1974. On the first visit, they were on their own, the Lincoln Section not being formed until the following year. When they brought it in 1974, there were members of the Lincoln Section to help build it. After that, the Lincoln FFN bought their own winehouse, in the form of a very large marquee, with solid front and back.

I well remember the first time we put it up on the Cornhill. Special anchoring holes had been set into the cobbled surface of the Cornhill and the tent was erected on a large frame. Having got the frame up, the next task was to cover it. Bear in mind that we had never done it before, or even seen the tent in its built up form. If you have trouble putting up a deckchair, then you might appreciate the problems we had. It was very heavy, but eventually, after several attempts, during which the ropes broke many times, we finally succeeded. Each time the ropes broke, the crowd, who had gathered to watch our antics, broke into applause. They reckoned it was the best free show in town. It was only when we had both sections of the cover in place that we realised the first section was back to front, so off it had to come. But we eventually got the hang of it and the Wine Festival opened on time.

We also had a stall at the Lincoln Water Festival each year and on one occasion, when we were selling wine in special souvenir glasses, one man bought a glass, but didn't want the wine, so he threw it into the Brayford. Unfortunately, he didn't hold on to the glass and it followed the wine into the water! We sold him an empty glass next time.

The Mayor's Parade which accompanied the festival also proved a busy time, when we entered a float. We had quite an elaborate design but on the day of the parade, it was very windy and proved impossible to build. A quick change of plan left major portions of the float laying on the ground at the South Common. We did a quick redesign and walked off with the first prize. There was certainly something to celebrate that evening at the Wine Tasting held at the Drill Hall. A few years later, I was involved in the Mayor's Parade again, this time through the Lincoln Asthma Swimming Group and it was quite a task trying to design a float in keeping with the theme which was chosen each year.

June was also a busy time for me at work. It was the month of the Lincolnshire Show, always a busy time for *Echo* photographers and we were always pleased when it was over and we could relax a little.

Lincolnian's Diary. June 20, 2000.

Happy days: Members of the Lincoln Section of the Feucht Frohliche Neustadter in a happy mood at one of their wine tastings.

Busy time: Lincoln's FFN Winehouse on the Cornhill.

Stirring Up Festive Law

DECEMBER is the one month of the year which probably has more customs associated with it than any other. We've just had 'Stir Up Sunday'. Yes, I know that it falls in November and is the last Sunday before the start of Advent. It is supposed to come from the collect 'Stir up, we beseech thee, O Lord…' It was traditionally the day when the Christmas pudding was made so many thought that the collect referred to stirring up the pudding.

There was a lot of tradition attached to this. To start with, it should contain 13 ingredients, representing Jesus and the 12 disciples. You had to stir it three times, anti-clockwise, with your eyes shut tight and then make a wish. I remember as a child doing this, but I don't think any of my wishes were answered. I'm still not a millionaire!

It was traditional to put silver charms and coins in the pudding, usually a silver threepenny bit or a sixpence. We don't have silver coins today, so what do today's youngsters expect from their pudding, that is if they can be persuaded to eat it. I would think nothing less than a pound coin would do today.

Another custom, early in the month, was the Christingle service, at any time during Advent. Children were given an orange, representing the world, carrying a candle (representing the light of the world). It was decorated with a red ribbon (the blood of Christ), and fruit and nuts for the fruit of the earth. Eighteen years ago, Lincoln held its first Christmas Market, based on an idea from our twin town in

First card: One of the first Christmas cards, sent in 1843, by 'John Washbourn and his wife'.

Germany and this has proved so successful that many towns and villages have followed suit.

Christmas cards date from 1843 and one of the first was sent by an ancestor of mine, Dr John Washbourn, of Islington. The Christmas tree was introduced from Germany by Prince Albert, consort to Queen Victoria. There were quite a few local customs and for many years. the Lincoln Christmas Fat Stock was held on the West Common. Another unusual custom in Lincolnshire when

women went 'mumping' or begging around the village. The name is thought to come from a Scandinavian word 'mompen' – to beg. It was usually elderly women who did this and they were given small gifts of food.

Then there were the events at Christmas. Traditional meets of packs of foxhounds were held on Boxing Day. I can remember when the Burton Hunt used to meet at the Sobraon Barracks, but now the venue is the Lincolnshire Showground. The Blankney Hunt meets at

Sleaford Market Place. And for the more hardy, or foolhardy, which ever way you look at it, there was the Christmas time swims, in the sea, at Skegness and Mablethorpe. There was, and possible still is, a swim across the docks at Grimsby. A few years ago, there was for a little while, an annual tug o'war between teams from Harby and Eagle, over a stream. The losing team had no alternative but to get wet. Competitors were tied to the rope! *Lincolnian's Diary. December 5, 2000.*

A Big Night For City Drinkers

THE BAR was full to overflowing. There was an air of excitement in the lounge. In pubs and clubs all over Lincoln, it was the greatest night of the year… It was the day when the Sick and Dividing Clubs paid out their annual dividends. And just how good a Christmas it was going to be in many a Lincoln household would depend on just how much money came out of the club and into the pockets of the regulars. These days, it is doubtful if any Sick and

Dividing Clubs still exist, but from the turn of the 20th century until the Swinging '60s, they played a major role in city life.

The idea was that the regulars paid in money throughout the year. Some of it would be used to help families at time of sickness or unemployment. The rest was shared out between the members. And what didn't go back over the bar the same night went to swell the income of the household at the most expensive time of the year. Back in December 1930, the *Echo* reported how some of the city clubs had experienced heavy calls on their funds because of sickness which had been prevalent during the year. But

despite all this, it looked as if most of the clubs would pay a share to each member of around £1. It might not seem much these days, but it was quite a big amount 70 years ago.

Among the fondest-remembered of Sick and Dividing Clubs is The Green Dragon, which in 1930 was paying out 15s 3d to its 535 members. The Monson Arms Hotel Tap was paying out between 23s and 24s. The Cornhill Hotel was paying 14s 3d to its 46 members and the Sloop Inn club – then established for 17 years – was paying out £2 10s 4d to its 19 double members and £1 5s 2d to its 26 single members. *The Gossiper. December 19, 2000.*

There have been few times when you could have walked under High Bridge, in the middle of Lincoln, without getting wet, but in the mid-1930s, repair and maintenance under the bridge meant that the river had to be drained. The tall building has an advertisement for Mumby and Son Ltd, who were wholesale clothiers. All of the buildings beyond and those on the left-hand side have been demolished. (Echo Ref RI-466)

Was This Lincoln's First Christmas Market?

FIFTY years ago, the war had only been over for five years and some food was still rationed, so the Mayor of Lincoln, Coun. Mrs Edyth Cowan tried to liven up the festivities with a barbecue. On Boxing Day, 1950, hundreds gathered in the Central Market car park to watch as venison was roasted over an open fire. The fires were lit at half-past-two and two hours later, were ready with 200 people on hand to cheer the chefs when they arrived to start cooking. But when the deer carcasses had arrived, there had been a bit of a panic! They had been quartered and the morning of Boxing Day was spent sewing the carcasses together with wire.

The 18th-century style spits had been made by Councillor W.J. 'Billy' Bell and at five o'clock, cooking commenced. Two hours later, the crowd had swelled and were ready for their venison sandwiches, at one shilling each and by a quarter to nine, 755 and been sold and although a halt was called to the sale of tickets, more sandwiches were provided with the pickings from the bones. But what was the opinion of those tasting the meat? One man sad it tasted 'like liver'. Others thought it was 'unusual but interesting' and some thought it was 'delicious'.

Entertainment for the evening was provided by the Lincoln Borough Silver Prize Band and there were even some couples dancing. The theme tune for the evening was *Rudolf, the Red-Nosed Reindeer*. Outside the market hall, members of the 62 HAA Regiment were kept busy selling roast chestnuts and roast potatoes and more than 500 people enjoyed these with part of the proceeds being donated to charity. Hot peas and drinks were also available.

It may have been 50 years ago, but surely, this was Lincoln's first 'Christmas Market'!

Lincolnian's Diary. December 19, 2000.

Christmas celebrations: Carving up the roast venison in Lincoln Central Market on Boxing Day, 1950.

It Was All A Load Of Whitewash

THE middle of April usually heralded the great Spring Clean. Between then and Whit-suntide, around a six or seven week period, every room in the house got a good 'going over'. Starting at the top of the house the three-ups and three-downs were turned inside out.

Can you remember the old lumpy whitewash which we used to do the ceilings with? I never got mine to the thick and creamy stage and usually splashed it all over. Some used the old blue dolly bags to make it whiter. The wallpaper was edged with a plain white strip at each side and we had to sit and trim it all off. If you cut too deep you couldn't get a match. Walls were uneven and it was terrible trying to keep the paper straight.

Many houses had no skirting boards and there could be a two inch deviation between the top and bottom of the wall. Mam always glue-sized the wall first to give it a smoother surface and as we only had starch or plain flour for adhesive you got a better bond. The starch and flour were first mixed to a paste with cold water. Then boiling water was poured over and you stirred until it turned into a gluey substance. When cold it was slapped on the paper and allowed to soak in before hanging on the wall. But before all this the chimneys were swept and the soot used for the garden. Most houses had a set of brushes but there always a chimney alight. Not very safe but they always had a good draw to the fire.

Country kitchens often had a dark blue ceiling which was said to deter flies but my Mam always used DDT – enough to kill the village by today's reckonings. Painting was a painful operation. First the surfaces were washed with sugar soap – guaranteed to peel the skin off your hands. Two undercoats and then a top coat of paint which contained lead. You could smell it for days and there were many remedies to get rid of it. Keeping straw in a bucket of water over night was one – and it worked.

Colour schemes rarely got beyond the serviceable brown, cream and green. Coco matting and rugs were thrown over the line and beaten. New clipped rugs were put in place and the furniture washed in a mixture of vinegar, linseed oil and water. Mansion polish gave the final sheen and the old red tiles got a coating of red Cardinal polish – which showed every footmark.

April or June brought blanket days when the sun was out or the wind blew. We never washed blankets in May under the old superstition that you washed one of the family away. Farming families moved into the outhouse kitchen which had white-washed walls and brick floors. The dilly man came and emptied the earth closets and they too were scrubbed with bleach and limewashed.

Moth balls were put into drawers and wardrobes to keep the moths at bay and if you didn't spray for flies you had one of the sticky fly papers hung in each room. But they also said leaving beer in saucers or wiping the window frames with paraffin also kept them at bay. A huge baking and preparation of food was done so that meals were on time. The male contribution was a very wise one – they kept out of the way.

Bette's Bygones. April 4, 2000.

69

St Peter-at-Arches had stood at the corner of High Street and Silver Street for 200 years before it was demolished in 1933 and rebuilt as St Giles' Parish Church. There was much opposition to the demolition of the building, for a street widening scheme, but it was Revd A.M. Cook (later Canon Cook, Sub-Dean of Lincoln) who suggested that it be rebuilt on what was a rapidly growing estate in the north-east of the city. Beyond the church is the Butter Market and the front of this building, which was demolished a few years after the church, was incorporated into the New Market which was built in Sincil Street. A new block, still known as St Peter-at-Arches was built incorporating shops, offices and some domestic accommodation (on the top floor). The main shop, now a booksellers', was at one time, universally known as 'The Fifty Bob Tailors', with suits costing 50s (£2.50 in today's money). Beneath the area is part of Roman Lincoln and a Roman fountain was found in the area about 50 years ago, during excavations below one of the shops.

Festive Fun – 1930s Style

IT IS almost Christmas, the time of year when people put on their party hats, play all sorts of silly games and generally do things that they wouldn't do at any other time of the year. Seventy years ago the festive spirit may have been just as strong, but the games people played might seem just a little strange to today's generation of youngsters. Now you can relive some of those times.

Stuck for some party ideas this Christmas? Struggling to find some ways of keeping the children amused? Then you could probably do little better than to follow some of the advice given to *Echo* readers in those innocent pre-war days. In December 1930, long before just about every home had television sets and video players, they made their own fun. And the *Echo* had some handy party tips. 'Simple, old-fashioned, but jolly games are often the most successful. The room should be well lit and nicely-decorated with holly, coloured streamers and Japanese lanterns. As each child enters, he or she should be handed a cracker and a small whistle, hooter or some noise-making toy. Children more quickly forget their embarrassment under the influence of these little surprises and the ice will be broken at once.'

If you were looking for some party games, then the writer had some suggestions. What about a game called Flying Feather? 'A sheet is held out so as to come just beneath the chins of the boys and girls. A light, vividly coloured, fluffy feather is placed in the centre and at a given signal, all the players start blowing as hard as they can. The game is for one side to blow the feather off the sheet and for the other side to prevent this.'

Or if that didn't appeal, what about Spoon Bluff? It was a game which had to be played without anyone making a sound – which must have made it a firm favourite among the harassed parents at least. 'One child is blindfolded and immediately all the others silently seat themselves round the room. Two spoons are thrust into the blindfolded person's hands and with these he has to feel for the faces of the other players – instead of using his hands. It is impossible for the onlookers to keep their faces straight while this is going on, but immediately one laughs or raises a cry, he must pay a forfeit. This goes on until the blindfolded players guesses the identity of the one he had caught, whereupon the captured player takes his turn as Spoon Bluff.'

And bearing in mind that Christmas is for giving and not just receiving, there was a game called Gifts for All. The writer explained; 'All sit round and are asked to think of gifts. The leader then pounces unexpectedly upon someone with the announcement 'Your gift is for the Prime Minister, what is it?' And the player must answer in a flash the thing he has been thinking about. If the answer is not forthcoming before the other players have counted to three, the player addressed pays a forfeit. The recipients mentioned may range from public personages to members of the family and the more incongruous the gifts, the more fun there will be.'

After that, Trivial Pursuit will never be the same again!
The Gossiper. December 19, 2000.

It Was Christmas Day In The Workhouse

NO, I'M not going to break into a monologue, especially one which many people know with naughty words, but just what was it like in Lincoln Workhouse, exactly 100 years ago?

Lincoln's Union Workhouse stood just off Burton Road, near its junction with Westgate and was a forbidding looking place. On Christmas morning, each inmate received a Christmas letter from Miss Leslie-Melville and cards were also distributed. Those that were able attended morning service and then settled down to a 'sumptuous dinner' of roast beef and mutton, with fowls and rabbits for the sick, plum pudding with rum sauce, beer, tea or coffee, according to the inclination of the diners.

The meal was 'heartily enjoyed and the appreciation was shown by the manner in which votes of thanks were accorded and the National Anthem sung'. The dining room had been beautifully decorated with evergreen and paper flowers, by the Master and Matron, Mr and Mrs Pettefar, with the assistance of inmates. After dinner, tobacco, tea and sugar, oranges and other fruit were distributed and at half past five, tea was served in the dining room. The menu was plum cake, seed cake and fancy cakes, in plenty.

The *Echo*'s report of the day stated that even then, the enjoyment was not yet over. At seven o'clock, an entertainment was given in the dining hall and 'after such a day, surely the inmates retired to rest with the consciousness of having thoroughly enjoyed the last Christmas day of the 19th century'.

I suppose for the inmates, it was a good day by usual standards and I would think that even today, some of the homeless living in 'cardboard cities' would find this fare a real treat.
Lincolnian's Diary. December 19, 2000.

Demolition: Lincoln's former workhouse falls to the demolition gang in the 1960s.

Walkabout: The Queen, accompanied by the Mayor of Lincoln in 1980, David Chambers, walks down a crowded High Street, despite the rain.

All Smiles... Despite The Rain

FOR MONTHS they had been planning it... For weeks they had been thinking about it and 20 years ago, this month came the day we had all been waiting for. The Queen was back in Lincoln for only the second time in her reign. Crowds waited eagerly during a dismal downpour in the hope of getting a glimpse, or maybe a word, with the royal couple.

Cheering crowds and streets decked with flags greeted the Queen and the Duke of Edinburgh when they paid an official visit to Lincoln in November 1980, for the first time in 22 years. Thousands were up and about early to get the best vantage points along the royal route. And from early morning, vehicles poured into the city centre full of people hoping to catch a glimpse of the royal couple.

The purpose of the visit was for the Queen to officially open the £5m new police headquarters at Nettleham and for the royal couple to attend a special cathedral service to mark the 700th anniversary of the Angel Choir. But if we had been hoping the weather would be any better than it had been when the Queen and Duke of Edinburgh were in Lincoln back in 1958 to officially open Pelham Bridge, then we would have been disappointed. Heavy rain and a strong wind greeted the royal visitors as they arrived at Central station, exactly on time. But what the waiting crowd didn't know was that the royal couple had arrived in the county the previous evening and the royal train had been parked overnight at Bardney.

As the Queen, wearing a red coat with black hat, shoes and handbag, had her first glimpse of the rain-swept forecourt, she may well have remembered the similar weather which had greeted her last visit to the city. But there was no mistaking the warmth of the crowd's greetings. Some people had been there from early morning, clutching flags in one hand and an umbrella in the other, while they looked down from surrounding offices in the dry. The Queen was given a black umbrella as she inspected a guard of honour, but Prince Philip, in a black morning suit, stood bareheaded in the rain.

It was a very proud Mayor, Councillor David Chambers, who presented the Queen with the Richard II sword. Minutes later, the nine-car procession set off for the cathedral. The route took them past the city bus station, where a newly-decorated double-decker bus was paying

Christmas Traditions

NO CHRISTMAS scene would be complete without a crib which dates back to 1224. St Francis of Assisi asked the Pope's permission to celebrate Christmas by recreating the nativity scene, complete with live ox and ass. They did not reach England until the 19th century and even then they were not common outside Roman Catholic churches until well into this century. And there is very little evidence to suggest that Jesus Christ was born on December 25.

In fact Christmas Day did not become official until the year 354 when Pope Gregory proclaimed December 25 as the date of the Nativity. In doing this he was following the Church's policy of absorbing, rather than repressing ancient pagan rites. This was the time of the winter solstice, which had been celebrated since early times. The Romans also celebrated Saturnalia around December 17, incorporating their tradition of feasting and revelry into what we now know as Christmas.

Carols date from the 12th century when they were simply songs to dance to on festive occasions. The church again soon took over these folk songs and gave them a religious significance by replacing the original words with sacred ones. But their heyday was short lived when the Reformation and Puritanism almost destroyed the carol tradition. But they were revived in the 19th century by folklore students, devoted to collecting the customs of 'Olde Englande'. They soon became part of the Victorian Christmas and the backbone of our Christmas festival. Christmas crackers were a late addition to the tradition. They were invented in the late 19th century by an enterprising young baker called Tom Smith, who got the idea from the way sweets were wrapped in France – with a twist of paper at either end. He set up a company to make these and put in the explosive charge.
Bette's Bygones. December 12, 2000.

its own tribute. There was a large crowd waiting outside the cathedral and a packed congregation for the 60-minute service which was conducted by the Bishop, the Right Reverend Simon Phipps. Afterwards, the Dean, the Very Reverend Oliver Fiennes, invited the Queen to sign the visitors' book and the Queen and Duke were shown the city's copy of the Magna Carta in the days before it had a regular home in the grounds of the castle. Then the royal car drove the visitors to the County Assembly Rooms for lunch.

Later, in the gathering gloom of the late afternoon, the royal car went on to the county police HQ at Nettleham. Crowds were waiting in the hope of giving the Queen a posy of flowers. And the *Echo* reported how at one time, the Queen had so many flowers that one of the posies slipped from her grasp and she had to stoop down under the Stonebow to pick it up. The walkabout – the first the Queen had made in Lincoln – followed a visit to the Guildhall. At times during the walkabout, from the Stonebow to St Mary's Street, the royal couple were 20 or 30 yards apart as the Duke stopped time and time again to talk to people in the crowd.
The Gossiper. November 7, 2000.

Lincoln has two pleasure fairs each year, one in April and the other, introduced during the Second World War, in September. This picture was taken at the April Fair, on the South Common, in 1958. (Echo Ref. RI-3709-2A)

It had once been a school – the old National School, but in later years, the building on the left of the old picture became the Lincoln Corporation Offices, and were decorated were for the coronation in 1953. Beyond these were the showrooms of the Gas Board and above them, Lincoln Register Office. This was a time when traffic was two-way in Silver Street. All of the properties left of the centre of the old picture were demolished and in 1981, the Stonebow Centre, a small shopping arcade was built. During the work, the wall of the lower Roman city was found and a postern gate, which opened out on to the river, was discovered. It is now preserved under the Royal Bank of Scotland's bank. In the distance, one of Lincoln's earliest banks, now the NatWest bank, has changed little on the outside.

Post Office History On Xmas Day

THE POSTAL SERVICES at Lincoln faced a dilemma. It was 1899 and Queen Victoria had directed that the mail from the men fighting in the Boer War should be delivered in time for Christmas. It meant a Christmas Day delivery, but even that wouldn't have been a problem if the railways had been running... But they weren't. Not surprisingly, the railwaymen wanted a day off, so there was no question of delivering the Christmas Day mail by train. If the post was to arrive on time, in a large part of the Lincolnshire Fens, desperate measures were called for. The answer? To take the mail from Lincoln to New York by car! That's our New York, of course, not the one on the other side of the Atlantic.

The story is recounted for me by Niall McSwiggan, formerly of Lincoln but recently moved to Holywell in North Wales. 'According to Charles Gilbert (1867-1939), it was Queen Victoria's wish that the mail from the men at the front in the Boer War should be delivered in time for Christmas and the GPO was asked to make a special effort. With winter conditions, no Tarmac roads or filling stations, the delivery of mail by car was quite an undertaking. It was thought to be the first in the provinces and it was perhaps the first in the country. The firm of Gilbert's was established in Lincoln in 1876.' And the company was asked to help. 'The company merged with another Lincoln distributor in 1980.'

Niall sends me a report of the Christmas Day delivery and it was not without its problems. It was the idea of Lincoln Postmaster, Mr J.T. Walker, to ask Gilberts for help. Although the car was then at King's Lynn and the company had only two days to make the arrangements, it agreed straight away. The car was a Daimler's Rougemont Waggonette and it was driven by Charles Gilbert. The mail was looked after by Alex Taylor, of the Post Office and it was given a cheerful send-off by Post Office workers at 7.40am on Christmas Day. With half-a-ton of mail on board, the car reached Wasingborough in an impressive 13 minutes. It then carried on through Heighington Fen and up an apology for a road, to Five Mile House. Here the car and its precious load were ferried over the Witham to Fiskerton. After leaving the village the deliveries continued at Short Ferry, Bardney, Southrey, Bucknall, Stixwould and Woodhall Spa, by which time it was 10am.

The car then carried on to Kirkstead and Martin Dales and back through Woodhall Spa to Tattershall where heavy mail for Tattershall Bridge, Billinghay, North Kyme were transferred to a rural postman with a horse and trap. For the car, the next stop was at Coningsby, where a large crowd of people were waiting to greet the rare visitor and to cheer the car on its way to Dogdyke, where the mail was dropped off for Chapel Hill and Holland Fen. It was 11.20am by the time the car reached New York having completed the 34 miles over some of the worst roads in Lincolnshire and at a time of year when they were liberally covered in loose stones. I am told that the Postmaster of New York, Mr S.J. Joll, invited the travellers to join him in his Christmas dinner and 'entertained them right heartily'.

On the way back to Lincoln, the car picked up mail from Tattershall, Coningsby, Tattershall Bridge and Billinghay, where a long stop was made for the mail to arrive from North and South Kyme. Mr A.C. Atchison, the sub-postmaster at Billinghay, warmed the travellers with a cup of tea. Then, the car was off again through Walcott and Metheringham to Lincoln where it reached the Post Office at 6.45pm – in time for the night mails. Then, the intrepid travellers went off home – to enjoy Christmas.
The Gossiper. November 9, 1999.

Different Clothes For Each Season

NEVER cast a clout till May is out is an old adage. Some say it means the end of the month, others when the May flower comes out. But every year when June dawned we went into summer dresses. What a relief. We covered our bodies with a mountain of clothes. First the interlock vest – those shapeless garments that drooped at the sides where Mum pegged them to the line. At school medical examination you were judged by the whiteness of your vest. It they were grey they said: 'She doesn't rinse them properly'. You needed sunglasses to look at others. Some Mums cheated by keeping a once washed new one specially for the day.

Then liberty bodices – what on earth use were they? Fleecy lined monstrosities with two loops back and front designed to hold stockings up. They rolled up round your middle and gave you a pot belly. Next came navy blue knickers – with a pocket on the right leg to hold your hankie. It they were fleecy lined you got a bit sweaty in PT (physical training) which was done in blouse and knickers. Underneath you still had on your vest and liberty bodice. A blouse, tie and gym-slip to cover the outer layer completed the indoor kit. Cardigans were worn in winter. Blazers in summer and a thick reefer coat or gabardine mac in the winter. Black wool or lisle stockings covered your legs in winter and white socks in summer. Dressing and undressing was a major operation, especially if you did it in a frosty-cold bedroom. Some even wore their vest in bed during the cold months.

The lads wore short trousers until they left school at 14. Then, it was usually an older brother's pair of cast-off long ones to start work in. Big stuff. And the young farm lads loved it when Mam bought them their first cap to go to work in.

Do you remember 'fustins'? Those dark grey stiff trousers that farm workers wore and which lasted a lifetime. 'There's cotton for all sorts of cloth and buttons for fustins'. Which meant that there is something to suit everyone. Their feet shod with hobnailed boots. Wellingtons came in after the war. Sacks were tied around their lower legs to keep them dry in wet and muddy conditions.

It was a great moment when they handed over their wages to Mam for the housekeeping. With their cap jauntily on the side of their head, a penny packet of five Woodbines and a five bob (25p) in their pockets they were men of the world.
Bette's Bygones. September 19, 2000.

The Obelisk, on High Bridge, Lincoln, had been a landmark for 200 years before it was removed in 1939, because its weight, combined with increased traffic, was thought too great for the safety of the bridge. On this occasion, it was decorated for the Royal Show, on Lincoln's West Common, in 1907.

Almost 100 years ago, Lincoln High Street was a hive of activity. Open-top trams, horse-drawn wagons, motor cars, cycles and pedestrians all thronged the city's busiest thoroughfare. The old picture of High Street was taken in 1907, when the city centre was decorated for the Royal Show. Hepworth's had their clothiers and outfitters shop on the corner of the Cornhill and the sign for the Black Bull Hotel can be seen on the left-hand side of the picture.

The modern scene still has decorations, but this time, they are for Christmas 2000. Most of the shops have changed use, but above ground floor level, many of the buildings are the same. There are still plenty of pedestrians around, but not a vehicle in sight. Hepworth's old shop still sells clothes, but is now part of the Next chain.

Crowds lined the High Street in Lincoln in April 1961, when the 2nd Battalion, East Anglian Regiment, marched through the centre of the city. On the right of the street is the Regal Cinema, which like the adjacent buildings of Fox and Co and Wakefields Army Stores, were soon to be demolished to make was for Littlewood's store. (Echo Ref. RI-4044A)

Personal Memories

A History Of Methodism

THE COUNTY of Lincolnshire has been a Methodist heartland for more than two centuries. A history sent in by Mrs Helen Ash of Bassingham tells of famous Methodists such as John Hunt of Fiji and also the staunch loyalty and faith of ordinary local preachers, class leaders, stewards and members who have supported Methodism over the generations. Preaching was the main aim of the Methodist societies and this worked in tandem with the Anglican Church. Methodism was involved with education and the name Sunday School meant exactly that.

The Weslyan Day School was housed in what is now the Bassingham Heritage Room had a large number of pupils and it was amalgamated with the Anglican day school in 1893. Bassingham also ran a lending library and magazine club. In some villages the Nonconformists were penalised for their faith and many meetings were disrupted. William Ash who lived at Carlton le Moorland gave the land for the chapel and then the vicar refused to baptise his children. William Lambe of Aubourn Hall was persuaded to allow a preaching service in the house of one of his tenants. He attended the service himself and soon afterwards 12 members joined to form a class. The Squire became class leader. His son, of the same name, continued the work and founded the first chapel at Aubourn and was also one of the first trustees at Bassingham.

Wesley began by preaching outside and his followers first met outside but soon efforts were made to find sheltered accommodation for classes and services. The new chapel was opened officially on January 14, 1840 by Dr Beaumont of Liverpool. It is inspiring to know that the chapel still continues.
Bette's Bygones. June 20, 2000.

Deadeye Harry Bowled 'Em Over

YOU DON'T have to think back very far to the days when just about any self-respecting garden fete or gala in Lincolnshire, would have you bowling for a pig.

Nowadays, it would be a different matter even in rural Lincolnshire, where the average householder could be just a little bit embarrassed if he arrived home from the village fete with a live pig under his arm. But in those bygone days, a pig was just the sort of prize many people would have wanted to win. And when it came to bowling for a pig, then there was a time when the hardest man to beat in Lincolnshire was Harry Rheams. Because in 20 years of accurate pitching, he won not one, but a whole herd of pigs. His skilful play and keen eye won him more than 300 pigs over the years.

Mr J.H. Kemp, of Alexandra Road, Woodhall Spa, tells me he remembers Harry well. 'I remember when I was a lad living at Martin, in the 1950s, there would be the annual church garden fete at Martin Vicarage, where the vicar was the late Reverend Jack Cooper. They don't make them like him any more. The first prize for the skittles or bowling was usually a pig. The cry would go up 'Here come Bateman and Rheams'. George Bateman was his 'partner in crime'. George usually won the skittles and Harry the bowling.'

Mr Kemp recalls that an article in *The Smallholder and Home Gardener* back in 1953 reported how Harry was spoken of in reverence in pig bowling circles. And it wasn't just pigs that he used to arrive home with. There were cash prizes and sometimes budgerigars and sheep as well. But don't think Harry was embarrassed about his wins. Farming a mixed holding of 20 acres, he always kept the best of his awards and sold the rest. The magazine reported: 'Bowling for the pig is no sport for either the short of sight or the unsteady hand. It involves pitching a four-inch ball through a five-inch hole set in a low board anything up to 24ft away. Six balls are bowled in succession and it is nothing for Harry to pitch each of them true without once touching the board.'

Harry, who lived at Kirton Holme, near Boston, was said to have won as many as 38 pigs during a single season. On one profitable Saturday, he went home with four weaners followed by three the following week and another four the Saturday after that.
The Gossiper. November 7, 2000.

Played Vital Part In *Tirpitz* Raid

WAS IT Denis Nolan's bomb which played a vital part in sending the German battleship the *Tirpitz* to the bottom of the sea? That's what his Number 9 Squadron colleagues believe and on the recent 56th anniversary of the raid, memories of that day came flooding back again.

Every November, members of No 9 Squadron Association, who were based at RAF Bardney from 1943-45, make the pilgrimage back to the village to attend a service and to place wreaths on the squadron memorial on the Green. One man who seldom misses the date, is Denis Nolan, who lives just over the county boundary, at Cottesmore. It was on November 12, 1944 that he and his crew took off in their Lancaster bomber to attack the *Tirpitz*. It was the RAF's third attack on the battleship within three months and it was a joint operation by two special squadrons based in No 5 Group and No 617 Squadron, both equipped with the 12,000 lb Tallboy bomb. Also at the memorial to share the day was Colin Cole, who recently moved to Bardney and was a wireless operator with No 617 Squadron, flying Lancasters from RAF Woodhall Spa and was on the same operation. They were introduced to each other by No 9 Squadron researcher, Roger Audis and it wasn't long before they were recalling that day 56 years ago.

Says Roger: 'The *Tirpitz* was seen to be a threat to the Atlantic convoys and over the years, many attacks had been mounted against it by the Navy and the RAF, but it had never been put out of action for any length of time. It was sighted during September 1944 in Alten Fjord, in Norway. It was out of range of direct flights from this country, so a force of 38 Lancasters flew to Russia and attacked the *Tirpitz*. The ship was damaged and it was taken to Tromso for repair. With the *Tirpitz* in its new position, it was calculated that with some modifications to the aircraft, it was now in range of direct flights from Scotland.

A second attack was planned and made. Forty aircraft left Bardney and Woodhall and landed at Lossiemouth, in Scotland, for refuelling. A long flight to the target was undertaken, but there was poor visibility and the raid was not a success.'

Denis Nolan recalls: 'We flew to the rendezvous point over Norway and met the main force. We were in the second wave and had to wait for No 17 to make their attack. We started our bombing run at at 14,600 ft, I activated the bomb release and out Tallboys fell towards its target. The ship had received several direct hits from aircraft and seemed to be on fire. Our bomb was observed as we left the area. It slid down the starboard side about midway along. There was a large explosion in the water and that was the last we saw. We arrived back in Scotland and we were told the *Tirpitz* had been sunk.'

Colin Cole recalls: 'We met up with the main force. We were in the first wave. We went in through the flak and dropped our Tallboy. Moments later, our rear gunner reported to the skipper that he thought it was a direct hit and by then, we were on our way home.' The crew returned to Scotland having completed at 13-hour, 2,400-mile trip.

Roger concludes: 'Over the years, each squadron claims it sank the *Tirpitz*, but it is now thought by some people that although there were direct hits, the one that went down the side and exploded on the sea bed could have caused shock waves that made the ship roll over.' 'So was it Denis' bomb that sank the *Tirpitz*?' 'No 9 Squadron think so.'

The Gossiper. November 21, 2000.

Medals Were Awarded For Long Service

IT WAS not uncommon 50 years or more ago to read of people receiving long service medals and some companies still award them today, but for much shorter periods of service. Long service in 1920 was just that for one workman, Mr Isaac Harley, a boilermaker, of Dunlop Street, Lincoln. The *Echo* reported that he was just celebrating the 55th anniversary of his entering the firm of Messrs Ruston and Proctor Ltd, which became Ruston and Hornsby Ltd. He entered the works in 1865 and in July 1915, received from the firm their gold medal for 50 years' continuous service. Since

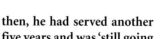

Award: The gold medal presented to employees of Ruston and Hornsby on completion of 50 years' service.

then, he had served another five years and was 'still going strong' having no thought of resigning!

Many people completed their half-century with this and other companies and my father's uncle, Ralph Dring, achieved such a distinction, at Rustons. Great-Uncle Ralph entered the company in 1905 receiving his medal in 1955 and I now have it. On the front are two views of the Ruston factory and on the reverse is a picture of a Ruston steam engine driving a threshing machine and details of the award. I also have his lapel badge which was given to 'gold-medallists'.

How many of today's youngsters starting their working career will clock up 50 years with one company? It's almost an impossibility these days, since most people will retire less that 50 years after they leave school.

Lincolnian's Diary. July 11, 2000.

For 100 years, a railway line was carried by a series of bridges over Lincoln's streets. The best known of these was 'Bainbridges Bridge', crossing the High Street. This picture was taken in 1950 and earlier, it had carried an advertisement for Allsopp's Ales. Later, it bore the name of Ruston Bucyrus, before being removed in the 1980s with the closure of the line. (Echo Ref. RI-662)

Grandfather Is A Family Legend

MEMORIES of a flamboyant and successful grandfather came flooding back for a North Hykeham man who spotted a story about Blakey's Oatmeal in the *Echo* the other day. One of Henry Blakey's grandsons, who did not want to leave his name, says his grandfather was born in 1866 and brought up in Lissington, near Market Rasen. He moved to Lincoln in 1882 and at 16 years old he began an apprenticeship with a local grocer which was to last nine years. It was in 1891 at the age of 25, Henry Blakey decided to branch out on his own and invented the locally famous Blakey's Malted Oatmeal. 'He did everything himself, making and selling the product,' said the grandson.

In 1896 Henry Blakey joined forces with the Cereal Food Company of Lincoln and then in 1912 he formed a partnership with premises in Oxford Street which was in the area now taken over by Pelham Bridge. In 1923 the firm registered as a limited company and was known as Blakey's Food Co Ltd. It then moved to premises in Hungate. The grandson says his grandfather was an amazingly fit man who cycled some 14,000 miles a year. 'Family legend has it, although I can't say for sure that it is true that Henry once cycled from Lincoln to Wainfleet, near Skegness and when he got there found my grandmother had forgotten her watch and so he rode back again,' he said.

'He certainly won a lot of medals. He was a fine athlete and principal of the Lincoln School of Physical Culture for many years. During his 20 years there he produced many of the day's leading lights in wrestling and weightlifting including: Charlie Cowling, who romped away with the middleweight championship of Great Britain; Joe King, the poplar and formidable wrestler; Gus Dawson, Charlie Crane and Seaman Claxton, all champion boxers in their class. In his heyday, Henry was Lincolnshire's strongest man. He was never one to sit back and be content to let things just go on. Even on the day of his death he was putting the finishing touches to new products which his firm hoped to introduce.'

Inventor of the famous Blakey's Malted Oatmeal, he cycled for miles to distribute his product to chemists and grocers both in Lincolnshire and neighbouring counties.

The grandson says he was approached in the 1960s by a lady who said her grandmother had cancer and insisted on eating nothing else but Blakey's Oatmeal.

Henry Blakey died in 1950. He was described in his obituary as: 'a man who had the looks and physique of a figure from an American story book and had, indeed, led a romantic life in business and sport.' He was 84 years old.

The grandson was prompted to get in touch after reading about Ivor Stewart Worth, who appeared in advertisements for the product, on the Gossiper page.
The Gossiper. September 19, 2000.

Modest Ron Was A Hit

IT MAY be some years since the people of Lincolnshire waltzed around the floor to the music of Ron Diggins and his Diggola, but for many, the memories came flooding back after reading a story in last week's edition of *The Way We Were*.

Mary Todd, who now lives in Faldingworth, recalls how Ron belongs to those days of good, clean, innocent fun. 'Any event you organised that had Ron and his Diggola, was always a sell-out. People would be almost falling over themselves for tickets. He was tremendous fun. But the thing I particularly remember about him was his modesty.'

Lincoln entertainer Mac Baker is another with fond memories of Ron and prompted by the article, he and a number of his friends were discussing some of the city dancehalls of bygone days.

They could well remember the Montana, the Court School of Dancing, the Co-op Ballroom in Free School Lane the dancehall above Burton's, at the top of High Street and the Castle Ballroom.
The Gossiper. December 12, 2000.

Campaigning Clarence Leads The Protest

PERHAPS he was ahead of his time... Perhaps his efforts sowed the seeds in the minds of politicians for future years... But Lincoln campaigner Clarence Hurst certainly had the people behind him when he took on the might of the 1972 Government in his bid to get a free television licence for old age pensioners.

Clarence is one of Lincoln's best-remembered characters of the '70s and there was never any topic too big that didn't merit his attention. His petitions and

Campaigner: Clarence Hurst (left) leaves for London with some of his supporters to present a petition at 10 Downing Street. (Echo Ref. RI-1342)

letters of protest frequently went off to the rich and famous.

In this *Echo* picture, he is seen on the left, about to leave with a group of supporters for Downing Street, with a petition calling for free TV licenses for the elderly. The picture was taken in Guildhall Street outside what was then Taverne House – headquarters of the city's Democratic Labour Association.
The Gossiper. October 3, 2000.

Hand packed: No sophisticated machinery, just simple hand packing at Blakey's, in 1956. (Echo Ref. RI-3622)

Dedication Of The Firm's Founder

THE ADVERTISING campaign screamed that 'My Baby Loves It' but did Henry Blakey, the founder of locally famous Blakey's Oatmeal, meet his death because of his dedication to his product and his business. Former salesman Richard Cobb thinks he might have done.

Richard read last week's story about how Henry – a keen sportsman and successful businessman who cycled some 14,000 miles a year to deliver product to grocers and chemists in Lincolnshire and further afield – was so committed to his company, he was working right up to the moment he died at the age of 84.

'I was taken on as a sales rep by Henry's son, Charles. At that time, we were about to launch two new products –

silver cake decorations and what they call hundreds and thousands today,' he said. 'Made of sugar, they were very popular because sugar was still being rationed in the late 1940s and early 1950s and people used them as sweeteners. These products were wrapped in the new plastic material. They were tubes about two inches thick, half an inch all the way round, but the plastic was not clear like it is today. Henry wanted to make the plastic clear and one night he was at the factory – I was there – and he put the plastic in the pressure cooker. Unbeknown to him, and me, he didn't realise that there was so much pressure in the cooker and it blew up. I'm sure that precipitated his death or started the illness that led to his demise, but I wasn't there when the accident happened. He was alone and the next day I heard he had died in a Lincoln hotel.'

Richard remembers driving the company's first van and some of the other successful products such as

Blakey's Malted Milk. He left the firm in 1953 but remembers Henry's son Charles very well. Charles Blakey was a Lincoln City goalkeeper. In the match against Middlesbrough in January 1920 he was described in press reports at the time as being 'masterly throughout'.

He saved a shot from more than six yards away and a later penalty. His performance in that match placed him at the forefront of the day's goalkeepers. Retford Town Football Club tried to tempt him away from Lincoln City but Charles' son thinks he declined the offer. He certainly went on to play for Doncaster Rovers and Boston Town. And Charles may be remembered by Gainsborough people as the man who developed Scotter Common.

When foresters finished planting their first trees on the Gainsborough to Scunthorpe road, a large area of scrub and moorland stretched out towards the villages of Scotton and

Scotter and Charles saw in this a possibility for developing the land for agricultural purposes. He built a bungalow for himself and then cultivated the land around it 'making the desert bloom' because others followed and in a matter of a few years, the Scotton side of Gainsborough Road was built up.

The Gossiper. September 26, 2000.

Advertising: A painted advertisement on the wall of a building in Canwick Road, Lincoln.

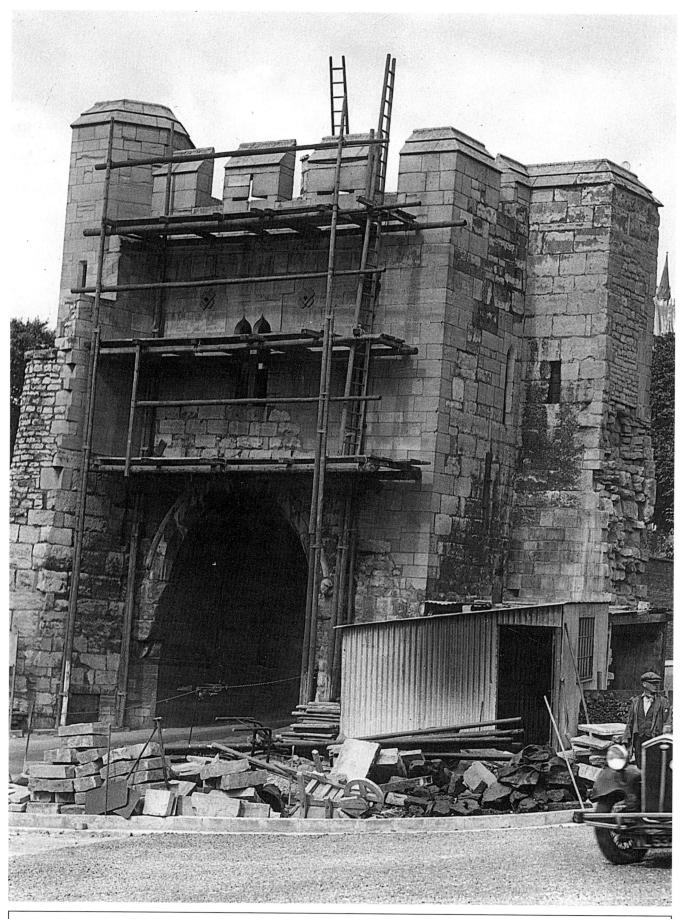

For centuries, traffic of all kinds has travelled through Pottergate Arch on their way down into the centre of Lincoln. Increasing numbers and double-decker buses meant that the arch was unsuitable and the road was altered to go around the arch, on the right side of this picture. Traffic travelling uphill had used a road on the left for many years. (Echo Ref. RI-222)

Childhood Days In A City Park

BY DAY, they played cricket and soccer between the trees. By night, they pitched their tents beside the lake and frightened themselves with tales of ghosts and the supernatural. In the winter, they trampled across the frozen lake and in the summer they raced and chased between the rhododendron bushes. Growing up in and around Hartsholme Park, half-a-century ago, was a time of innocence for the area's children who enjoyed it all, made their own fun, in a way that present and perhaps future generations may never be able.

In recent times, there has been controversy over the prospect of felling some mature trees in the park and talk of the level of water in the lake being reduced. And prompted by all this, Derek Newton, who now lives in William Street, Saxilby, wrote to recall those happy childhood times in Hartsholme Park. 'Going back nearly 50 years, we used to play cricket and football on the old caravan site. In the autumn, the park's chestnut trees were full of conkers. In the winter, there might be thick ice on the lake and you could possibly walk across to the island. You could travel the length of rhododendron lane without touching the ground, by climbing along and among the bushes. Behind one side of the lane were the ferns where access could be gained to the pine woods on the edge of the old Skellingthorpe airfield. The airfield was like a magnet to us and many an hour was

Playground: Hartsholme Park, Lincoln, bringing back memories of childhood days.

spent in the old buildings that still remained.

'In the park, there was the promontory behind Shearwater Road that we called the tunnels, created by large rhododendron bushes reaching up and across to form tunnels where you could climb and play hide and seek. Also here, there were punch trees – trees with soft trunks that you could strike with your fist without hurting yourself. The park was used for all-night camping (not an official campsite) and in the days when I was interested in angling, I fished from every spot around the lake and up the river. Dark nights never deterred us from entering the park to play. Armed with torches we would still play hide and seek, but this was eventually abandoned after we were frightened by 'ghosts' while playing in the old greenhouses behind the old hall. I think, that night, we could have had a serious claim to the 440-yard world record!

'One thing that we did treat with respect was the old hall itself. In those days, it was still being used occasionally by the Civil Defence. But some brave (or foolish) people still managed to enter although it was in a very poor state. Some of my courting was done in the park and later I had the pleasure of walking my own children around the lake and reminiscing on where I had been and what I had done in my childhood days. Unfortunately the youngsters of today do not have the same opportunities we had back in the 1950s.'
The Gossiper. February 22, 2000.

I Crowded The Queen Mum

DURING my years as an *Echo* photographer, I only had one opportunity to photograph Queen Elizabeth, the Queen Mother. It was when she visited RAF Scampton to meet the Red Arrows, which she did quite frequently as their Commander-in-Chief. After all the formal (or with the Queen Mum, informal) proceedings and lunch, she went out to meet families of airmen at the base. There was just one problem.

Press photographers were kept some 15 yards behind the Queen Mum during her walkabout, with a line of cars in between. No amount of protesting would make the powers-that-be change their minds. Getting pictures seemed pretty hopeless until I spotted a TV cameraman actually in the crowd where the Queen Mum was talking to the people. So I thought: 'What's good enough for him is good enough for me.'

When I thought no one was looking, I left the press party and sneaked over to the crowd, joining a group of waiting children. A few minutes later the Queen Mum arrived and when she spotted my camera, she stopped and chatted to the children, giving me some lovely smiles and even time to change cameras for both black-and-white and colour. It made my day, but a few minutes later I felt a hand on my shoulder and I was escorted back to the official press party. I didn't care. I had the pictures which I wanted!
Lincolnian's Diary. August 5, 1999.

All smiles: The Queen Mother during her RAF Scampton visit.

You might think that the historic heart of Lincoln does not change much from one decade to another. But you would be wrong, as these two pictures show. Gordon Road links Bailgate with St Paul's Lane and is used by residents and tourists alike. Sixty years ago, there were cottages in the street, behind the shops which fronted on to Bailgate. At the end of Gordon Road William Elderkin had his baker's shop and on the other corner of this narrow street was Mrs Lucy Horton's toy shop, which also dealt in wool and needlework materials.

It looks like a different world today, the old cottages have been replaced by modern shops and a café and the whole street springs into life during the tourist season, especially at the time of the Christmas market, when thousands of visitors trample over its cobbles.

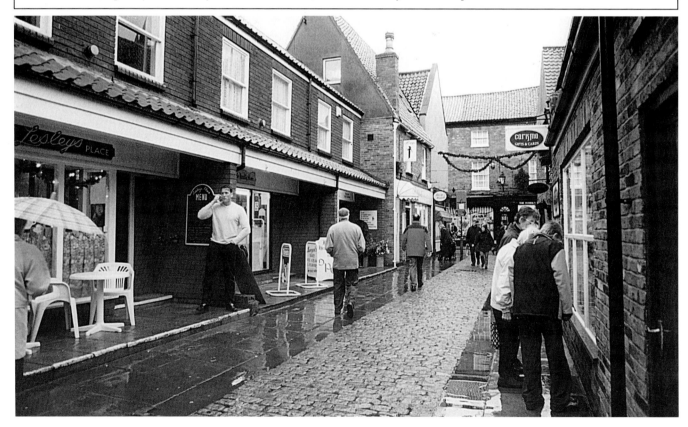

Great Man's Links With Our City

THERE has been a lot of discussion lately as to who was the person who was most influential in the 20th century. The person who comes very near the top of the list, if not the top, is Winston Churchill, who died on January 24, 1965. It was Churchill who, despite being First Lord of the Admiralty, was a prime mover in the invention of the tank as a fighting weapon in the First World War.

Winston Churchill came to Lincoln three times. His first visit was in 1902, when he gave a lecture in the Corn Exchange, about his experiences as a news correspondent in the Boer War, where he was taken prisoner. Eight years later, as the Liberal Home Secretary, he called in at Lincoln on Election Day. He attempted to speak to a crowd assembled below the Liberal Club balcony, despite an agreement between the Liberals and the Unionists (Conservatives). He was howled down by the crowd and someone pointed out to Churchill that the Unionist candidate, Sir Robert Filmer, was standing nearby. Churchill went to speak to him and on the way back, was struck over the head by a woman wielding an umbrella. It was rumoured that when the time came for Winston to leave the club, he was smuggled out using a cape and policeman's helmet as a disguise. This was, many years later, denied by the great man.

His third visit to the city came during the Second World War. In September 1939, Churchill was back at the Admiralty and once more, could not help interfering

Childhood Days At The Northern

CLEMENT ATTLEE was taken up with the place, a teenage Peter Scott called in with his mother and the huge Italian heavyweight Primo Carnera made the floorboards groan. But it's not these VIP guests that Denis Long remembers from his childhood days at the Great Northern Hotel in Lincoln High Street. It's the larger-than-life guests like Harold Cannon, who had a permanent suite at the hotel.

'He was a man of huge girth and an appetite to match. He was of independent means and did no work. He played golf and breakfasted on porridge, two kippers, at least two eggs, bacon, sausages, liver, kidneys and several rounds of toast,' recalls Denis, whose father and mother, Charles and Annie Lang, managed the hotel from 1919 to 1948. 'He and my father didn't get on. Although neither had any interest in the practice of religion, they were Roman Catholic and Protestant respectively and they quarrelled. Poor Cannon suffered greatly from wartime rationing and I was told, he became a shadow of his former self.'

Prompted by my recent items about the old hotel, Denis got in touch from Newcastle-on-Tyne. 'The sombre fact is that I must be among the few people who remember the hotel between the wars. The trains ran past the hotel. My father's office was on the first floor by the railway side. Here he would sit, writing up his books for head office when a train would pull up and the engine, below his window would whistle or let off steam. The noise was considerable. It was difficult to think or to speak. Up would go the window and a shouting match would take place between my father and the engine driver. The driver would vainly try to explain that he personally wasn't responsible for the noise the engine was making. It had a mind of its own. But there was no malice in any of this. It was a kind of ritual exchange between manager and driver and it frequently happened.

'My mother was a kind and considerate person who put herself out, especially for the well-being of service personnel who came to the hotel, airmen in particular. One night, I was home on leave and two young Canadian airmen sought a bed for the night. The hotel was full, so they were very grateful when my mother made up two beds on our upstairs sitting room floor. At about 11pm, wondering if they were warm enough, my mother took two blankets up to the room and knocked on the door. Unfortunately, they had two girls with them. My mother was a Northern Irish Presbyterian with a moral code to match. The girls fled. Even now, nearly 60 years on, I recall in detail what she said to them.'

The Gossiper. March 7, 2000.

Prime Minister: Clement Attlee, speaking in Lincoln, who visited the Great Northern Hotel. (Echo Ref. RI-422)

with land warfare, thank goodness. He wanted some means whereby Allied troops could advance in safety on the Siegfried Line. His idea was for a trench-digging machine to be operated under cover of darkness. Ideas flowed and a model was made. After a successful demonstration, the task of making the full-sized machine was given to Ruston-Bucyrus and a section of the factory was bricked-off to maintain secrecy. It was

during this period of construction that Winston Churchill paid a visit to the factory to see the progress on the machine. He watched tests of 'Nellie', as the machine came to be known and it proved a success. But it never went into action. By the time that enough could have been built, the Allies were no longer within a night's crawl of the Siegfried Line.

Churchill had one other link with Lincoln. While at

Harrow, he was, for a time 'fag' to the head boy, Frederick Cyril Nugent Hicks, who became Bishop of Lincoln in 1942. There is a story of Hicks giving Churchill a 'whopping', for some misdemeanour. Churchill said to Hicks 'I shall be a greater man than you', to which Hicks replied 'You can take two more for that' and landed a couple more in the same place.

Lincolnian's Diary. January 18, 2000.

Family group: The Eccleshare family pose for a group photograph.

Perfect Partners In Business And Love

THE STORY of Frank Eccleshare starts in the last century and his mother's family, the Reeds, who farmed at Eagle Barnsdale. The boys worked on the farm and the girls went into service. They started in the kitchen and climbed the ladder to be 'my lady's maid'.

Lillian worked at the 'big house' Morton Hall, the home of Captain Torr whose daughter Rosetta Forbes became the lady explorer. His father Hal was employed by a local decorating firm working at the hall and when they met, Hal Eccleshare and Lillian Reed fell instantly in love. He decided to go to America to seek his fortune and when he was settled, Lillian, in spite of dire warnings, followed him. She sailed from Southampton and enjoyed a fair crossing. 'The food was not very good.' She told her son. 'And the conditions for the lower deck passengers appalling.' She landed in Boston and married her beloved Hal in a dress made by her mother. They worked for four years but became homesick and returned to Lincoln.

Lillian and Hal decided to set up a shop in the High Street where they combined his trade with a hardware and wallpaper shop. Without any doubt she was the brains of the business. Hal got contracts to paint local pub signs and Lillian stocked the shop with pots, pans and 'gusunders' (chamber pots) as well as decorators' items.

Frank was born above the shop called The Star Bazaar and he recalls those days as being very happy. His job was to edge rolls of wallpaper for his father's customers. 'My fingers got sore with pushing them through the scissors handles,' he grumbled. But as more work came in Lillian bought a cutting machine. 'Mother's business brain showed in her offer of giving every customer free trimming for the first four rolls. This wouldn't paper a whole room so they had to pay something,' he said.

The shop stood between Ozzie Duncan's Herbalist Shop – considered a bit risque – and Swales, one of the most popular drapers in town. 'We used to watch as the ladies went into Ozzies for a packet of 'pink' pills. They always spoke in whispers and pushed the packets into their handbags and scurried away.' He laughed. The children would wait with a bucket and shovel to pick up the manure left by horses delivering to the pubs and shops. 'You could get up to 2d (less than 1p) from keen gardeners for a bucket full,' he said.

Bette's Bygones. May 23, 2000.

Early days: Frank Eccleshare with his mother outside the Star Bazaar.

Lots Of Fun On The Cricket Pitch

A LETTER from an old friend Nev Needham asked me if I remembered the time, in the 1950s and '60s, when the Lincoln YMCA had a pretty good cricket team, but no home ground to play on!

Nev says, 'All our fixtures were away, we did not have our own ground. We played at all the local village grounds and some top-class fixtures, such as the Guest Eleven at Belton Park, played on the green in front of Belton House. Most of the Belton Eleven would be Cranwell Officer cadets and the local gentry. It made something for the visitors to see, the quick procession of our team going in and out at very regular intervals.'

Memories: Nev Needham.

Nev lists the names of the team and some of the names are very familiar to me: Cliff Proverbs, Phil Schofield,

Tony Bosworth, Dick Horner, Norman Horner, Dennis Carter, Newton Loynes, Larry Mosedale, Maurice Storr, Pat Shillingford, Fred Reed, Charlie Banks, Jack Ancliffe. Nev himself was wicket-keeper and the team's travelling umpire was Sid Proverbs, who sometimes would play if the team was short of players.

At that time Nev had an A55 van, number 297 BFW, which the lads in the team said stood for 'Big Fat Wicketkeeper'.

Another incident recalled by Nev concerns the time when he played clarinet in the City School Orchestra. The rest of the woodwind section included Derek Storr and Frank ('Baggy') Palmer, who died recently. During one school service, in the cathedral, with the orchestra under the baton of Canon Ozzie Jones, there was a part of the service when the orchestra wasn't playing for some time. I would think it might have been the sermon or something like that. However, to while away the time, the trio decided to play Three Card Brag! Nev tells me that he did not win, so 'Ozzie's boss' could not have been too pleased with him.

I can recall the time in the late 1950s when the *Echo* had a cricket team and like the YMCA, had no home ground. We used to play our 'home' games either on the

West Common, or on the Post Office sports ground on Wragby Road, if it wasn't in use. There is one incident which will always remain in my memory from a game against our sister paper, the *Grimsby Evening Telegraph*. One of our team was an *Echo* photographer who was persuaded to play to make up the team. As he stood at the wicket to face the bowler, he called a halt to play and walked up to the bowler and said 'I've not played before, please don't bowl too fast!'

Does it come as any surprise that he was out first ball?

Lincolnian's Diary. September 19, 2000.

Content To Live A Simple Rural Life

M ORE memories from the writings of Horace Spencer. Pungent smell of strong tobacco wafted across the field of frozen Brussels sprouts.

The man smoking the pipe some 70 years young said, 'Let's go into the house, I want to talk to you'. I only wanted to discuss a small parish matter but was content to stay a while. He lived alone in his cottage which stood in two acres. In the living room I sat in an old high-backed chair with a cushion tied to the back. On one side of the room a flitch of bacon hung from the ceiling almost obscuring a picture of Lord Roberts in the Boer War.

The year was 1931, but as I talked to the old man I seemed to slip back to 1900. He put his

hand on the oven door, satisfied it was hot enough and then fetched a piece of bacon and a basin full of meal paste. He covered the bacon with the paste before placing it into the oven.

'If a man has a pig, some flour and some apples, he can live,' he said. This business of living was becoming very difficult. The old man was apparently content to live in the fashion of 1900. I asked if he read a newspaper and he replied that he read the local weekly and one sent by his brother from New Zealand. I drew a contrast in my mind of life on Lincolnshire soil in 1900 and 1931. The man of the soil in 1931 could buy a second-hand car for £5 and he already had his pig, flour and apples.

But something had gone wrong. The economists had got things mixed up. The unemployment figures had risen to two million, bringing widespread suffering and distress while at the same time thousands of tons of good potatoes had gone rotten in the piles and many

farms had become derelict. But this new world had not yet reached the cottage. I listened as he talked of crops, prices and large white pigs. I was comparing his life with mine. He had no domestic responsibilities. I had a wife and two children. He had never known unemployment while I had to struggle for a job. He had no one constantly telling him every month that his figures were very disappointing.

It seemed there was something to be said for a pig, flour and apples.

There was an inde-pendence and contentment. 'I want to tell you something,' he said. 'I don't know whether to buy a horse or get married.' I didn't know what to say. He looked worried as he pondered his problem. I asked his age. '72' he replied. I was unable to advise him and when I met him a year later and without mentioning the subject I found out that he had neither a horse or a wife.

Bette's Bygones. May 16, 2000.

They Fell In Love In A City Park

SHE WAS 13 and he was 15, but from the first moment they met, they knew they were in love. Teenage dates were spent in Boultham Park, walking round the lake and carving their initials on a wooden seat.

Then came the war. He joined the Royal Navy and sailed away, while she stayed in Lincoln. They thought they would never see each other again but, two years after the war, fate took a hand. They bumped into each other in Lincoln. Two years later they married, and they stayed together until his death 35 years later.

The story is recounted by Lorna Nicholls of Thorpe Avenue, Lincoln, prompted by our recent items on those bygone days in Boultham Park. 'My late husband, Len, and I first met in Boultham Park,' she writes. 'Some people might think it is impossible for a girl of 13 to fall in love, but I took one look at this handsome boy and fell in love. I was still at school but he was working, at Bracebridge Brick Works. I think he liked me too as we were in a group of boys and girls, but we picked each other.

'He was a very shy boy and even though we went out together for three months, we only ever-held hands or he would put his arm around me. We spent many happy hours in Boultham Park and we used to walk round the lake or sit on a seat near to the boathouse. I remember we carved our initials in that seat.

'When he was 17 I learned that he had joined the navy and I really thought I would never see him again. The war started and in the years that followed I had many boyfriends and he must have had girlfriends, although he sailed all over the world. He told me in later years that he had been to South America and South Africa. I never thought we would meet again, although I still thought of him sometimes.

'Fate must have taken a hand and it was our destiny to meet again because, in November 1947, I was going home from work one dinnertime, walking along Canwick Road and who should be coming towards me but the boy I had loved so long ago. Of course, he was now a man, but I recognised him instantly. He still had the same blue eyes and lovely smile. We looked at each other and then we spoke. Neither of us could believe that this meeting had happened, and we were still attracted to each other. For the next 18 months we were inseparable. We saw each other every lunchtime, teatime and evening, and in July 1949 we were married.

'Our marriage lasted for 35 years until the death of my husband. This is why Boultham Park will always be a special place to me. My husband and I went back there on several occasions after we had met again, and after we were married. Sometimes I think I would like to go there and walk once more round the lake and through the trees, sit in the summerhouse and see if our initials are still on that seat. But then again I know it would not be the same. In my mind I will always have a picture of the time when we first met and fell in love.'

The Gossiper. February 1, 2000.

Aggi Always A Tonic To The Community

I WONDER what that stalwart army of early District Nurses would think to all the modern techniques and methods of today! They and the local doctor dealt with all the ailments of the people living in villages and the remote surrounding areas. They cycled miles in all weathers to minister to the sick and dying or to bring yet another life into the world. And in the village of Ingham on the limestone escarpment Aggies' Cottage is a lasting memorial to Nurse Agnes Donoghue Gill, who for many years was the district nurse for that area.

Aggi (as she became affectionately known) was born in Yorkshire and decided to follow her sister into the nursing profession. On completion of her training she travelled down to London and qualified as a midwife, going on to work and deliver babies in the tough East End of the city. In 1935 she moved to Ingham on a five-year contract as district nurse and midwife. She stayed until retirement. At her funeral service Dr John Alwyn related these memories of Aggi who was know as a 'character'.

'Agnes was an ecumenical Catholic lady who always supported local jumble sales or fetes, irrespective of denomination. She was a very astute lady and would be found searching through the stalls looking for a bargain'. And once she had gathered all her 'goodies' together Aggi would pleasantly renegotiate the asking price – and usually won. But there was much more to Aggi. She was very tough and considering the terrain most district nurses covered, it was part of the criteria of the job. 'In the Second World War she would be seen on her bicycle at all hours of the day or night, riding through the villages to stitch up a cut or bring a new baby into the world,' said Dr Alwyn.

She married a local lad by special licence and lived in her cottage until in her 90s. District nurses were expected to set an example and be pillars of society. They had to be calm in extreme emergencies and have the professional insight to know when to seek help. They sat with women in labour and by the bedside of the dying, giving comfort to the relatives. But they were firm and patients did as they were told! Aggi Gill lived up to those expectations and became a staunch member of the community. She was a founder member of the Women's Institute and a keen whist player.

There are many stories of her hair-raising journeys, in all weathers, either on her cycle or on the back of her husband's motorbike, to visit her patients. Among her belongings was her uniform – immaculate and complete with celluloid collar and cuffs. 'Her midwifery bag was beautifully maintained, even after all these years,' said Dr Alwyn. 'And it was also extremely adequate for her work.

From that one can perceive that she was a meticulous practitioner. The medical profession owes a great debt to the Agnes Gills of this world.' And a great many people also owe them their lives.

Bette's Bygones. November 2, 1999.

Westgate is one of those streets in Lincoln which has changed over the years without really changing at all. It was an early morning in the mid 1950s when the old photograph was taken. Prominent are the triple towers of Lincoln Cathedral and on the left, just beyond the line of houses, is the tiny spire of St Paul-in-the-Bail church, which was demolished some 25 years later. On the right is the Strugglers Inn and beyond the block of houses in the centre of the picture was an agricultural implement repairers. And prominent, on the left, is a police pillar used both by the police and for the public to make emergency telephone calls.

Today, the Strugglers Inn is still there, but the adjacent cottages have been replaced by a public toilet block and the police pillar has gone in this day of mobile radios and telephones. The road has been realigned and a new mini roundabout installed at the Burton Road/Union Road junction.

Ornamental: One of the two fountains which were at the ends of the terrace in the Arboretum.

Heyday Of The Arboretum

THE FLOWERBEDS were always a talking point… The conservatory was a joy to behold… And the peacock was one of the most popular residents. Most Lincoln people have happy childhood memories of the Arboretum. This special article, on one of the city's most popular parks,

has been written from information supplied by Eileen Rankin, whose father, Mr Charles Shambrook, was park superintendent for many years from April 1936 until his retirement.

It was the Second World War which put an end to one of the most popular features in the Arboretum. Until then, the one place families would visit again and again was the conservatory – the home of all sorts of flowers, plants and shrubs. For youngsters, another big attraction was the

Spring sunshine: Sunshine filters through the overhanging branches and tempts people out for a walk in the Arboretum. (Echo Ref. RI-4272)

Winters tale: Even in winter, the Arboretum was still a favourite place for a walk.

ornamental pond and fountain in the middle. It was here where the family of goldfish used to live – until that fateful Sunday afternoon when a lone German bomber attacked the city.

Eileen Rankin recalls: 'An enemy aircraft was high-tailing it for home and loosed

its last three bombs in a string. They hit the nurses' home, but no one was injured because the shift was changing over. A bomb fell on Sister Swan's home which had been commandeered by the Army. It should have been empty but one officer, who had returned to continue his

92

Victorian delight: An old picture postcard view of Lincoln Arboretum a century ago.

work, was killed. The conservatory in the Arboretum was shattered beyond repair. The pond in the middle was cracked and lost its water, but amazingly, when the glass was cleared out of it a few days later, the fish were still alive. They had been trapped in a bit of water under the broken glass. They lived out their lives in the pond that Dad had made in the Lodge's own garden.'

But what happened to all the plants and palms that used to be a feature of the conservatory? Recalls Eileen: 'After the shattering blast, they were the first things to be removed, because of their temperature needs. They were taken to the large glasshouses in Boultham Park.' Another vivid memory that Eileen has of those bygone times in the Arboretum happened sometime afterwards. 'There was

once a wigwam of tall wooden poles, rather like telegraph poles, stored in the Arboretum for some reason. Children often used to use them as a wigwam and one day, some of them thought it would be fun to light a fire inside. You can imagine the result. Fortunately, the children were on the entrance side of the fire, so they were able to get out.'

If you remember the

peacock which used to live in the park, then you probably remember the bantams. 'Dad kept chickens in our own garden by the Lodge, regularly supplying some local shops with eggs. A family friend gave me the bantams as a birthday present but they did not get on with the chickens so they were rehoused with a bird they had to be more respectful to.'

Eileen, whose home is now in Ruskington, also well recalls those special flower beds which used to be a feature as you entered by the main gate. Special occasions were marked over the years and thanks to the skill of Mr Shambrook and the park's staff, few events passed by unnoticed. Among those you may remember were the initials of successive mayors and a display for the coronation of King George VI in 1937.

Why one bed formed the picture of an elephant, with the name Jumbo underneath, isn't – at first glance – very obvious.

The Gossiper. November 14, 2000.

Gateway: The Monks Road entrance to Lincoln Arboretum. (Echo Ref. RI-4272)

Changes In Style And Methods

Talking about the 1950s seems like yesterday but is half a century ago. A lot of things have changed and perhaps one of the greatest differences is in hairdressing. Carousel Coiffure of North Hykeham is a reputable and popular hair salon opened by Hans Nettesheim more than 28 years ago, but his experience and career goes back much further. Hans wrote and told me that the picture of the curling tongs featured in *The Way We Were* brought many memories of his hair-dressing apprenticeship which start in Germany in 1954.

'One of my first tools of the trade was a pair of curling tongs. In those days, we used to do a Marcel Ironwave different from the fingerwave. Marcel waves were done on dry, long hair and usually had an end perm at the back of the head.

When we became proficient we used to check the heat of the tongs on our upper lip by almost 'smelling' the heat. Unfortunately, too often the nose got in the way and we got some nasty burns. In Germany it was compulsory to train in both men's and ladies', which has stood me in good stead.'

Having worked in large salons, including in Cologne, Hans decided he would like to come to England to learn the language. He set off on a world tour and visited Sydney, New Zealand, India and London. While in London he met his first wife who was a local Lincoln lass. On first coming to England he worked in London earning £10 a week, £4.50 of which went on board and lodging. In those days it was cubicle work – very private – but the cold perm had been introduced. Before that the hair was attached to a machine by electric wires and plugs.

During his time in London Hans coiffured the hair of Maria Bueono, the winner of the 1959 Womens' singles at Wimbledon. He also worked for Mr Ronald who did the hair of the competitive ballroom dancers. 'The salon was closed for the day when we styled the dancers. Violet Barnes, Nellie Duggan and Valerie White were among those I did.' Hans laughingly added that they were 'very catty'.

He worked in many well-known salons and in 1962 opened his own salon in the East End of London. But as children came along the daily travelling became too stressful and in 1972 Hans came to Lincoln. At that time a wash and set was between 4s 6d (22p) to 7s 6d (37½p) and a perm between two and three guineas (£2.10, £3.15).

His advice after all these years of experience is not to over-process hair or over condition it.

'One of the best setting lotions in my young days was light ale but we had to give it up because we drank too much.'

Bette's Bygones. July 25, 2000.

Driver Went Down With His Tractor

I HAD a letter a few weeks ago from Mrs Steph Ingamells, of Saxilby, reminding me of an incident in 1963, involving her father, Ray Miles, during the extremely severe winter of that year. Ray was the licensee of the Anglers Hotel, Saxilby and during conversation in the pub one evening, someone recalled that a few years ago, a horse and cart had been driven over the frozen surface of the Foss Dyke Canal. Ray thought that he could drive his 35cwt tractor from Saxilby, along the canal, to the Pywewipe Inn.

Bales of straw were placed by the side of the bank and the tractor was gently driven on to the ice. Wearing a hat and with his pipe clenched between his teeth, Ray drove the tractor for a mile down the canal and then reached the railway bridge. Unfortunately, the ice here was only five inches thick. A crack appeared and then, when everything seemed to be going OK, the tractor slipped backwards and the back end of the machine, with Ray aboard, disappeared under the surface. For a while, only Ray's straw boater could be seen bobbing about on the surface, then up he came, spluttering, but still with his pipe between his teeth. As one onlooker commented, 'He went down like a true ship's captain – with his ship.'

Afterwards, wet and bedraggled, but still smiling, Ray told how his leg had been trapped and he showed a bruise to prove it. People believe that if he had been able to start from near the chemical works, he would have made it, but unfortunately it was not possible to get the tractor on the ice at that point. Mrs Ingamells tells me that the 'drive' was not done as a bet, as many people thought, it just came up in conversation and Ray thought he could do it. It made the headlines of the front page of the *Lincolnshire Echo* and chief photographer Ken James was on hand to record the whole incident.

Lincolnian's Diary. March 14, 2000.

Breaking the ice: A newspaper cutting from the Lincolnshire Echo in February 1963 showing pictures of Ray Miles' tractor falling through the ice on the Foss Dyke Canal.

Imps Legend Hit Six Goals

FOOTBALL transfer fees are in the news at the moments with moves to limit the huge fees that are paid when a player moves clubs. But 50 years ago, Lincoln City paid out a fee in the region of £3,000 to bring a player to the club who was to become a legend and hero in the eyes of many supporters. It was on September 21, 1950, that the *Echo* reported that the Imps had signed Andy Graver, Newcastle United reserve centre-forward, after a month's concentrated effort by manager Bill Anderson.

The *Echo* report read 'Andy, who is 22, weighs 12 stones and is 5ft 10ins tall came to Lincoln's notice before the season opened and while they were making enquiries for a leader to replace Jock Dodds. Manager Bill Anderson went north to watch him as soon as football started and decided then that Graver was the man who could turn the goal-shy City attack into a promotion proposition. Newcastle declined to talk transfer business about Graver. They did not want to part with a player who was doing well in their Central League side. Mr Anderson persisted and was rebuffed, but he never let up. Finally, at Tuesday's board meeting it was decided that the chairman (Mr C.W. Applewhite), Mr Edgar Gilbert and the manager should go up to Newcastle yesterday. This they did, permission was finally given for them to approach Graver and the deal was completed, Lincoln paying something like a £3,000 fee.'

Andy had played prev-iously with Willington, who had won the FA Amateur Cup and Annfield Plain before signing for Newcastle as a professional, but he only played one game in the First Division side. Bill Anderson's move paid off. That season, the Imps finished fifth in the Third Division (Northern Section) and the following season, were promoted to the Second Division after finishing the season as champions. But Andy's early days at Sincil Bank saw him so homesick that after every game, he caught the train back home to be with his friends and family. It was only the intervention of manager Bill Anderson, a fellow northerner that kept Andy at Lincoln.

Andy did leave the club, twice, but came back each time and in his three spells with the Imps, he made 274 appearances and scored 143 goals. But it was on September 29, 1951, that Andy made probably his biggest impact at Sincil Bank, when the Imps played Crewe Alexandra in the FA Cup. City won by 11 goals to one, with Andy scoring six of them, before a crowd of over 11,000. I am proud to say that I was in that crowd and saw Andy play on many more occasions.

Little could I have known then that I would get to know Andy much more, as just over 20 years later, we were both members of the Lincoln Section of the Feucht Frohliche Neustadter and spent many happy moments serving wine at numerous wine tastings.
Lincolnian's Diary. September 12, 2000.

Footballing hero: Lincoln City's Andy Graver, a six-goal scorer.

Britain's First Disco DJ

WHATEVER happened to Ron Diggins and his Diggola? That's the question I asked in The Gossiper column the other day, when I mentioned the man who used to provide the music and games for many an annual dinner dance and works function. Well, the good news is that Ron is still alive and well and living not far from Boston. And although he's now approaching his 84th birthday, it's still less than six years since Ron spun his last disc.

Of all the DJs who have ever sat behind a disco unit, Ron was the first. It all started back in 1946, when he was working at his radio and electrical equipment shop in Boston. One day, the following year, along came some Land Army girls and asked if he could play the records for their dance in nearby Swineshead. Armed with a stack of 78rpm records and a wind-up gramophone, Ron loaded everything into the back of his Hillman Minx shooting brake and off he went. He quickly realised that if he was to start appearing at dancehalls regularly, he would need something more elaborate. So, with some brand new public address equipment, twin turntables, a 12 volt amplifier and a control panel, Ron's first Diggola was born. It was to be the first of several and every new Diggola would be more impressive than the last. The front panel would change colour. Stage curtains would provide a backdrop. There would be a mirror ball and the whole thing had a mark of showmanship about it. 'So where did the name Diggola come from?' I asked.

'The first four letters came from my name and because it looked like a miniature cinema organ and they were called organolas in those days, I joined the two words together to make Diggola,' explained Ron. He built a total of seven Diggolas in his workshops and when the demand exceeded more than one man could meet, he employed other DJs with other Diggola units. 'We covered an area from Scunthorpe and the Humber, to St Neots and Nottingham.' To cater for the non-dancers, Ron made sure his evening's programmes included a number of games. 'Most of the games were my idea and we never did anything that was too embarrassing', he recalls.

But although Ron has taken almost 22,000 bookings for his Diggola units, he is the first to confess he's no dancer himself. 'I have done one or two old-time favourites, but I have never done a quickstep in my life,' he says. Three of Ron's Diggolas survive.
The Gossiper. December 5, 2000.

A Character Of The City Is Missed

EVERY town and city has its characters, some better known than others and Lincoln has been no exception to this in the past. A lot of readers will remember 'Briggy'. He could be seen almost every day in Lincoln High Street and I can recall him from the time when I was a schoolboy. In the 1940s and '50s, his favourite haunt was Woolworth's tea bar and woe betide anyone who had just ordered a cup of tea and then looked away for a moment. The cuppa had mysteriously emptied and I watched this happening many times with amusement. His favourite words were 'Got a fag, mate?'.

Everyone knew him, but little about him and as schoolchildren, we were scared of him and would run a mile if he appeared. In later years, he was employed by Lincoln City Council as a road sweeper, well to be politically correct, street cleansing operative. I remember going to his retirement presentation at City Hall. You just could not recognise him, instead of the overcoat which he invariably wore, he arrived in suit and tie and you felt that this man was overwhelmed by the occasion.

Of course, he was referred to throughout as 'Briggy' and it was not until later, when I was writing the caption, that I realised that no one had used his real name. A phone call to City Hall and they had to admit that they did not know it, but it would be in the records. They rang me back. 'His name is Leslie Briggs,' I was told. After his retirement, 'Briggy' could still be seen in the High Street, sitting on a bench, but he now had a new trick up his sleeve.

There were at that time, quite a few buskers in the street, earning a few bob with their music. So 'Briggy' bought a mouth organ and sat playing it. Well, to say 'playing' was a bit of an exaggeration. He just blew up and down the holes, making a sound. But there were always a few coppers in his cap, beside him, which no doubt would provide him with a few more of his favourite Woodbines.

He died a little while ago and left the city a little sadder at the passing of one its characters.

Lincolnian's Diary. November 9, 1999.

Our Singalong While Cycling

WE ALL have different memories of the war years – of childhood games, family life and of the aftermath of war.

These memories, sent in by readers, cover some of those years. They are part of our history. We are delighted to hear from you.

Mrs Mary Capp of Doddington Park, Lincoln, recalls her dancing days in the 1940s. 'I can remember we used to leave our cycles in Saltergate garage, walk to the Drill Hall and after the dance finished pick up the cycles and ride home again – in the dark as it was in the blackout. But we never bothered. We would ride along singing our heads off. I wonder if anyone else can remember? I still go dancing – but not with my bike!'

Lewis Reynolds, of Gainsborough, writes to tell me of the days before computers and television. 'Memories came flooding back of the games and things we did to occupy our young lives. Mind you, it was a time when we were not afraid to stop a man in the street and ask: 'Any fag cards mister?' And he would stand there while he opened his Park Drive packet to find us a cigarette card and hand it to us. For the boys it was a time for Rally (Relive) O'Rusty Bum, marbles, Snobs and can anyone remember the game Peggy – mind the windows? The girls had their hopscotch and together we all had our whips and tops with chalk on the top produce lovely patterns. We would go to the fruit shop to buy a penny orange rope and boys and girls would get together to have a good all in skipping: 'All, in, a bottle of gin, all out, a bottle of stout'. And how many remember the sedate game of Pin'a'Prick Book. I remember one girl had such smashing pictures in a book and with my mother being a dressmaker, I was able to get a good few pins so I could have a good number of goes to try to win some of her treasures. To please children nowadays seems to cost parents a lot of money to purchase the things they think they need. It did not cost anything at all for the enjoyment we made ourselves but looking back we were happy with what we had and it kept us all very busy. That is until Mum called out: 'Come on, it's bedtime'. And then it was fine tooth comb through the hair and off to bed – tired out. Happy Days.'

And Billy Hoe, a Burma Star Veteran of Bracebridge Heath, says he reads our articles on the good old days and current affairs and can relate to both, but his opinions differ somewhat. He does not agree with all the whingeing and says: 'It seems that anyone born about 1930 in general is full of whinge. We now have the poor pensioner and the poorer pensioners.

'The threshold set to ensure all creature comforts can be met, is probably a little low. But add on benefits, allowances and wonderful help given by the voluntary services and no one need be more than a little deprived. The poor will always be with us.'

Bette's Bygones. November 7, 2000.

Personality: Leslie Briggs.

Our Man At St Mark's

WHEN I started as a pupil at the City School there was one teacher's name I knew even before I stepped through the door. My cousin, a former pupil at the School had 'warned' me about Ozzie Jones! Canon Arthur Oswald Jones was a teacher at the school and the school chaplain as well as being vicar of St Mark's Church, Lincoln. Having a singing voice that was much better then, I was soon 'recruited' into the school choir and taking up the violin soon met up with Ozzie.

He was respected by all and feared by a few. Anyone showing a lack of understanding of the subject he was being taught was soon labelled by Ozzie as a 'blithering idiot'. Ozzie took us for Religious Instruction, music and, if my memory serves me right, maths. I remember once during a music lesson, he asked if any boy could sing the notes of the Cathedral quarter chimes. I offered and won a three-penny bit for my effort. After I left school, I lost touch with Ozzie for a while, until I started taking photographs for the *Echo*.

Ozzie had the ability to fill St Mark's Church when he held services. These were not just for people. Many will remember the annual Pet's Service, when the church was filled to capacity with animals and their owners. Whenever there was a wedding at St Mark's and we were due to take photographs, we knew we were in for a long wait. Ozzie made sure the couple really knew that they were married. During his wedding sermon, if he saw someone in the congregation he knew, he would speak to them and tell any story about them he could recall. It was a sad loss to Lincoln when he died and he would have been even sadder to have known that his beloved St Mark's was to be demolished.

My memories about Canon Ozzie Jones a few weeks ago has prompted Mrs Jane Hayes, of Lincoln to write to me with more memories. Jane tells me that her father was very nervous as a child and going to the City School was very different to his earlier schooldays at St Botolph's School. Ozzie was not only vicar of St Mark's Church, but also a teacher at the school. His great loves were music and cricket.

Jane's father was a good cricketer. Ozzie got to know of this and one morning, at assembly, he stood on the stage in front of the whole school and shouted 'Where's Plumley?'. Young Plumley went to the front wondering just what he had done wrong. 'Now, Plumley', said Ozzie, 'will you tell the school how many runs you scored at cricket yesterday?' Jane doesn't know how many runs it was, but it must have been quite a lot otherwise Ozzie would not have called him out. 'Now, school,' he said, 'will you tell Plumley what you think to this cricket score?' and the whole school, staff and pupils broke into applause. It was a memory which remained with him all his life.

In later years, Jane worked with a Mrs Marshall who lived next door to the Joneses. Ozzie did not have a television set and he regularly went round next door whenever a Test Match was on. Ozzie was a wonderful colourful man, says Jane, but her father didn't think much of him.

Lincolnian's Diary. December 7, 1999. and March 7, 2000.

Workers Defied A New Man's Way

WAY BACK in the early 1930s holidays on most farms consisted of a day off for bank holidays and one for the County Agricultural Show. Each year it was held in a different place. It was the highlight of the year for the men who rarely left the villages. They saved in a club all the year round so that they could pay the bus fare and have enough to sink a pint or two and eat. It cost around £1 and anything extra was a bonus. One year the new estate accountant Jerry Wishart called the foremen together and informed them to tell the men who intended going to the show they would lose a day's pay.

'Why can't you tell'em, unless your ower frit,' Bill Thompson challenged. 'There'll be a note in their pay packet.' Jerry Wishart was not afraid of anyone – least of all a few country bumkins. It caused a riot and local feeling ran high. That night the Joiners Arms was full and the subject was the 'new chap' and his 'new ways'.

'Lets go and to hell wi'em' shouted George Clark. 'I've got five kids. I can't lose a day's pay.' 'Nor me!' echoed around the room. 'We need a spokesman. Someone to put our case,' Herb Grey said. Reluctantly he agreed to take it on but only with supporting signatures. When he presented it he was treated with scorn. 'Does Maäister know about this,' he asked. 'Maäister doesn't need to,' was the mocking reply. 'I'll teach you lot that money doesn't grow on trees'.

Another note in the pay-packets said that any more disruption would result in immediate sacking. The Squire and the blacksmith got on well but as he rode into the smithy he felt the unpleasant mood. 'Something the matter blacksmith?' he asked. 'Aye, you could say that, Sir.' Blacky replied and told him the tale.

The accountant was told that profits came through the workers and each man would get paid and 5s (25p) extra in their pay packets. As the accountant went to work on show day he was disconcerted to see the men taking down little white sweet bags from the branches of old chestnut trees. 'Money does grow on trees mate. If you go the right way about it,' shouted Herbie Grey. Moneybags Wishart was never allowed to forget.

Bette's Bygones. June 20, 2000.

Respected: Canon Arthur Oswald Jones at Gift Day at St Mark's Church.

Unusual Personalities In Our City

When you look around today, there don't seem to be any replacements for the odd characters who were a regular sight on the streets of Lincoln not so many years ago. I remember only a few years ago, there was a man we used to call 'Saluting Sam'. He could be seen in the High Street marching backwards and forwards and pausing every few steps, then saluting. Who or what, I don't know, but there is a postcard and a guide book showing High Bridge, with 'Sam' sitting on a seat with his hand raised in salute.

Torksey Ned: Edward Makins.

Another High Street regular was a character who winter and summer alike, always wore a khaki overcoat and a scarf wound round the lower half of his face. Wellington Boots completed this outfit, even on the hottest days. I once saw him tramping along the road between Lincoln and Horncastle.

One of the most 'chronicled' of Lincoln's characters was Torksey Ned, even to the extent of being the subject of a picture postcard. Edward Makins was a big man; his attire was a large felt hat, tied with string under his chin, an old overcoat, with loops of string instead of buttonholes and boots. His only possession seemed to be a stout stick. His hat was his store cupboard and he often carried his dinner in it. Local youngsters would try to knock it off, but this was where the stick came into use. Many a lad felt its strength when they misjudged Ned's dexterity with it.

He was reputed to frequent the yards of local pubs looking for beer barrels. If there was anything left in them, he would drink the contents, then take the empty cask back to one of the local breweries, where he would no doubt be given a pint and a few coppers for his trouble. It is said that he was a drover, from Torksey, who came into Lincoln and lived at one of the lodging houses on the Waterside although he was at various times, an inmate of the Lincoln Union Workhouse, where he died in 1886.

There were a lot of other names from the past who I hope to find more about one day. Parson Billy, the Revd William Osbourne, Pyewipe Annie and Cuckoo Smith are just some of the names I have heard of.

Albert Dealt With A Desperate Situation

A FEW weeks ago, I wrote in this diary about Christmas being a busy time for press photographers. It prompted an old acquaintance of mine to write and tell me of one very busy Christmas which he experienced when he was head of the plumbing department, at Simons, the Lincoln building company. Mr Albert Roberts was in charge of a staff of 30 plumbers in 1981, which was a very severe winter and one of the rare White Christmasses.

After finishing work on Christmas Eve he received an SOS message from a nearby Methodist Chapel. Water was pouring through the ceiling of their kitchen and they were due to serve lunch to 120 people in the hall the next day. Sections of the heating system in the schoolroom above the kitchen had burst and the leakage of water had brought down half of the ceiling, leaving water dripping off the light fittings.

Despite this, the ladies of the church were continuing to prepare the meal for the next day!

A decision had to be made

Busy at Christmas: Albert Roberts with the van presented to him in 1989 after 38 years with Simons building company.

quickly. Draining off the heating system would mean putting out the boiler, which would result in no Christmas lunch next day. To repair the burst cast-iron pipework would take at least two days so the only solution was to drain down the top section of the heating system and hope the boiler would work with a very low water content. By 9.00pm, the work was done and the boiler lit. Albert then had a very worrying and uncomfortable night wondering what he would find the next morning. He returned to the church early on Christmas morning to find that the water had stopped dripping and that despite a very low water content, the boiler had kept working and both the church and schoolroom were warm and comfortable.

A desperate situation had been dealt with and 120 people enjoyed their lunch in warm and comfortable surroundings.

When Albert retired, in 1989, after 38 years with the company, he was presented with a replica of 'Nellie', the three-wheeler van which he drove for many of the early years he spent with the company.

Lincolnian's Diary. February 8, 2000.

Boy's Priceless Painting My Favourite

OFTEN, when I have been giving talks about my time as a Press photographer with the *Lincolnshire Echo*, has the question come up 'What is your favourite photograph?' One of my favourites was a picture of the Queen Mother, taken at RAF Scampton and this was used in the first Lincolnian's Diary back in August last year.

There were others, but I think my all time favourite has to be one taken about 15 years ago, at the start of the school summer holidays. A holiday play scheme was started at the King George Playing Fields, on St Giles Estate, Lincoln. I went along at lunchtime, on the first day to find youngsters painting the entrance walls before work got under way to provide a recreation centre on the field. The first thing that caught my eye was a young boy, about five years old. He was covered, head to foot, in green and white paint. It was not that he had been mistaken for the wall, but that his efforts had been a little too enthusiastic and he had ended up with more paint on himself than on the wall. All I can remember about him now is that his name was Philip. It was something that just called out for a picture

Splashing out: Philip's play day proved unforgettable.

and my only regret is that in those days, we only photographed in black and white.

A couple of years later, we met again. I had gone to photograph the opening of the centre and drove in across what I thought was a gravel path, to park the car. The axle sank into the gravel and I realised that it was a gully, filled with gravel, to prevent people from driving on to the field. As I got out of the car, a young voice said 'What's up mister, are you stuck?' I looked round and there was, Philip, a couple of years older, but I still recognised him. I wonder where he is now? Perhaps married and doing his own decorating. I just hope that he learned from his early efforts and now gets more paint on the walls!

Oh yes! I did get out of the gravel, with a little help from a few strong young men at the opening.

Lincolnian's Diary. October 10, 2000.

Skipper Ross, Maestro Of The *Mary Gordon*

I AM delighted to see that the old pleasure boat the *Mary Gordon* is back again in Lincoln and hope that it will once again be giving pleasure trips along our waterways.

I remember it well from my early days at the *Echo* and I remember too its larger than life 'captain' character known to all as Skipper Ross. If you look in the *Echo*'s *Memory Lane – Lincoln and Lincolnshire* book, you will find a picture of Skipper Ross, in his dungarees and straw boater, about to set off along the Fossdyke with a boatload of passengers from his boat station at the bottom of Lucy Tower Street.

But I remember him better from the time when he had been involved in an accident.

Brayford celebrity: 'Skipper Ross' was a character famous for his Mary Gordon *boat trips in the 1950s and 1960s. He is pictured here before setting off on a trip with a boatload of young passengers.*

He was returning home late one evening, having been to the local 'chippy' to get his supper, when he was involved in a collision with a car on Carholme Road. After treatment, he was confined to bed and I went along to take a photograph of him recovering, such was the interest in him in those days. He lay there in a bed downstairs in his living room and his words to me as I got ready to take the picture were: 'Make me look pretty – if yer don't, I'll get up and bash yer!' And I think he would if the picture had not been to his liking. Anyway, it must have been OK, I never received a visit from him.

Lincolnian's Diary. August 5, 1999.

An historic event in an historic setting. In 1958, the Territorial Army in Lincoln was celebrating its Golden Jubilee. After a service in the Cathedral, 400 men and women marched across Castle Hill to the Castle grounds. (Echo Ref. RI-1871)

Poet's birthplace: Somersby Rectory, birthplace of Alfred Tennyson.

Alfred, Lord Tennyson.

Anniversary Of A Famous County Poet

'Men may come and
men may go,
But I go on forever.'

Words from Tennyson's poem *The Brook* and appropriate for the poet's works; also a reminder that August 6 is the anniversary of his birth in 1809. Alfred Tennyson was born in Somersby, near Horncastle, the son of the local curate and he rose to become Poet Laureate to Queen Victoria. At his brother's wedding, in 1836, he met and fell in love with Emily Sellwood, but her father did not take to the Bohemian, pipe-smoking poet, and Emily's father banned her from speaking or writing to him. However, in 1850, when he was appointed to Poet Laureate, Alfred resumed his courtship and quickly married Emily.

They settled on the Isle of Wight, where Queen Victoria also had a house and Tennyson's works now gained in popularity. He eventually turned his hand to verse drama and a play, but it was his poems for which he is best remembered. Many of his works were inspired by his native Lincolnshire. *Come into the garden, Maud* is said to have been written after a visit to the gardens of Harrington Hall. *The Brook* is about a stream near Somersby and the Lincolnshire coast inspired a number of his works. The family used to rent a cottage in the summer, at Mablethorpe and it is still there today, named appropriately Tennyson Cottage. His home on the Isle of Wight was at Farringford and there is an area of the island known as Tennyson Down.

After his death, in 1892, he was buried in Westminster Abbey and among the mourners at the funeral were many eminent Victorians, among them, Sir Arthur Conan Doyle, Henry Irving, J.M. Barrie and Thomas Hardy.

Alfred Tennyson is one of the few British men to have had a set of postage stamps issued in his honour. A set of four stamps was issued in March 1992 and depicted portraits of the poet and paintings of four of the ladies remembered in his poems.
Lincolnian's Diary. August 8, 2000.

Cranwell Days Of Charles The Joker

RECENTLY, Prince Charles, the Prince of Wales, visited Lincoln and Gainsborough. For a while, in 1971, he became a resident of the county when he spent five months as a student at RAF College Cranwell, with the rank of Flight-Lieutenant, taking an intensive course to gain his wings.

During his time at the college, Prince Charles acquired something of a reputation as a joker. He managed to make an announcement on the college tannoy system that a fault had been found in the basic design of the shoes worn by officers and would they please hand them in at the Porter's Lodge. Quite a few fell for it and duly handed in their footwear to a puzzled porter. It was three days before it was realised that it was a hoax and the joke was confirmed by Buckingham Palace.

During the Prince's time at Cranwell. The annual charity cricket match took place, against a Lord Taverners team. I remember being there and when it was time for Prince Charles to come out to bat, he did so mounted, in cricket whites, in the saddle of one of his polo ponies, shouldering not a cricket bat, but a polo stick, much to the amusement of the crowd of spectators.

Another time when Prince Charles caused some amusement was during a visit to Lincoln Cathedral. I was in the press party covering the visit but at this particular time, it did not attract as much press coverage as it would today. We were waiting in the Cathedral Workshops and in walked the Prince. 'Hello,' he said, 'I see the Press Gang have got here before me.' Later in the visit, he was to tour the roof of the Minster and as we made our way up among the timber. There was a rather narrow passage which had to be negotiated. One of the press party was the late Cyril Middleton, not a small man therefore it was easy for the Prince to notice him.

Now it is the recognised thing for the press to work ahead of the royal visitor, so that they can get good pictures, but this time Prince Charles stepped in and good humourdly said to Cyril: 'I think I had better go first, I don't think you're going to make it through the gap.' He was right, poor Cyril had to go back down the stairs and make his way through the Cathedral, climb the stairs at the west end and meet the party back in the roof, where there were no more narrow passages.

Lincolnian's Diary. October 26, 1999.

Royal pitch: Prince Charles, dressed in cricket whites, takes to the field in the game at RAF College, Cranwell.

Tom Could Tell A Story Or Two

TOM BELL was a natural story teller. 'He could yarn for years without tekking breath,' they said. He would sit by the fire, in the Ferry Boat Inn and delight regulars and visitors with his tales. 'Tell 'em the one about…', they would say to get him going. And over and over again he would tell them stories – each time with a little different twist in the tale. A favourite was when the old parson dies and they were looking for a new vicar.

'You know ow'd Pomfret's dead – well I reckon he is unless Rural Dean buried him suspicious last week. He were a nice gent. Bit standoff-ish, not a lot of conversation. Called with the magazine every month.

His funerals were a real treat. Made all the women cry. 'Cept when he buried Tom Pearson's missus – crabby ow'd bat. Vicar allus said, 'Ashes to ashes, dust to dust', as he flung earth on coffin.' But Tom added: 'If the Lord weren't hev you the devil must,' and they all cracked out laughing.

'His sermons were a different thing. I nivver understood a word. If he got a bit excited he spluttered and spit like an owd tomcat. He were so glad when Miss Greeney got wed. She'd been trying to hang her hat on his peg for years. He pronounced them man and wife three times.

Rural Dean asked village what kind of man they wanted. By gum he'd ha' been a cross twee'n Errol Flynn and King and angel Gabriel.'

'We want a human man,' said choirmistress Ella Jones, 'not like that one ower at Claxby who goes to the pub and drinks beer – bold as brass. I don't know what the Church of England is coming to. Mrs Smith (her wi' nine kids) said they wanted someone good with children cos Sunday school gives you a chance of a bit of a rest after dinner if you get my drift. Her Ted reckoned an hour's not long enough. Mrs Bustard-Popham – stuck up wench – was furious cos he chucked her little James out of choir. She said it were onny high spirits when he cut holes in the organ bellows and stuffed the pedal with peanuts so they stuck when Jack Wilson tried to strike up the *Bridal March* at squire's wedding.

'They were missed when they stopped going to church. They'd bin regular every harvest festival for years. She reckoned vicars should be wed 'cos she don't hold wi' this celibacy of clergy. Says it aint natural. They also wanted one wi' a bit o'brass. Councillor Jackson said you couldn't expect him to keep 22 rooms at the vicarage and live on £320 the state pay him. He said there's already too many parsons in the church neutralised industry. Pub landlord wanted one who'd keep things short and snappy. Get his customers out an hour afore dinner. Bishop sent a man from Claxby. He were like them on wireless – quarter of an hour and that was your lot.

Didn't last long though. Not after his bike were spotted outside schoolteacher's door at six one morning… But that's another story.'
Bette's Bygones. August 22, 2000.

Leader's Temporary Role Lasted 15 Years

AS LINCOLN Kirke White Club celebrates its first 100 years, readers have been responding to our plea for memories and pictures of the club's earlier years. Today, thanks to one-time club leader Ken Turner, there's a chance to look back at some of those bygone days with a host of memories from the late 1960s to the mid-1980s.

Ken Turner arrived at a bad time in the history of the Kirke White Club. The swinging '60s were drawing to a close. 'The full-time leader had resigned. Membership was at an all time low and the leaders were dispirited,' he recalls. 'The club was beset with vandalism. I was working part-time at St Giles Youth Club, as a weight-training instructor on Monday and Friday nights and also doing Wednesday nights at the Kirke White Club. I was asked by the then youth leader for Lincoln, Peter Wright, if I would be prepared to take over as caretaker leader in charge at Kirke White until they could appoint a full-time leader.'

But it was to be a short-term leadership which was to last 15 years. 'The first thing I did at the club was to set up a canteen with my own money', recalls Ken. 'I also wanted to bring some discipline back into the place and to raise the morale of the leaders. The club ran so well that the education authority, on the advice of Peter Wright, decided to leave well alone and with the help of the leaders, I continued to run the club. During my time at the club, we worked with the Ugandan and Vietnamese refugees, both at the club and at the refugee centres in Lincolnshire. Members would go round doing repairs for the residents and cutting hedges and things. At one time, they were fitting security chains which had been supplied by the Care of the Elderly, on the doors of the old people.'

The club re-opened after Easter 1969 and used to have a junior section for children up to 14 years, who would go along from 6.30 to 8pm. The seniors then took over from 8pm to 10pm. 'To my mind this is what Henry Kirke White would have wanted. We are still keeping the young ones off the street. The senior ones would work with the younger ones and this gave them a sense of responsibility. The junior members would eventually graduate to senior ranks. When I took over the club as caretaker, there were no funds and few members. When I left in December 1984, the club had its own mini-bus, two disco units and around £1,000 in the bank. There were times when we had as many as 100 members in the club on a single night.

'When the new authority came into power, the younger members were kicked out to roam the streets. What would Henry have thought about his club getting rid of the youngsters he had started it for? The club's success was not due to me alone. I had a good team of leaders and – with the members responding to a firm leadership – we cut out the violence and swearing. The boys were taught to respect the girls and any hint of racism was quickly stamped out.'
The Gossiper. October 19, 1999.

Glitz and Glamour

50th Anniversary

DRAMA has been filling Lincoln Theatre Royal for many years. Everything from *Floradora* to *Barnum*... From *The Desert Song* to *Grease*... From *My Fair Lady* to *Annie Get Your Gun*... If it's available to amateur groups, it's got a large cast and it's likely to be a winner at the box office, then the County Amateur Operatic and Dramatic Society has done it... at least once.

Now the society, which has been filling Lincoln Theatre Royal annually for longer than many people can remember is celebrating a landmark in its history. It is 50 years since it was formed, and two of the original members are still very much involved today. One of them, Sheila Buckthorp, tells me 'I was in the Clayton Babcock Society which restarted after the Second World War. We did *The Desert Song* at the Theatre Royal in 1947, but after the production there seemed to be some unrest among the members. Some of them were unhappy about the way things were going, so a meeting was held at Ye Olde Crowne. The upshot was that the Clayton Babcock Society folded and in 1949 the County Society was formed.' And before the year was out, members had presented *When We Are Married* and *On Approval* to appreciative audiences.

The County Amateurs had arrived and they were here to stay. But it wasn't always a success story. Sometimes the productions failed to pay their way and members had no choice but to roll their sleeves up. If you are looking for a landmark production in the society's history, then you have to go back no further than 1995 when members broke with tradition to stage the ambitious circus musical, *Barnum*. It was no longer a matter of singing, dancing and acting. Members of the cast suddenly found they had to learn a whole new range of circus skills.

'It's getting progressively harder to choose the right show every year,' say Sheila and the society's chairman, Mary McMurray-Herbert. 'A lot of the newer shows aren't really so popular because there are fewer parts. These days, professional theatre doesn't want large casts but we do, a lot of the newer shows aren't practical for us to do.'

Every year it seems to cost more than ever to stage a production. At one time, the bill for putting on a show would be in the region of £3,000. Today its a nearer £40,000, and that's a lot to get back through the box office. The hire of the theatre for two weeks, sets, props, an orchestra, royalties, back stage crew, rehearsal rooms, costumes, professional fees, insurance and publicity all have to be paid for. But somehow the society manages to cover its costs and raise a bit of money for charity at the same time.

At present, they are hard at work preparing for their next production, *Fiddler on the Roof*, which opens at the Theatre Royal on November 1. And hardly will the curtain have gone down on the final performance two weeks later, than the society will be thinking ahead to its first production of the new Millennium. 'By the end of January we should know which show we are doing', say Sheila and Mary. 'We hold auditions and start casting in June and then we begin the singing rehearsals.'

As first night approaches, rehearsals are held on up to five evenings a week and on Sunday afternoons as well. And although not everyone is involved in every rehearsal, it still adds up to a big commitment in time and effort. But you would be hard pressed to find anyone involved in it all who doesn't enjoy every minute of it.

The Gossiper. October 5, 1999.

Ooh-la-la: Members of the County Amateur Operatic and Dramatic Society at a French evening held at the Green Room Club in 1960. Sheila Buckthorp is second from left, at the back. (Echo Ref. RI-1816)

On stage: Lincoln Theatre Royal stage manager, Art Walker, on stage with the whole of the auditorium behind him.

City Theatres Had Their Troubles

AS LONG ago as 1732, Lincoln had a theatre in the form of a small playhouse, built under the castle walls in a street which came to be called Drury Lane.

Some sources believe that the street was so named because of the theatre, Drury Lane in London is the heart of theatreland. Others believe it takes its name from a family surname; Richard Drewery (1536), Emma Drewrye (1548) or Richard Drewrie (1612). Whatever the origin of the street name, the theatre

remained there for almost 30 years until the manager built a new theatre, in 1763, in the King's Arms Yard, off Clasketgate. This was rebuilt in 1806.

In 1892, this theatre was destroyed by fire. Smoke was seen coming from the roof and soon the fire took a very firm hold. The stage manager, Mr Matt Hall arrived and closed the iron door separating the main building from the dressing rooms but this did little to save the building, which was owned by the Lincoln wine merchants, Whitton and Ashley. A large explosion ripped through the building, caused by the fire reaching the compressed gas tank used in connection with the lime-lighting apparatus. It was impossible to save the

building and the fire brigade concentrated their efforts on saving adjoining properties. Within a year, the theatre had been rebuilt, almost half as large again as the old one, and opened on December 18, 1893. The auditorium was on three levels with four private boxes, two at each side of the stage. A large pair of doors at the rear of the stage opened out into Swan Street to enable scenery to be carried in without the need of it being folded up.

In the 1950s, it looked as if Lincoln might lose the Theatre Royal. Plans were announced to convert the building into a dance hall, but the Lincoln Theatre Association was formed and purchased the building, saving it from closure. But this was not the end of the

troubles. In February 1976, the association voted to go into voluntary liquidation and although a bid was put in by Lincoln City Council, of £27,500 to buy the theatre, this was rejected as not high enough. A subsequent bid in April saw the theatre pass into the council's hands.

During the 1960s, Lincoln Theatre Royal had a repertory company and many of the actors and actresses who played with the company are now familiar names in theatre and television.

Some that I remember are Penelope Keith, Jean Boht (from *Bread*), Freddie Jones, Anna Carteret, Georgina Hale and John Savident, who plays Fred Elliott in *Coronation Street*.
Lincolnian's Diary. June 27, 2000.

Giant Visitor Draws Crowd

IT WAS one of the most unusual things ever to go on display in the centre of Lincoln.

In November 1970, Lincoln was gripped by 'whale fever'. Adverts had described how Jonah – could it really have been named anything else? – the giant whale was visiting Lincoln for four days. It was dead, of course, but the creature was 68ft long and would have weighed, when it was swimming around in the sea, all of 58 tons. We were told that its heart would have pumped 25,000 gallons of blood a minute around its vast body. Everyone wanted to see it.

The whale, being transported around Britain in a small convoy of vehicles, was coming to the High Street to help raise money for the World Wildlife Fund. And the site was a temporary car park created by the demolition of some of the buildings, which were on the route of the proposed Wigford Way. Today, the High Street pedestrian subway is more or less on the exact site once occupied by the whale. The whale was on view from 10am to 10pm, but it was all just a little disappointing. It didn't really look like one of the giants of the ocean at all. It looked like a massive tarpaulin which had to be sprayed regularly with some sort of chemical or preservative to stop it from becoming just a little bit smelly. There has never been another one in the city and if one were to appear under similar circumstances in the future, you can't help wondering what sort of a stir it would create.

The Gossiper. November 7, 2000.

Cheers: Lincoln's It's a Knockout *cheerleaders at Nice in 1972.*

Knockout Programme Makes A Comeback

LOVE or hate it, there's no getting away from the fact that, 30 years ago, *It's a Knockout* dominated our television screens. Channel 5 has started screening a new series of the games which glued millions of people across Europe to their screens. In Britain it was called *It's a Knockout.* The international version was *Jeux Sans Frontieres* and the idea was to win one of the home games and go on to play in one of the European countries taking part.

Lincoln's first involvement came in 1972 and I was adopted by the squad as its photographer. Only trouble was, it meant training with the team in order to be able to keep up with them. Team manager was Lincoln's publicity officer, Robin

Rushton and team coach was county youth organiser Peter Wright. The first game was at Nottingham, when Lincoln, captained by Olympic canoeist Lawrence Oliver, beat them thoroughly, by 14 points to eight.

Then on to Nice, France, in the middle of July. Due to Lawrence's Olympic duties, captaincy was taken over by Bob Price here. Lincoln didn't do quite so well in the south of France, but were only three points behind the eventual winners. However, they did make sure everyone knew they were there. Fifty cheerleaders and supporters followed the team to France to help vocally and visually for the team.

The second brush with *Knockout* came six years later, when Lincoln took on Cleethorpes and Gainsborough in a three cornered battle. We finished just one point behind the home team, so lost out on the international heat. Cleethorpes took part in *Jeux Sans Frontieres*, from the Lincolnshire Showground.

The Lincoln team played guinea-pigs for these, demonstrating the games to the teams before the event.

There was yet a third encounter with this madcap game, remembered for Stuart Hall's laughter and Eddie Waring's Fil Rouge, the game which ran like a mini-marathon through each event. Lincoln took part again in 1980, but this time under the name of Lincolnshire, in the winter *Jeux Sans Frontieres*, played at Cortina, in Italy. All of the games involved ice-skating and as there were no facilities for this in Lincoln, the squad had to travel to Sutton-in-Ashfield twice a week to train. It's not surprising that they didn't win, but they put up a good fight and gave one or two scares to the teams more used to ice-sports.

It remains to be seen if the city will ever feature again in this mad set of games remembered best for its enormous costumes which the competitors had to wear.

Lincolnian's Diary. October 19, 1999.

Horses hooves echo between tall buildings and cart wheels rumble across the cobbled street. There is no motor vehicle in sight and very few pedestrians. This scene is in the centre of Gainsborough, in 1937 and although Pillard House Lane still exists, it doesn't look anything like this today. (Echo Ref. RI-374)

LINCOLNSHIRE: THE WAY WE WERE

Presentation: John Jones receives his prize from the Rolling Stones. (Echo Ref. RI-2429)

Rolling Stones At ABC

SCREAMING teenagers were surrounding the Lincoln cinema hoping for a glimpse of their pop idols before they went on stage. But inside the ABC, the Rolling Stones were coming face to face with a young man who would have admitted he wasn't a particularly keen fan. It was

35 years ago tomorrow. The Rolling Stones – who had already had hits with *Not Fade Away* and *It's All Over Now*, were appearing in Lincoln, as part of a nationwide tour. And before going on stage, they had a special duty to perform.

They had to present John 'Eddie' Jones with an amplifier and microphone he had won in a national competition.

In those days, John lived in Lincoln Road, North Hykeham. He was an apprentice

draughtsman at Ruston's and a keen songwriter playing around the Lincoln clubs and pubs at various times with the Johnny Jones Trio and the Impalas.

John's meeting with the Rolling Stones started the day he entered a competition to write a song for Joe Brown. John's entry called *Angel* – was judged third.

'I met the Rolling Stones for about 10 minutes in the foyer, on the night of the presentation,' he recalls. 'It was a bit nerve-wracking at

the time.' I wasn't a big fan of them – but I was diplomatic enough not to tell them.' So did John's competition entry change his way of life? Well, not really.

His winning entry was never recorded, but John carried on his own musical interests with the Impalas until the mid-1960s appearing at venues like the Naval Club, the Liberal Club, Ruston's Club and Monks Road Club.
The Gossiper. September 21, 1999.

The Ritz Put Up A Fight

News that the Odeon is to go ahead with the long-awaited plan to build a nine-screen 2,000-seat complex on the edge of Brayford, has been welcomed by many. And it has revived memories of the days when another Odeon operated another cinema in the city centre.

If ever a Lincoln cinema had its good days and its bad, it was the Ritz. It opened in a blaze of glory; delighted audiences for decades, changed its name to the Odeon and fell on hard times. The lights went out; the doors were locked and barred and the 'for sale' signs went up outside. It looked as if it would only be a matter of time before the developers moved in. But the story of the

Lincoln Ritz was about to take an unexpected turn.

Stage producer and director, Barrie Stead found himself in Lincoln. He looked up at the 'for sale' sign and tried to visualise how the cinema would have looked in its prime. Then the thought struck him. Could it open its doors once again? In a bold venture, Barrie and his wife Brenda, decided to try to succeed where the mighty

Rank Organisation had failed. They bought the decaying building, renovated it, brought back its original name and got the first film back on the screen in time for the school holidays.

The crowds flocked back. In those first heady days, queues formed right down the side of the building and well into First Road. And this was only the start of the story. Encouraged by the support,

Golden days: The Ritz Cinema, Lincoln, before its conversion to a three-screen cinema.

Barrie and Brenda began to turn their attention to their first love in showbusiness – big name live shows. A stage was added and in the final decade of the 20th century, a procession of international and national stars began to arrive at the Ritz. Roy 'Chubby' Brown turned the air slightly blue with his humour. The Chippendales took off their clothes and drove the women wild. Daniel O'Donnell created one of the biggest rushes to the box office that the Ritz had ever seen. Ken Dodd had them rolling in the aisles until well into the night.

Lincoln was seeing stars like it had never seen before. But it couldn't last. There were never enough live shows for the Ritz to exist on them alone. Between times there had to be film shows and in the eyes of the film renters, the Ritz was a dinosaur.

A cinema seating around 1,200 people with a catchment area of around 100,000, just didn't seem to make sense to them. They were more used to the studio cinemas where the seating capacity could be numbered in dozens or scores and where a film could run quite happily for weeks on end. At the Lincoln Ritz, even the biggest of the biggest blockbusters frequently ran its course after a week. The Ritz had to change and change it did. Barrie and Brenda reluctantly decided to divide their cinema into three. The film renters were happy but it meant the people of Lincoln had lost their only opportunity of seeing the biggest stars without having to travel long distances.

Hardly had the Ritz settled down to its new role as a triple-screen cinema, than Odeon returned to Lincoln with a new multi-screen cinema in Tritton Road. It may have been further away from the city centre than the Ritz, but what it lacked in convenience it made up for in car parking. The Ritz put up a good fight, but even its most enthusiastic supporter could see things couldn't go on. Its closure was only a matter of time and it wasn't long before the building was revamped and turned into the bar we all know today.

The Gossiper. March 14, 2000.

Turning Out For The Circus

YOU NEVER quite forgot your first visit to the circus. Like your first day at school or your first pantomime, it was a memory that stayed with you for a very long time. Now, as the Circus Olé pitches its Big Top on Lincoln South Common, we take a look back at some of those circus visits in bygone days.

The crossing gate keeper at Lincoln Central could have faced a bit of a dilemma that Sunday afternoon back in March 1955. Normally, he would have felt no qualms about bringing the city centre to a halt to allow the odd train to go over. By this time he might have thought twice if a train had been on its way. Because bearing down on the

Pleased to meet you: One of history's best remembered clowns, Coco, at Bertram Mills' Circus in 1956. (Echo Ref. RI-2600A2)

level crossing were more than a dozen elephants, with exotically-clad young ladies on their backs. And behind them came a convoy of brightly-painted lorries and trailers, bringing one of the nation's largest circuses to town.

Back in 1955, in the days long before just about every home had a television set with an almost unlimited choice of channels and no one had thought of video recorders and computer games, a visit from a travelling circus was the signal for the whole city to turn out. Most of the circuses would parade through the city centre on the day they arrived, taking herds of elephants, groups of horses and exotic animals, from the Central Station to the South Common. Crowds lined the pavements and if you happened to stumble across the scene before the parade had arrived, you might have been forgiven for thinking that a member of the royal family was on the way.

Circuses have been pitching their Big Tops on the South Common since at least the 1930s and possibly for some years prior to that. Even in those dark days of the Second World War, the circus still came to town, providing much needed entertainment for civilians and service personnel alike. An *Echo* advertisement shows that Reco Brothers Empire Circus was on the South Common for three days during May 1943. The following year, the patriotically-named Victory Circus and Zoo paid its first, and possibly only, visit to the site during the Whit holiday, staying for just two days. We were still getting over the celebration parties when

Parade: Circus elephants parade through Lincoln carrying advertisements for National Savings in 1950. (Echo Ref. RI-657)

Rosaire's Royal Command Circus and Zoo arrived on the South Common for three days in September 1945. With admission prices ranging from 2s to 5s 9d, the circus was said to have the largest Big Top travelling and it was capable of seating 3,000 people.

The years immediately after the end of the Second World War were a boom period for British circuses. Many were born, rose quickly in size and content and then disappeared. But three of the exceptions to the rule made regular visits to Lincoln. Bertram Mills Circus, with its elephants, tigers and teams of well-groomed horses, was the type of show where you wouldn't have felt properly dressed, if you weren't wearing a tie and a jacket. It travelled almost entirely by rail and even if the special

Animal magic: Crowds turn out in March 1955, to see the circus parade when Billy Smart's Circus came to town. (Echo Ref. RI-1674A)

trains came and went in the middle of the night, there were usually people around to watch as the animals and equipment were loaded off and on again.

Chipperfields Circus was the oldest-established British circus and it reached a peak in popularity during coronation year of 1953. It brought a 6,000-seat Big Top to the South Common for a week in May that year and a programme which included Roman chariot racing around a perimeter track which surrounded the sawdust ring. But perhaps the best-remembered circus to visit Lincoln in post-war years, was Billy Smart's. It was big. It was brash and when it came

to Lincoln in 1955 it brought with it a staff of 250 including veterinary surgeons, chefs, interpreters and its own police and fire services.

There were more than 1,000 costumes and a school for the artistes' children. The circus even boasted its own soccer team and around the tent you would have heard at least six languages being spoken. When you think that the circus gave 14 performances during its Lincoln visit, that meant there were up to 84,000 seats to sell – enough for the entire population of the city to go to the circus once, with room to spare!

The animals may have gone these days from many of

Clowning about: One of Chipperfield's Circus clowns mingles with the audience in 1961. (Echo Ref. RI-2693)

the nation's travelling circuses. The tents may be more compact. Seating, lighting and music may be

more sophisticated, but a lot of the atmosphere is still the same.

The Gossiper. May 23, 2000.

Men Who Brought Laughter To Lincoln

HEARING the other day of the death of actor Deryck Guyler reminded me of when I met him in Lincoln. He is perhaps best remembered for his portrayal of the long-suffering caretaker in *Please Sir* and as Korky, the police-man, in *Sykes*. He was appearing in a play at the Theatre Royal, Lincoln and a publicity stunt had been arranged in Lincoln High Street. Deryck was to appear in his policeman's uniform, but unknown to him, we had arranged to have two real policemen standing by and he was handcuffed and 'arrested' for impersonating a police officer.

Eric Sykes was another comedy actor who appeared at Lincoln, frequently with Jimmy Edwards. I remember them giving a press conference at the White Hart

Hotel, Lincoln. We were sitting in a room, enjoying a bit of hospitality and chatting. At 7.25pm they looked at their watches and said, 'Oh dear, we are due on stage at half past,' or words to that effect. So what did they do? They ordered another round of drinks and a taxi. I don't know what time the curtain went up that evening, but no doubt they would have had an excuse for the audience.

I met Jimmy Edwards on other occasions and rem-ember one at the Lincolnshire Showground when he was presenting riding awards. Jimmy was a Master of Foxhounds and in his inner pocket was a hunting horn. He asked me, as we walked across the showground, had I ever heard the National Anthem played on a hunting horn and he proceeded to play.

One of the first funny men I met was Norman Wisdom. He was appearing at Skegness at the time when the County Police was separate from the Lincoln Police. The county constabulary held a families

day each year and on this occasion it was held at the Lincoln School. Now Norman wasn't very tall and couldn't see beyond the front row of the crowd, so he climbed on the shoulder of a police inspector to perform the opening ceremony. I got the impression that there wasn't any occasion that Norman couldn't turn into a funny event.

Once, I was able to help a very funny man find his way in Skegness. I was just about to get into my car parked near

the Embassy Centre, when I saw a man looking lost. I recognised him as Frankie Howerd, who was appearing at the Embassy that night. I asked him if I could help him find his way and minutes later, we were both on stage with the director of entertainment. Frankie turned on the comedy for a picture. But up to then, he had been discussing seriously the arrangements for the show.

Lincolnian's Diary. October 19, 1999.

Joke: Deryck Guyler is 'arrested' by Lincoln policemen for impersonating a police officer as part of a publicity stunt.

Since the mid-1930s, a cinema dominated Saltergate. Initially, it was The Savoy, then changed about 1960 to the ABC. It then became the Cannon Cinema. It was eventually altered to become a cinema upstairs and a bingo hall where the stalls had been. The Co-operative Bank occupied adjacent premises, on the left, and during the Second World War, the National Restaurant had been in this section. Beyond had been a milk bar, wine merchant's and the Navy and Royal Air Force Recruiting Offices. The whole block was demolished in the late 1980s and in its place rose the Waterside Shopping Centre, incorporating the old Woolworth's building, which had entrances in both High Street and Saltergate. Beyond the Waterside Centre is The Still, public house, a reminder of Pratt's Still, which occupied this site together with their cellars, bottling premises and shop.

For generations, Magpies Bridge has been a vital part of the city's network of roads. Today it is one of the busiest bridges in the county, carrying traffic on the Broadgate/Melville Street route. But back in the 1930s, when the old picture was taken, it was far narrower than it is today. The bridge was rebuilt and widened just before the Second World War. On the left of the picture, you can see Harrison's, which combined the businesses of tobacconist's with radio dealer's. The gable ends of what was to become the Green Dragon can just be seen behind the tree on the right. The photographer was standing on Waterside North, looking in the direction of High Bridge.

Today, the new bridge is now called Thorn Bridge, its original name six centuries ago. A pedestrian footbridge rises high above Melville Street and the old buildings have been replaced by shops and a bus station, with car park above.

Early in the 1950s, Lincoln High Street still had two-way traffic and the Saracen's Head Hotel was still open. F.W. Woolworth & Co's shop had a mock-Tudor frontage and no one had thoughts that one day, the area would become a pedestrian zone. (Echo Ref. RI-421)

For years, there has been a road bridge across the River Witham in Lincoln, linking Boultham Avenue with Coulson Road. But it has not always been the same one. McDakin's Bridge started out as a wooden structure serving what was a private road to Boultham Hall. Originally intended to carry only horse-drawn traffic, it served the area well until the 1960s. Then it was taken down and replaced by today's concrete structure. It was possibly named after the engineer responsible for building the bridge, or it might have been the name of the bridge keeper, as records from 1856 show that there was a Capt McDakin living in Boultham Cottage. Visible in the background is the old mill building, now converted to residential accommodation.

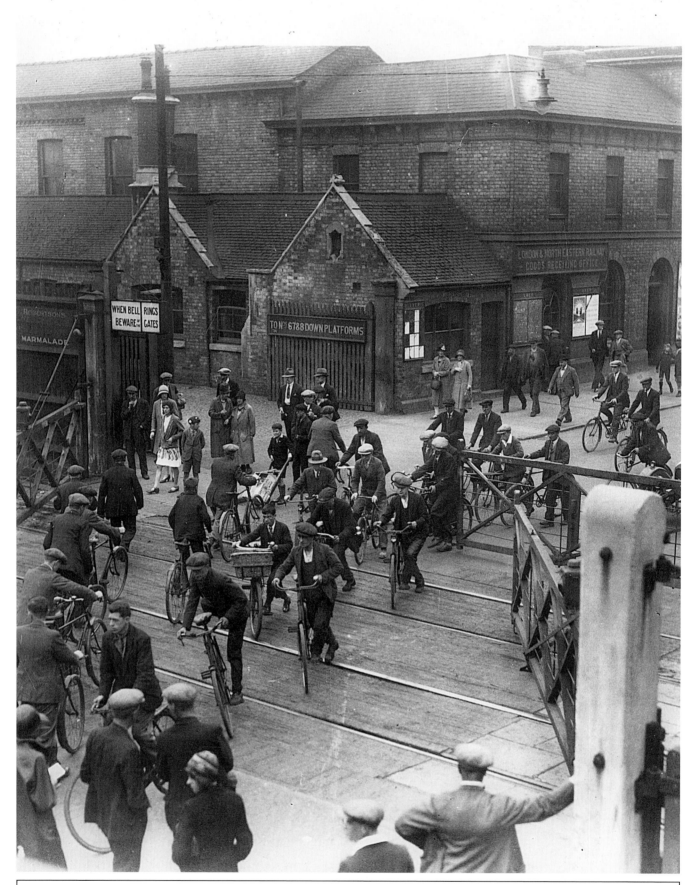

Lunchtime saw busy scenes in Lincoln High Street when hundreds of Lincoln factory workers would cycle home for a meal and negotiate the level crossing gates in the High Street and at other locations in the city centre. And they didn't always wait for the gates to fully open before continuing their journey, as this picture taken in the early 1930s shows. (Echo Ref. RI-14)

History that's not bunk

Big Chapel Is Part Of Lincoln History

SO MANY of our chapels and churches have disappeared from the scene through lack of attendance and planning. It is rather sad when you read of the sacrifice devout Christians made to bring faith to the city. Women feature high in this list. Sarah Parrot is well known in Lincolnshire Christian folklore.

This poor woman of Bracebridge had such concern for the well-being of the city that she walked 10 miles every week to Sturton village to meet in class. One night in 1778 the members were discussing how their Methodist witness might get into the city. It was agreed that it could be achieved if some good Methodist would go and live there and make a home for preachers. Sarah Parrot knew that Mrs Dorothy Fisher who lived at Great Gonerby near Grantham was of ample means and so she walked the 27 miles to invite her to move to the city to make a home for Wesley's preachers. She was convinced as she prayed about it that it was God's call. That call was honoured when Dorothy Fisher moved to Lincoln and with two others, Hannah Calder and Elizabeth Keyley, formed the first Methodist Society in the city.

A chapel was built on the Waterside housing between 500 and 600 people which became too small for the growing congregation and members and so another one was opened in St Swithin's Lane. The one that will stay in the memory of Lincoln's history is, of course, 'Big Wesley' – the House of Prayer – built on the corner of Flaxengate and Danesgate which, in Danish times, had been one of the fortified city gates. On either side climbed Lindum Hill to the Minster above. It was an ideal site for the new big chapel in which they were to preach the Old Gospel.

The Festival opening was on June 30, 1836 and the preparations were done well ahead. In good ow'd Lincolnshire style the Ladies were requested to provide two or three whole rounds of beef, two or three hams. Just the stuff Methodist feasts have become famous for. The proceeds from public breakfast amounted to £502 and this was followed by dinner and tea. They really made a day of it!

The first Sunday must

Soon to go: Roadworks in Clasketgate, Lincoln, outside 'Big Wesley' which shortly after this picture was taken in 1959, was demolished. (Echo-Ref RI-2810)

have been a truly wonderful occasion. Every chapel in the Lincoln circuit – some 40 villages – were closed and people came from near and far to rejoice in the opening of 'Big Wesley'. In the book *One Hundred Years* covering the period 1836-1936 there was a Sunday School, Women's Work, Girls' League, Overseas Missions, Women's Meetings, Church Sewing Meeting, Men's Committee, Wesley Guild, Young Leaguers' Union, Guides, Scouts and a Badminton Club.

Sadly 'Big Wesley' and many of those organisations have long vanished from sight – but never from memory.
Bette's Bygones. August 15, 2000.

From Derelict To Delightful

IT'S 10 years since The Lawn Visitor Centre opened its doors for the first time. And to mark the occasion, we take a look back at how the former mental hospital became one of the city's biggest tourist attractions and at some of the many events which have taken place there since.

What do you do with a redundant mental hospital close to the historic heart of the city? That's the question they were asking back in the 1980s when the whole future of The Lawn was in the melting pot. The treatment of the mentally ill was changing and the hospital, which dated back to 1820, was no longer needed. The patients were moved out, the staff left and the 'for sale' signs went up. The asking price was £450,000. But just who would buy the buildings and their extensive grounds

and what would they do with them?

By the early summer of 1986, we had the answers. The *Echo* announced the city council had ambitious plans to spend £2.5m on turning the redundant hospital into a major leisure complex. The blueprint, revealed by Lincoln architects Scorer and Pilling at a special presentation at City Hall, would transform the hospital site into one of Britain's most impressive recreation centres, we were told. By combining existing buildings with two new ones, it would be possible to house a conference centre complete with outside dining terrace for 150 people, vintage cars, the restored Lincoln Flirt tank, the National Cycle museum and a sports hall. The gardens would be redesigned and visitors would be encouraged to take a stroll around them.

Council leader Derek Miller – who did so much to promote the scheme in those early days – said it would be financed partly with grants from various organisations

Tropical: The interior of the conservatory, at The Lawn, Lincoln, filled with tropical plants.

like the Government and the EEC, with more money hopefully coming in from the private sector. Many parts of the scheme were to come about. Others fell by the wayside. And some, like the suggestion of moving the National Cycle Museum from its home in Brayford Wharf North, came about but were relatively short-lived.

As the months turned to years, we all watched with interest as the high wall which used to divide the hospital from Union Road was pulled down, opening up new and impressive views. We saw landmarks like the old hospital water tower being demolished and we saw photographs and artists' impressions of the indoor tropical garden, aquarium and concert hall. Opponents of the scheme said it would never work, but supporters were convinced the council had no alternative but to buy

Façade: The south façade of The Lawn, a former mental hospital.

Touch of the Orient: The Tangshan Chinese garden at The Lawn.

the hospital and make the best possible use out of it.

The first event took place on September 29, 1990 and – appropriately enough – it was the first Family Fun Weekend, which was a joint venture between the *Echo* and BBC Radio Lincolnshire. Hundreds poured through the gates for the event and to see for the first time all that had been going on at The Lawn. Councillor David Jackson, who was then Mayor of Lincoln, opened the event and said 'This is a great start for The Lawn complex.' But even he might have been just a little bit surprised at the wide range of activities which have been taking place there ever since.

The biggest crowds ever to visit The Lawn for a single event have got to have been seen at the Christmas Market. Once the old west gates of the castle were reopened to provide a new link, The Lawn became a natural extension to the market. Stalls filled the main hall and the grounds and this year there is talk of making greater use of the grounds during the market, with perhaps a circus and more fairground attractions to be sited there. The Lawn has become the home for another of Lincoln's most popular annual events – the Great Australia Day Breakfast. On a Sunday morning in late January, many hundreds of people gathered there for breakfast, which traditionally includes a host of local and national celebrities serving up bacon and egg.

The main concert hall has staged performances by the famous and the not-so-famous. Comedians Cannon and Ball have appeared there. Royalty has set foot in the building. Visitors have flocked to The Lawn from all over the world to learn more about our past. There have been vast open-air concerts, galas and firework displays in the grounds. But perhaps the event that will never entirely be forgotten, came just five years ago. Hundreds packed the grounds for an event held as part of the celebrations to mark the 50th anniversary of the end of the Second World War.

Perhaps in some respects things at The Lawn could have been busier and better, but it has come a long way in the first 10 years and it looks destined to be an important part of city life for decades to come.

The Gossiper. October 3, 2000.

Descriptions Of City That's Lost In History

READING through books about Lincoln often makes me wish I could have been a 'fly on the wall' centuries ago – with my camera, of course.

There is a wonderful description in the late Sir Francis Hill's book *Tudor and Stuart Lincoln* of the city seen through the eyes of traveller John Leland more than 400 years ago and of how he found the state of the city. Approaching from the south, Leland would have passed between St Katherine's Priory and the Malandry hospital (on the site now used by the pleasure fair). Lower High Street would have been a causeway across a very marshy area between the River Witham and the Sincil Dyke.

The road crossed the Witham by the 12th-century High Bridge, on which stood the chapel of St Thomas of Canterbury, before entering the walled city by means of the Stonebow. The upper part of the city was a separate part of Lincoln, The Bail, including the castle, being under the manorial jurisdiction of the Duchy of Lancaster. The cathedral, of course, was in another separate area, The Close. North of the Bail, outside Newport Arch, was the medieval suburb of Newport.

He recorded some evidence of the decay of the city, with many houses empty and falling for want of repair. It was forbidden by the common council for private individuals to pull down houses or export building material from the city. It was common practice in those days to recycle building materials and it is interesting to see houses today which have been built using recycled bricks. I think that many of these look better than 'new' houses, especially in villages. Leland found 11 churches in the suburb of Wigford, to the south of the walled city, with one in 'clean ruin'. In the rest of the city, there were 13 more.

Also in Tudor and Stuart Lincoln is a description of Lincolnshire at that time. It was the most north-easterly county directly governed from London. Beyond the Humber, shires were administered by the Council of the North, at York. In the north-west, there were areas at Thorne and Hatfield, which were often flooded and the River Trent was un-banked. Add to this the vast area of the fens and it made Lincolnshire almost an island. There were 16 creeks along the coast, a smugglers' paradise. Travelling along the old north road from London, it was a three day journey on horseback. When the traveller reached the county, he had a choice of routes to Lincoln. He could continue up to Newark and take the Fosse Way, or turn off through Peterborough, Crowland, Spalding and Boston before journeying to Lincoln. There is little wonder that Henry VIII called it one of the most brute and beastly shires in the whole realm.

Whilst I would love to have seen Lincoln and Lincolnshire at this time, I would sooner have been around in Roman times. What a grand place Lincoln appeared to have been, judging by the reports which have come down through the years. Thankfully, today we have cameras, so the images of our city and county are recorded for future generations.

Lincolnian's Diary. October 3, 2000.

Royal event: The Queen and the Duke of Edinburgh at Lincoln Cathedral, in 1980, for the service on the 700th anniversary of the Angel Choir.

Two Kings Paid Hugh Homage

EIGHT hundred years ago, on November 17, 1200, Hugh of Avalon, the seventh Bishop of Lincoln, died at the Old Temple, London.

Hugh became Bishop in 1186 after being Prior of the monastery at Witham, in Somerset. He was born in Burgundy, in 1140 and his mother died while Hugh (or Hugo, as he should properly be called) was still a child. He was educated in a convent of regular canons and at the age of 19 was taken by the abbot to Chartreuse. The solitude and deportment of the monks appealed to Hugh and returning to Chartreuse, he was admitted to the habit. He spent 10 years in a private cell before being committed to the general procuratorship of the monastery.

King Henry II, of England, founded the first house of Carthusian monks at Witham, in Somerset and asked for Hugh to take charge of it. Hugh thought that he was unfit to take up this appointment, but he was ordered to England and

through his humility and the meekness of his deportment, soon won over even the enemies of the foundation at Witham. The bishopric of Lincoln became vacant in 1167 and remained so until 1183. The king nominated his son Geoffrey Plantagenet, to the post, with no intention of him taking it up, but receiving temporalities for the king's use. Geoffrey never became bishop or even took up holy orders and resigned.

In 1183, Walter de Coutances, Archdeacon of Oxford became bishop, but later in the same year was promoted to be Archbishop of Rouen. It was to be two and a half years before the post was filled by Hugh. A year before his installation, an earthquake had destroyed much of the cathedral, so Hugh's task was to rebuild it. Hugh was afraid of no one, not even the king and many times chastised his monarch for his wrong doings. In 1200, with his cathedral still unfinished, Hugh went to France, to try and ratify the peace treaty between France and England. He became ill and returned to this country, where on November 17, he died, in London.

His body was brought back to Lincoln and six days

later, arrived in the city. A great Council was being held in Lincoln at that time, with the King of Scotland and King John of England being present. The two monarchs, with other nobles carried the body of Hugh to the entrance of the city (this would probably have been Bargate). The bier was carried through streets knee-deep in mud up to the cathedral and on November 24, was laid to rest in the chapel of St John the Baptist. Hugh was canonised in 1220 and a new extension to the choir of the cathedral, now known as the Angel Choir, was built to house his shrine. The Angel Choir was completed by 1280 and the saint's remains were translated into the golden shrine, with the head being buried in a separate shrine. No doubt the authorities thought that more people could give gifts of money if there were two shrines instead of one!

One hundred years ago, the *Lincolnshire Echo* reported on the celebrations taking part to mark the 700th anniversary of the death of Bishop Hugh of Avalon. Special medals, or badges, showing the figure of St Hugh, were provided for the Cathedral choirboys to wear at the special commemoration service in the cathedral. The report stated 'The four choristers will be habited in new copes and lead the procession. It is believed that the black gowns, so well known to all Lincoln people, are the only instance of the wearing of copes by others than those in holy orders'.

The day of celebration (November 17) started with a choral celebration in the cathedral, at 8.45am, followed by a public service, at 11 o'clock, with Matins and a sermon. The choir was augmented for the occasion

by the Lincoln Musical Society and members of the Diocesan Training College, bringing the number of voices to over 150. Following the service, the Dean and Chapter hosted a luncheon at the County Assembly Rooms attended by other clergy and the Mayor and Corporation of Lincoln. In the afternoon, there was an organ recital in the cathedral by the cathedral organist, Dr Bennett. More commemorations were held at the city's St Hugh's Church, on Monks Road where a solemn high mass was celebrated. The *Echo* reported that the church was full for the services and at one of them, 'there was scarcely standing room in the church'. The altar was decorated with flowers and lights and it was said that it would be a long time before the celebrations 'are forgotten by those who were privileged to be present.'

Diana Lyons then sent me some more information about the Bishop of Lincoln who became a saint. Diana has sent me some extracts from two books which she has read recently and they provide some very interesting and provoking thoughts. *Lincoln – The Cathedral and See*, published in the Bell's Cathedral Series, in 1898, describes the scene, on October 6, 1280, when the saint's remains were moved to their new shrine. King Edward I was present and supported on his own shoulder the remains as they were carried to their new resting place. The King and his Queen, Eleanor, who was soon to have her own memorial tomb in the new Angel Choir, were accompanied by the Earls of Kent, Gloucester and Warwick, the Archbishop of Canterbury and the bishops of Lincoln, Bath, Ely, Norwich, Worcester, Llandaff, Bangor and

Bishop's mark: The seal of Bishop Hugh, from Lincoln Cathedral.

St Asaph, together with the bishop-elect of Exeter and 250 knights.

Soon after the translation of the body, the head was removed and enclosed in a separate metal case, enriched with gold, silver and precious stones. A keeper was appointed to guard the relic, yet, it was stolen in 1364. The head was thrown into a field and the case sold in London, for 20 marks. On the way back to Lincoln, the thieves were robbed of their ill-gotten gains and later convicted of the crime and hanged at Lincoln. The head was found and returned to the cathedral.

A recent book, *The Head of God, the Lost Treasure of the Templars*, by Keith Laidler, published in 1998, tells of how several clerics, later canonised themselves, used rather grotesque methods of obtaining saintly remains to produce revenue. And it seems that even St Hugh himself was not above this. When visiting the reputed body of St Mary Magdalene, at Fécamp, in Normandy, Hugh bowed over the remains as if to kiss them but to the horror of onlookers, bit two pieces of bone from the arm.

He argues that as he took Jesus' body and blood into his mouth during the Eucharist, why shouldn't he do the same with with the bones of a saint?

It would seem that centuries ago, many so-called saint's remains were not always genuine and if those of St Mary Magdalene were real, she would have possessed six separate bodies. The book also throws light on the fact that Hugh might have been an undercover Templar, coming from Avalon which has strong links with Templarism.

Lincolnian's Diary. November 2000

Information On Days Past

OLD PARISH maga-zines and recorded histories are a great source of information about life as it used to be. In a *History of Billinghay*, Stuart Wilson recorded that in 1663 'John Cood of Billinghay was given three months' imprisonment because he and members of his family over 16 years of age had not attended the parish church for the space of three Sundays, contrary to the form of the statute.'

The Annual Cricket Match planned for Bank Holiday on August 1, 1861 was played between 'eleven of Billinghay and eleven of Timberland and Martin'. 'Wickets will be pitched at 10 o'clock' said the notice.

'After the first innings refreshments will be served for the players and at the close of play a public tea will be provided in a com-modious booth erected on the premises of Mr Ely Bailey. A variety of rustic sports will be introduced until 9 o'clock.

The 9th Lincolnshire Rifle Corps Saxhorn Band is engaged for the occasion. Gentlemen's tickets are 3s (15p), Ladies' 2s (10p).'

In a Lincolnshire Show catalogue of 1926: In class 6, Charles Abbot of Spilsby was awarded £4 because he was the Labourer in Husbandry who had brought up and placed out the greatest number of children without having ever received par-ochial relief and not having occupied more that half an acre of land.

He had 12 children born and 12 brought up with 11 placed out. In class 7 George Allit was the married man or widower who had lived or worked exclusively and continuously in the service of one family or their suc-cessors, or on the same farm for the greatest number of years and not having occupied more that half an acre of land and not having received parochial relief.

He received £5. George was aged 70 and had been with Captain J.S. Reeve and family for 51 years.

This must have been the forerunner of the long-service awards.

Bette's Bygones. June 27, 2000

History Behind The City Fairs

IT WILL soon be time for the September Pleasure Fair, on Lincoln's South Common, but anyone thinking that the September fair in Lincoln is a com-paratively recent event would be mistaken.

In the reign of King William III and Queen Mary, the city was granted a fair by the king after a royal visit to Lincoln during a tour of the kingdom. As this was at harvest time, it is unlikely that many people would not have visited the fair, so it became known as the 'Fools Fair'.

Fairs, many years ago, were not for pleasure purposes, but as a means of buying goods not produced locally and most places had these two or three times a year. No fair could be held without the permission of the king and for this privilege the king had to be paid. To recoup this fee, the city would charge tolls on everything bought or sold. Who says that VAT is a modern invention? Of course,

disputes sometimes arose, and special courts were set up to deal with these im-mediately, during the period of the fair. These courts were called the 'Pie Powder' courts, from the French words 'Pieds poudrés' – meaning dusty feet, which is what the people would have had if they had travelled from afar.

In the 14th century, there was St Botolph's Fair, which extended from June 17 until July, a total of 25 days. A second fair, dating from the early 15th century, until 1803, was held starting at the feast of St Hugh, on

November 17 and originally lasting for 30 days. Was this the forerunner of the Lincoln Christmas Market? Lincoln also had two other fairs from a later date. These were in April and September, but only lasted for a few days. The present April fair is a survival of the one granted by King Charles II, at which horses and sheep were sold in the city streets. The present day April Pleasure Fair was supplemented with a second fair during the years of the Second World War.

Lincolnian's Diary. September 5, 2000.

Just a mere 20 years divide the time span of these two pictures, but they could be a century apart. Beevor Street, in the 1980s still had factories, at its Firth Road end with the former boiler works of Ruston, Proctor and Co and the sign above the street with the name Jones, Dewey and Turner Ltd, in large letters. Beyond was the old level crossing and in the distance, the Beevor Rooms, the dining and function suite for Ruston Bucyrus. On the right-hand side of the street were a number of terraced houses and a corner shop. What a contrast when you look at today's scene. The shop is now Pressgang clothes care centre. The houses are still there, but everything else has been swallowed up by modern development, with trading centres on either side of Beevor Street and the roadway in the foreground carries modern street furniture.

Lincolnshire's Monuments To Pilgrims

MOST of us have heard of John Bunyon's book, the *Pilgrim's Progress* and there is a carving on Lincoln Cathedral of a medieval pilgrim on his journeys. But mention the word pilgrim in Boston and apart from the football club whose nickname it is, it generally brings to mind the group of religious separatists better known as The Pilgrim Fathers. This group came from an area consisting of villages where Lincolnshire, Nottinghamshire and Yorkshire meet beside the River Trent.

Their religious views were developed in the comparative freedom of the reign of Queen Elizabeth I, in the late 1500s. But their church was

Separatists: The Pilgrim Fathers memorial at Scotia Creek, Boston.

Liquorice Park Has A Long History

THERE can't be too many large areas of land close to the city centre which can boast that they have never been built on. But the allotment site on the north side of Yarborough Road, is one of them. And it's likely to stay that way.

The allotment is in the area we have now learned to call Liquorice Park. And according to the newly-published Lincoln Civic Trust annual report, it has a long and varied history. The site has belonged to the City Council since 1573 when, as a much larger area, it was sold to the area by Thomas Grantham.

In a Civic Trust article, Mary Lucas writes 'The decision to name the current scheme Liquorice Park, is based on information from 1631 when the lessee Benedict Anton, died. His probate inventory valued at £24 11s 6d and described it as two

outlawed by King James I, in 1604, so they planned to escape and join other exiled separatists in Holland. Their belief was that religion was to remain 'pure' and so became known as The Puritans. The first attempt to get to Holland was in 1607, from Boston, where they had bribed a ship's captain to take them to their destination.

At Scotia Creek, down river from the port, they went aboard the boat, but were arrested and taken back to Boston where they were imprisoned in the Guildhall. After a month, they were sent back to their homes, but their leaders were put on trial at Lincoln. Later, they too were

orchards wherein the deceased had grafted many young trees and planted liquorice.'

The area underwent one of its biggest changes in the 19th century, mainly thanks to the efforts of solicitor and alderman Richard Carline. He wanted to improve the city and one of his worries was that the principal route from uphill to the city centre, was Lindum Road and it was difficult for horses drawing heavy loads. Mary writes 'Carline proposed to the council in 1854 that a route, following a more gradual slope be built.' He suggested it should go 'from the junction of Far Newland, through the fields below the Asylum and thence under the hill to Burton Road.' The idea eventually led to the construction of Yarborough Road and Carline Road – which was named after him.

'Once these roads had been built, by 1860, all the land above Carline Road and below Yarborough Road down to West Parade, was sold off for housing, leaving the steepest part in the middle as open land. In the

released and allowed to return home. A year later, they tried again, this time from Killingholme, north of Grimsby and while the men managed to escape, their wives were left behind. However, the women eventually managed to reunite with their menfolk, in Amsterdam. It was to be another 11 years before they set sail for a life in the New World. They left Holland on the *Speedwell* and joined up with the *Mayflower*, at Southampton. But the *Speedwell* proved to be unseaworthy and put into Dartmouth and Plymouth. It was from here that most of them travelled to a new life in

early years of this century, the land became allotments. By 1910, the day-to-day running was taken over by the allotments committee.' The site was laid out in 31 uniform plots. In 1929, a gents toilet was built by the gates on Alexandra Terrace and in 1934, allotment holders were allowed to put up small wooden sheds. 'During the Second World War, allotment gardening was boosted by the Government's Dig For Victory campaign, when everyone was encouraged to grow as much fruit and vegetables as possible. One person was given permission to erect a loft on his Yarborough Road plot 'to be used for the housing of pigeons for war purposes'!'

But the 1960s brought a time of change. Few people wanted allotments until there was just one sitting tenant on the site. The site is still owned by the council, but is leased to the Trust for 999 years. And Mary says 'It is to be made a pleasant and accessible space for the enjoyment of all the people of the city and elsewhere.'
The Gossiper. April 25, 2000.

America aboard the *Mayflower* and in December 1620, they founded the Plymouth Plantation.

There is a monument to their first attempt to leave England at Scotia Creek and there are also memorials to be found in St Botolph's Church, in Boston.

The Pilgrim Fathers also had a connection with Gainsborough, where there was a group of more than 50 Separatists. They worshipped secretly at the Old Hall, where the owner Sir William Hickman and his mother, Rose, were both former religious exiles.
Lincolnian's Diary. July 25, 2000.

Monument Rebuilt After The Civil Wars

IN THE year 1290, King Edward I was holding council at Clipstone, in Sherwood Forest, when his wife, Queen Eleanor was taken ill. She was moved to the home of Richard de Weston, at Harby, just over the county border, in Nottinghamshire. Medicines were sent from Lincoln, but without success and the queen died in November 1290.

Effigy: Queen Eleanor's tomb in Lincoln Cathedral – a replica of the one in Westminster Abbey.

Her body was brought to Lincoln for embalming before its journey to London for burial. This task was performed by nuns at St Catherine's Priory and the viscera (the stomach organs) were removed and buried in Lincoln Cathedral.

Every place where the body rested on its journey to London, an Eleanor Cross was erected and the body was finally laid to rest in Westminster Abbey.

The Bishop of Lincoln, Oliver Sutton, performed the burial service in London, in the absence of the Archbishop of Canterbury. Bishop Sutton was present when the king and queen attended the opening of the Angel Choir, in Lincoln Cathedral, to house the shrine of St Hugh.

Memorial: The Eleanor Cross, only one of three remaining, at Geddington, in Northamptonshire.

The remains buried in Lincoln Cathedral had over them, a tomb, which like so many, was destroyed in the Civil Wars of the 17th century.

Fortunately, in 1641, drawings were made of this and other important tombs. Just over 600 years from the death of the queen, a replica of the monument was built, thanks to the generosity of Joseph Ruston, a great industrialist and benefactor in Lincoln and in January 1892, it was blessed in a special service. This tomb is a replica of the one in Westminster Abbey and has a full sized bronze effigy of the queen on top.

I have been fortunate to

Excavations Led To Imprisonment

FIFTY years ago, when I was a pupil at the City School, Lincoln, my history teacher wrote on my report, 'Not suited to this subject'. I had just come 20th in my history exam.

There were 20 pupils taking it! When I left school and started working as a photographer, I soon came into contact with the late Mr Tom Baker, who was then Deputy Director of Libraries, Museum and Art Gallery, in Lincoln. He got me interested in archaeology and I soon joined the Lincoln Archaeological Research Committee and the first 'dig' I took part in was to search for the line of the Roman south wall of Lincoln.

We dug in the grounds of the old Sub-Deanery, south of Lincoln Cathedral and although we went down more than 25 feet, we never found it. We realised we had been digging 50 feet to the north and we found it the next year, in the grounds of the Bishop's Old Palace.

At that time, the mid-1950s, a section of the castle banking behind Union Road had been excavated to expose stonework of the Roman Westgate, buried when the castle was built more than 900 years ago. Professor Ian Richmond was the country's leading authority on Roman matters and he asked if I could take some pictures of this stonework for him. There were only the stones of the archway and a small portion of the wall visible and they had been uncovered to see if it was possible to excavate the whole arch, which it wasn't, because of the cost. I did not know then the full story of the collapsed stones, but I have since found out.

In April 1836, a man called Philip Ball, who owned the building which is now The Strugglers Inn, bought land behind the building and in order to fill up the castle ditch, excavated soil from the castle bank into the ditch. This exposed the western gate and much of the stonework above it and it is recorded in a drawing by Samuel Tuke. The stonework, now exposed to the air for the first time in several hundred years soon began to collapse and the whole thing was filled in again, to prevent further collapse.

Poor Philip Ball! He was 'lodged in Lincoln Castle' for endangering the fabric of the castle walls. He was released a year later but could not resist the temptation to carry on his excavations and in 1840, he started digging again, but in 1841, he was committed to the Fleet Prison, in London, for ignoring the previous injunction.

After a total of 18 months in prison, he was returned to Lincoln.

Explorations of the gateway have taken place in recent years and I would love to see it restored, giving Lincoln not one, but two, Roman gateways. But I expect the cost will prove, once again, too great.

Lincolnian's Diary. July 11, 2000.

have seen both tombs and also all of the remaining Eleanor Crosses, of which I now have a photographic record.

Lincolnian's Diary. April 25, 2000.

There was a time when, if you travelled down Yarborough Road towards the city centre, the skyline would have been dominated by one of Lincoln's biggest parish churches. St Martin's, on West Parade, was a substantial stone building with a square tower. It had served the community for almost a century but just over 30 years ago, it closed and was demolished. The site today is occupied by an office block with the name Lancaster House. Traffic could park freely in the days when this picture was taken and yellow lines did not decorate the sides of the road. The houses on either side of the road have changed little today, but the street lamps, lit by gas in the old picture, have been replaced with modern electric lamp standards and the motor car is much more in evidence.

Owler's haunt: The New Inn, at Saltfleetby, was a favourite meeting place for 'owlers'.

County Was Home To An Illegal Trade

WHENEVER I hear about smuggling today and the big business which it is for some, I always conjure up a picture of men in rowing boats, pulling into rocky coves and hiding their illicit haul into caves.

But did you know that Lincolnshire was once a smugglers' paradise?

Smuggling was perhaps at its greatest height during the 18th and first half of the 19th century, when not only spirits and tobacco were highly taxed, but also tea and silk.

There was also a tax on exported goods, especially wool and with Lincolnshire being situated ideally for this trade with the continent, much of it was carried out from our beaches.

Under an act of 1672, wool exporting was prohibited, but there was a demand from the continent and with Lincolnshire being a county with plenty of sheep, there were people, known as 'owlers', who were prepared to take the risk.

They operated at night and the coastline, with its gentle sloping beaches and numerous creeks was ideal for this illegal export and import.

Of course, there were men employed to try and prevent this. They were called Riding Officers, but even they were not always totally loyal and a well-placed bribe could often find them turning a blind eye to the smugglers. There used to be an old saying 'put a guinea in each of my eyes and I shall see nothing'. It is reported that at the start of the 20th century, a skeleton was found in the brickwork of the Vine Hotel, Skegness, with brass buttons carrying the royal insignia.

Could this have been an officer who refused to take the bribe?

Goods were brought ashore and often buried in 'caves' dug into the sandhills. Later, a man with a barrow would dig in the sand and shingle, on the pretext of taking the material for road repairs and remove the smuggled goods.

Various ways were devised to cover up the operations. Carts used in the recovery had their wheels wrapped in straw, so as not to make a noise on the roads which had to be crossed and they often carried sacks of sand in case the straw wore off. Lights were often strapped to the leg of a horse, which would then be walked up and down the beach, away from the real action, to appear like a boat riding at anchor to anyone on watch.

One man, Thomas Paine, was appointed Alford Outride, in 1764. His office was in the Windmill Inn, still there today in the Market Place, but 12 months later, he was dismissed from the service. His 'sacking' however, was unjust and he was reinstated as Excise Officer, in Sussex.

He emigrated to America in 1774 and for three years, held the post of US Secretary for Foreign Affairs and became a close friends of such famous men as George Washington, Thomas Jefferson and Benjamin Franklin.

In the village of Saltfleet, the New Inn is a reminder today of one of the 'owlers' haunts.

Lincolnian's Diary. December 14, 1999.

The price of honesty: A skeleton with brass buttons carrying the royal insignia was found in the brickwork at the Vine Hotel, in Skegness.

Brick Buildings Are Not Such A New Idea

A ROSE, is a rose, is a rose. Somebody wrote that, but I can't remember who. Some people might think also that 'A brick, is a brick, is a brick', but they would be wrong. There are many kinds of bricks and a book I have about brick building in Britain, lists at least 40 different kinds. I would think a visit to the brick library in a builder's merchants might reveal many more.

We often tend to think of our old buildings as being made of stone, with brick being a comparatively new building material, but we would be wrong. Thornton Abbey, in the north of the county, was built in the 14th century and the gatehouse and barbican both have bricks in their construction. Since there was a flourishing brick-making industry at Hull at that time, it can be assumed that the bricks came from there. Tattershall Castle was first built in 1231, but the structure we can see today was begun in 1434-5 and used brick as its building material. The magnificent keep, which we see today, has walls 20 feet thick at the base and rises to a height of 110 feet, all made of brick.

Gainsborough Old Hall also dates from the 15th century and the four

Look out: The Tower on the Moor at Woodhall Spa.

projections on the outside of the west wall, brick built, contain chimneys, garderobes and cabinets, dating from the late 15th century. Wainfleet All Saints, perhaps better known for its brewery, has a magnificent brick structure, the Magdalen College School, built in 1484. Today, it is a public library. Three remains of brick houses can be found in Lincolnshire. The Hussey Tower, at Boston, is 15th century (1450-60) and part of a large tower house building with three floors. Not far away, at Fishtoft, is the Rochford Tower, of the same date, another tower house with three floors.

Tor o Mor, the Tower on the Moor, at Woodhall Spa, was built in the 15th century by Ralph Cromwell, of Tattershall and may have been a hunting or look out tower. Some of its bricks were used to build Tattershall Castle after the demolition of the tower. Lincoln's oldest brick building is The Chancery, in Minster Yard, dating from 1480-90, with a frontage of brick in which is set a large stone oriel window.

Lincolnian's Diary. June 13, 2000.

Carving Out History Of Village

J UST a couple of miles to the west of Lincoln is the village of Skelling-thorpe, only a hamlet about the time that Lincoln Cathedral was being built and the Domesday Survey made.

In the *Domesday Book*, the village is listed as Scheld-inghope. It has been interpreted as meaning a 'Shield-shaped hill enclosed by a marsh'. The hill is not very high, but the area was certainly in an area of marshy ground.

Much of the village's history is recorded on its sign. It was erected by the village's Women's Institute to mark their Diamond Jubilee, in 1982.

It was designed by John Atkin and carved by an old friend of mine, Graham Stringer, who was a representative for a photographic company. He learned the art of wood-carving especially to make

Back: This side of the sign shows the Domesday spelling.

signs similar to the ones in Norfolk, where he lived for some years. He also carved signs for Nettleham and Potterhanworth.

The sign is double sided and on one side, the name is spelt as in the *Domesday Book* and shows a Viking or Danish raider, Lincoln Cathedral with spires on the west towers, rabbits and a duck decoy.

Skellingthorpe Duck was a London delicacy, so this and the many rabbits in the area, not uncommon in Lin-colnshire, the villages would have been able to make a living.

The village's Old Wood is said to be part of the Sherwood Forest.

The other side of the sign shows a more modern Skel-lingthorpe. A passing train is a reminder of the time when Skellingthorpe had a railway station. Behind the railway is St Lawrence's Church and over head flies a Lancaster bomber, recalling the Second World War airfield, now taken over by Lincoln's Birchwood Estate. Also on the sign is the coat of arms of Christ's Hospital, London.

In 1693, Henry Stone, who

Front: Skellingthorpe's carved sign telling the history of the village.

was lord of the manor, bequeathed the land to the hospital and this coat of arms also appears on the wall of the public house, the Stones Arms.

Lincolnian's Diary. February 15, 2000.

It was the summer of 1953 when this picture was taken in Sincil Street and the country was celebrating the coronation of Queen Elizabeth II. T. Cook's chemist's shop was still open and the litter in the street was cleared away by a street sweeper with a brush. (Echo Ref. RI-823)

Puzzle: St Mary's Guildhall in the High Street in Lincoln gives no clue as to its purpose.

Mystery In The High St

ONE THING which has puzzled historians for many years is why was St Mary's Guildhall, in Lincoln High Street, built?

It is known that the building was constructed sometime in the second half of the 12th century, but there is no real evidence as to why. Although it was obviously a domestic complex, it was on such a grand scale that it may have been built originally as the king's house for his visit to Lincoln, at Christmas, in 1157. During the visit, there would have been a crown wearing ceremony and since monarchs were superstitious of the belief that whoever wore his crown in Lincoln's walls would have a stormy reign, as had happened to King Stephen, it is likely that this ceremony would be in the suburb of Wigford. There are records that the king stored some of his wine in the property and then the building passed on to the ownership of the Great Guild of St Mary, in 1251-2.

The Guild was the principal social and economic guild in the city and even the king himself was a member. It continued in use as a guildhall until the middle of the 16th century, when it was given to the City of Lincoln on the abolition of chantries and religious guilds. Then followed centuries of different uses. A school, a hospital and then into a number of commercial uses, including a chimney sweep and a maltster. The large paddock behind the property was used by the military for exercising and then from 1884 until 1895, was the first home of Lincoln City Football Club.

Just after the turn of the century, it was taken over by a local building company as their store and remained with them for many years. In the 1970s, part of the complex was used once more for storing wine, this time by the Lincoln Section of the Feucht Frohilche Neustadter. But the Guildhall was by now, in a very sorry state and in 1981, the Lincoln Civic Trust took out a lease and set about organising a restoration programme. The south range was restored and is now used as a church hall. The west range restoration then followed and now houses a complex of meeting rooms and the Trust's offices. Restoration of the north range still has to take place.

One thing is clear, it must have been a very important building since it was allowed to have been built on top of the Roman Fosse Way. Perhaps only the king would have been allowed to do this. *Lincolnian's Diary. November 9, 1999.*

Intrigued: Visitors to St Mary's looking at the Roman road under the glass floor.

Signs Of Suffering Are On The Walls

ONE OF LINCOLN'S old buildings is amongst the most important medieval remains in the county, yet it is probably visited by tourists more than Lincoln residents.

The Bishop's Palace, in the shadow of Lincoln Cathedral, was started in the 12th century during the bishopric of Robert de Chesney. Building continued for many years and in 1329, Bishop Burghersh obtained a licence from King Edward III to crenellate and turrellate the walls of his palace. Crenellation was a status symbol showing the importance of the building's owner.

During the later episcopate of Bishop Alnwick more building took place, including a gate tower, still standing today. But by the middle of the 16th century, the palace was only used occasionally and was in a poor state of repair. Some repairs were carried out and in 1541, King Henry VIII and Queen Catherine Howard stayed in the palace. Another royal visitor was King James I, in 1617.

In 1536, the palace had suffered at the hands of the rebels in the Lincolnshire Rising, it suffered again in the Civil War of 1648, when parliamentary troops had to retreat into it. Royalist troops broke in and overcame the parliamentarians, setting fire to the buildings. Reminders of the fire can still be seen in the stonework today.

After this, much of the stone was from the ruins was used for repairs to the cathedral. Some restoration work took place in the first half of the 19th century and when the size of the diocese of Lincoln was reduced, Bishop Wordsworth's main residence

Impressive ruins: The remains of the Bishop's Old Palace, in the shadow of the cathedral.

at Buckden, Hertfordshire, was moved to Riseholme Hall. The bishop wanted to sell the hall and build a house on the site of the old palace, but nothing came of the idea. It was Bishop King who sold Riseholme and built a new residence next to the palace. It remained as the bishop's residence until 1945.

Today, visitors can get a good idea of the majestic building it once must have been, when the ruins are open to the public during the summer months. For me, one of the most impressive parts is the vaulted east hall, partly cut into the hillside. And in a garden below the walls of the palace is the Lincoln Vineyard, planted by the Feucht Frohlice Neustadter, to commemorate the 900th anniversary of Lincoln Cathedral.

Lincolnian's Diary. April 11, 2000.

Important part of history: The vaulted east hall of the Bishop's Palace is partly cut into the hillside.

Murder: Road, rail and river all come together at Saxilby. On the right is the Sun Inn, the scene of some macabre happenings.

Friendly Village Has A Grisly Tale To Tell

SAXILBY is a village near to Lincoln and has the distinction, in Lincolnshire, of being very easy to get to. It is one of the few places in the county where you can arrive by car, bus, train or boat.

Its waterway, the Fossdyke Navigation, was cut by the Romans to connect Lincoln with the River Trent at Torksey and opened up a route for boats into the north of England. One date in the village's history came in the mid 1930s when the marchers from Northumberland passed through the village on their way to London in a bid to persuade Parliament to save their shipyards. The weary men, with worn out shoes, stopped in Saxilby for the night. They were provided with blankets and washing facilities and the village's two shoe repairers mended their boots overnight. Next morning, they were sent on their way with food and good wishes.

Saxilby also has a grisly tale to tell. In 1805, Tom Otter, a local poacher-cum-labourer married a local girl and then murdered her the same day, killing her with a blow from a hedge stake. Then the story takes on something of a legend. He had been seen by one John Dunkerley, who, frightened that he would be blamed, ran away without telling anyone.

The body when found was brought to the Sun Inn but as there was no proof that Tom had been the murderer he was not charged.

One day, the following year, the village constable looked through the windows of the Sun Inn and saw Tom sitting there with what appeared to be a patch of dried blood on his shirt. He was arrested, charged, tried and found guilty. Following his execution at Lincoln, his body was hung in chains on the gibbet near to Drinsey Nook – a warning in those days to other would be wrong doers.

But this is not the end of the story. The hedge stake was

Unusual: The village of Saxilby sign is also a memorial.

kept at the Sun Inn and each year on the anniversary of the murder, it would disappear, only to be found again at the site of the murder. Eventually, the Bishop of Lincoln ordered it to be burned, but it was not

until John Dunkerley lay on his death bed that he confessed that the ghost of Tom Otter appears to him every year commanding him to take the stake to the murder scene.

Today, the lane is called Tom Otter's Lane and a plantation nearby is named Gibbet Wood. Saxilby also has an unusual village sign. It is carved in wood and shows the church, a poacher, a sailing barge and the head of a Lincoln red bull. It was erected in 1984 in memory of Geoffrey Ford, who had served as a councillor for many years.
Lincolnian's Diary. October 5, 1999.

Lincoln's Part In Aviation History

IT SEEMS hard to believe that in this day and age when aeroplanes can travel at twice the speed of sound, or more, and spacecraft orbit the earth, it is still less than 100 years since man first flew in a heavier than air machine.

The Wright brothers made that first historic flight, in 1903 and it was less than nine years later that the first aircraft flew into Lincoln. The pilot was Mr W.H. Ewen and the flight was from Peterborough. On the way, he had to put the plane down in a field near Scopwick and ask the way to Lincoln, where a large crowd had assembled to watch the landing, near to Wragby Road.

Less than three weeks later, another pioneer aviator, Mr B.C. Hucks landed his plane on the West Common, Lincoln and it was estimated

that some 20,000 people turned out to watch his flying display of aerobatics. This was to be the start of a long connection between Lincolnshire and flying. On April 1, 1918, the Royal Air Force was formed, although there had been military airfields in the county at Skegness and Cranwell operated by the Royal Naval Air Service.

In 1964, planes similar to the ones flown by Hucks and Ewen were seen again in the county, but this time the aircraft were replicas, made for the film *Those Magnificent Men In Their Flying Machines*, part of which was shot on location at Skegness.

Several years ago, I visited the Shuttleworth Collection, at Old Warden, in Bedfordshire, on a number of occasions. This collection of aeroplanes and vintage cars was started by Richard Shuttleworth, a relative of Joseph Shuttleworth, the founder of the Lincoln company which carried his name. Some of these replicas are in the collection, including a Bristol Boxkite, which is still able to fly,

Those magnificent men: A Huck's Starter, at Old Warden, being used to start a Hawker Hind.

providing the air conditions are almost calm.

There is also a most unusual vehicle in the collection, connected to the aviator B.C. Hucks. Basically, it is a Model T Ford and on a 'tripod' like construction on top of the car, is a long shaft, connected to the drive shaft by a chain. This type of machine was known as a Hucks Starter. At the time when aircraft engines were getting more powerful, in the First World War, it would often need three men to swing the propeller to get the

engine started. The shaft from the starter would be engaged with the hub of the propeller and when the clutch was released on the car, would turn the propeller and engine.

Also in the collection is a Sopwith Triplane, built for the collection and similar to the ones built in Lincoln by Clayton and Shuttleworth and also an Avro Tutor, which saw service with RAF Cranwell and the Central Flying School.
Lincolnian's Diary. May 9, 2000.

Heyday Of 1¾ Mile Tram Link

THERE are proposals to widen Tritton Road and make bus lanes and I can remember a couple of years ago that someone suggested that a tramway should be introduced along this road. Seventy years ago this year, trams disappeared from Lincoln's streets after having been a system of public transport for almost 50 years. I'm not quite old enough to remember them but I can recall seeing the old tramlines being dug up to provide metal for use in the Second World War.

I did once ride on a London tram, before they were scrapped. I think it was in the early 1950s. Since then, I have ridden on trams at the National Tramway Museum at Crich, in Derbyshire. It's a wonderful day out and the opportunity to ride on as many trams as time will allow.

From 1880 and 1882, the first recorded public transport service between the city and Bracebridge, was a horse-drawn omnibus operated by Jacksons and Sons. In 1882 trams were introduced to Lincoln, with the horse-drawn service replacing the buses with tram-cars. A total of 10 cars were eventually used on the track, only one and three-quarters of a mile in length, from St Benedict's Square to the Gatehouse public house at Bracebridge. Lincoln's first tram system ended on July 22, 1905, when the horse-drawn vehicles were removed from service, but it was to be almost four months before electric trams replaced them. The power system was for an electric supply to be fed to the trams via a stud in the road.

In November 1905, the first, No 1, carried the Mayor and Corporation officials and it was decked with flags and bunting. The daily service ran from 5.25am in the morning with the last tram leaving the Bracebridge depot at 11pm. The fare for the journey was one penny. During the four months when no trams ran, wagonettes were used over the route for public transport. Lincoln's tram system ran after electrification, but not without its problems.

The original open-top cars put into service in 1905 were covered in 1907, and in 1908 plans to extend the route east and west of the city centre were proposed but not put into operation. The stud pick-up system for the electric supply was also not without difficulties and had also resulted in a number of accidents. It was decided in 1918 to convert the supply to overhead wires and the first cars to use this system ran at Christmas 1919. But the trams had only 10 years to live, before they were finally scrapped.

Petrol-driven buses had appeared on Lincoln's streets in 1920 and by 1929 it had been decided that Lincoln trams had had their day. With the introduction of buses, citizens now had a public service over many more routes than the one High Street/Newark Road route taken by the trams. The electric trams, described by many as noisy and slow (but of course, without pollution) finally ran on March 4, 1929, with as much ceremony as when they had been inaugurated 24 years earlier. So ended an era, but Lincoln kept its place in the record books. The first system to use the Griffiths-Bedell stud contact system and the shortest tram route in the country, just one and three-quarters of a mile in length.

One amusing tale is told that when the horse trams were withdrawn, one of the horses was sold to a Nottingham taxi driver, but the horse was so used to following the line in Lincoln that it would only follow the lines in Nottingham. It is a shame that one of Lincoln's trams has not been preserved. Several eventually saw duty as summerhouses in gardens and the last one in the area, at Waddington, was inspected a few years ago to see if it could be preserved. Unfortunately, it was beyond preservation.
Lincolnian's Diary. Oct 26, 1999.

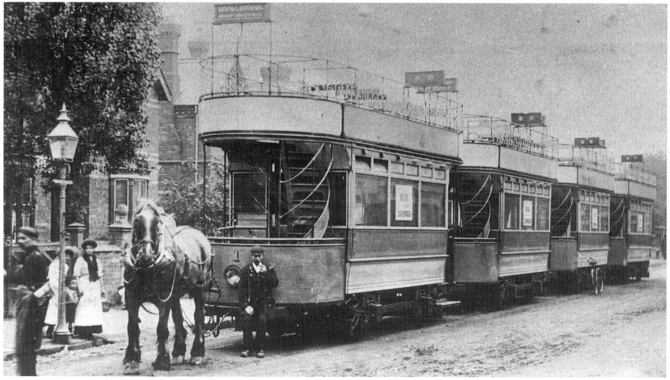

On track: Electric trams being delivered to the depot in Bracebridge in 1905. (Photograph from the Maurice Hodson Collection)

Lincoln in the 1930s wasn't on the tourist trail as we know it today, but it had an old-world charm of its own. Shoppers, not tourists trudge up and down the hill and a delivery boy, with large basket on the front of his cycle, takes a breather. Judging by the number of ladders, it looks as if it was window cleaning time. (Echo Ref. RI-58)

Exhibition: A London street scene in the Blitz. A display at the RAF Museum, in Hendon, in the 1990 exhibition.

Anniversary Of Battle Of Britain

I'M NOT quite old enough to really remember the Battle of Britain, being only four years old at the time, but I do have memories of some events in the air over Lincolnshire during the Second World War.

I can remember seeing two planes collide in mid-air over the city. One crashed on houses in Oxford Street, the other on houses in Drake Street. I can also remember seeing hundreds of planes going over at night for one of the thousand bomber raids and I will never forget the sound of a 'doodle-bug' going over Lincoln.

This year, it is the 60th anniversary of the Battle of Britain, but 10 years ago, there was a special exhibition, the Battle of Britain Experience, at the Royal Air Force Museum, at Hendon. I visited the exhibition and took photographs for an article in the *Echo*. The exhibition told the story of the battle through a labyrinth of tableaux, depicting the peaceful, but uneasy days just before 1939. This was followed by a scene showing Prime Minister Neville Chamberlain waving his famous piece of paper. Further tableaux showed families preparing for war and the evacuation of children to safer areas of the country. One of the most impressive scenes was that of a street after a bombing raid. Amidst the rubble, a Cockney mother tells of the problems. It was so real, you really thought someone was stood there talking, but it was all achieved with a plastic head and a hologram. Another hologram showed Winston Churchill delivering his 'finest hour' speech.

The military side of the experience took you through typical scenes to be found all over the country: a watch office, an ops room and the aircraft involved. The second Battle of Britain was not forgotten. This was later in the war when Hitler's V1 and V2 weapons brought a new type of pilotless attack on the country. Lincolnshire had only one airbase which could be truly described as a Battle of Britain airbase and this was RAF Digby, a few miles south of Lincoln. It flew Hurricanes and Spitfires in support of the 'Big Wing' squadrons of East Anglia. Later, RAF Digby came under the control of the Royal Canadian Air Force and 11 squadrons from this force used the base.

Lincolnian's Diary. September 12, 2000.

A horse-drawn wagon makes its way carefully across a snow-covered Castle Hill, while a weary pedestrian thankfully reaches the top of Steep Hill. Only the sandbags around the bottom of the lamp standard in the middle of the square give a clue to the fact that this is a wartime scene, taken in 1941. (Echo Ref. RI-421)

Legends May Not Be All That They Seem

I SUPPOSE legends are the things which often bring history into our homes and some of them do have an element of truth, but often, they are 'inventions' from the past which somehow have stuck.

Almost everyone knows of King Arthur, Merlin and the Knights of the Round Table, after all, there have been enough films made on the subject. Another story, which may be true or may be legendary, is that of St Oswald, who was killed in AD 642. His body was dismembered and years later, his remains were brought to

Bardney Abbey, but the monks would not allow it in their buildings and closed the door. A pillar of light appeared from the night sky and was regarded as a miracle warning them of their foolishness and after that, the door was always open. Ever since then, there has been the saying, if you leave the door open, 'Do you come from Bardney?'

One of the earliest legends concerning Lincoln hangs on the rhyme. 'The first crowned head that enters Lincoln's walls, His reign proves stormy and his kingdom falls.' King Henry II was obviously a superstitious man, for during his visit to the city, in the 1150s, he was crowned for the second time, not within the walls but in the suburb of Wickenford, below the Stonebow.

The legend of the Lincoln

The truth is out there: The legend of Robin Hood is a dubious one.

Commercial: The legend of the Lincoln Imp was an invention of local jeweller James Usher.

Imp was an invention of a local jeweller, James Usher, who saw commercial possibilities in making the tie pins and spoons bearing effigies of this carving which can be found in Lincoln Cathedral. The legend and there are several similar versions to this, says that one day, two imps were playing around the cathedral, when one went inside to do mischief. He annoyed the angels in the Angel choir, who warned him that if he did not leave, they would turn him to stone. He ignored them, so was petrified and placed high up in the choir as a warning. The second imp was told to leave the city and not look back. He could not resist one last look at the cathedral and was turned into salt and blew away in the wind. Personally, I think the carving is that of a workman who dropped a large block of stone on his foot. Holding his injured leg, he uttered a terrible oath and was immediately transformed for his blasphemy.

But my pet attack against any legend involves Robin Hood, although he was

reputed to come from Nottinghamshire, it still has local connections. Robin Hood was the sworn enemy of the Sheriff of Nottingham, who was a supporter of King John. Now King John died at Newark, in 1216. The Sheriff of Nottingham first appeared more than 200 years later, Lincoln had its first sheriff 1408, before his counterpart from Nottingham.

So how come there are two centuries between these 'facts?' Of course, there might have been a Sheriff of Nottinghamshire, but this title was just shortened by the story makers. And one more thing, Robin Hood is always shown wearing Lincoln Green. But Lincoln Green should really be Lincoln Grain, the colour of the cloth used for making sacks and this was a reddish-brown colour.

Oh well. I suppose this will stir up a hornet's nest so I'd better get my disguise on and climb back into the branches of the nearest tree and wait for the arrows!

Lincolnian's Diary. September 14, 1999.

Home Sweet Home

A Good Housewife's Work Was Never Done

IN THE days when cleanliness was considered next to Godliness each day had a set routine which the housewife followed slavishly – that is if she wanted to be considered any good.

Monday was traditionally wash day. If you couldn't afford to hire a washerwoman (and who could) you did it yourself.

Monday was chosen because in the average home there was less cooking to do. Sunday's joint was usually served up cold and so the time was devoted to the laundry. But if the laundry was to be done properly then preparations were done on the Saturday or Sunday.

The clothes were sorted into piles. Whites were put into soak before being washed and boiled. Coloureds followed and then the really dirty things like working overalls and clothes. By the time they were finished the water, in spite of being changed two or three times, was as black as the ace of spades. Two or three tubs were needed. The dolly tub for swirling the clothes around.

The wooden washing tub for scrubbing and a bowl for the starch, which was made with a powder and boiling water.

The copper was lit around six o'clock in the morning and once it boiled the battle started. All the whites were boiled for around 20 minutes until they dazzled. Lifting them out of the boiling water with a copper stick to put them in the tub for rinsing was a work of art. In the winter you could hardly see across the wash-house for steam and condensation.

The whites were then rinsed in blue water coloured with what they called a dolly bag. This made them look whiter. Linens such as shirts and pillowcases were starched and so were net curtains. But never silks.

You were judged by the colour of your clothes and the time you hung them on the line. A good housewife had her first lot of clothes out before nine o'clock in the morning. And all hell broke loose if the line sagged and dropped the clothes on the garden.

Then the whole procedure had to start again.

A huge iron mangle was used to take the water out of the clothes and also to press dry sheets, towels and tea towels which then did not need ironing. Ironing with only a fire for heating was all right in the winter but the summer months could be scorchers.

Before ironing it was mending. Socks and woollens which were washed by hand, were darned, sheets turned sides to middle if necessary, buttons replaced, laddered stockings repaired and worn for housework then patching and general repairs. Mending was considered the art of a thrifty housewife. A careless housewife hung woollens up by their shoulders or the ribbing which dragged them out of shape.

Frills were pressed with a goffering iron but if this was not available then the goffering was done with hair tongs which were placed in the fire, tested on newspaper and used to curl hair. Ears often bore fiery scars from red hot tongs being used. In a small household the laundry took one day to wash and another to iron.

Mending was done at night – long before the days of television. Ironing was done on the edge of the kitchen table on an old sheet and blanket.

Today's crafts were born through the necessity of yesterday's housewife who made rugs, clothes, cakes and soft furnishings. Baking day was usually Thursday when the tins were filled with something to 'cut at'. Visitors often arrived uninvited on Sunday and word soon went around if you couldn't provide a good table for tea. Some tables were so full the legs creaked under the load of meat, pies, cakes and bread – all home-made. It was a gourmet's delight.

Shoes were cleaned every night ready for work and school the next morning. No handy machines – just hard graft and a lot of elbow grease.

But, in spite of all the work they seemed to have more time in those days.

Bette's Bygones, March 7, 2000.

Letters Helped To Recall Past Times

WHAT memories your letters and calls evoked. **Reckitts blue bag which we used to make whites whiter.**

Do you remember Rinso for heavy solid clothes and Sylvan Soap Flakes which we used for hand washing? When Tide, the first detergent came out in the 1950s the doctors surgery was full of women with skin rashes because they had used too much. We had to dip our hands in the water in those days. There was no escape. My Mum used to donkey stone the step every morning and God help you if you stepped on it before it was dry. When her white net curtains had gone a bit grey she dipped them in a yellow dolly bag to make them a lovely cream colour.

Homemaking and decorating was simpler. The bedroom, living room, sitting room and kitchen curtains were the same colour and material. Brown and thick for winter and flowered and thin chintz for summer. The grapevine was speedy. If anything untoward was happening the lace curtains would twitch as everyone took a peep. I remember one neighbour saying: 'Mrs Kerry is so nosy I've been watching her all day peeping through her curtains.'

At night Dad repaired the shoes and Mum the clothes. Mrs Stephenson reminded me that, as youngest it was her job to clean the shoes. Her dad was a Grenadier Guardsman who told her to make sure the backs of the shoes shone as much as the front because more people saw the backs.

But we had love, as Mr Lewis Reynolds of Gainsborough said in a beautiful letter about his wife. He recalled the little house they lived in which they called The Shack. Earth toilet, no taps in the house, no electricity; and only one gas mantel. 'But we didn't care, the one thing in that house that was not missing was our love for one another'. And that was the way it was. We worked for what we had and we may not have had all we wanted but we certainly had all we needed. We had love.

A respect for our neighbour and a helping hand in trouble.

I remember when a young wife in our street received the dreaded telegram to say her husband had been killed at sea. Within minutes of the telegram boy leaving there was somebody there. Arms were placed around her as she cried. A cup of tea was made and the children taken by another neighbour. She was alone but to say she had no one to turn to was wrong. She had friends and neighbours and that was worth more than silver or gold.

Bette's Bygones. March 14, 2000.

Spring Water

'MAKE a cup of tea', Dad asked. **I looked around the kitchen for the sink and taps. Nothing. Dad sighed heavily 'Water's outside', he said. I had been used to a white sink – two chrome taps – one marked hot and one marked cold. All I could see was a wooden contraption with a long arm sticking out. It was the pump. This was the running water. I took the kettle and held it gingerly under the iron trunk that protruded from the wooden box. Nothing happened.**

'Push it up and down – pump it – that's what it's for'. Dad was losing his temper. I pumped the handle up and down and all of a sudden the water gushed out. It went all over my feet and almost drowned me but not a drop hit the kettle. I was mortified – more so because I caught the eye of a rather nice young man standing at the gate watching me. Perhaps Laughton wouldn't be too bad after all. He smiled and hung a bucket on the gate.

'Try hitting this', he laughed and I took the bucket and pumped it full of clear, cool water. It was spring water and tasted so good – in fact it made the best cup of tea I have ever drunk.

Bette's Bygones. September 14, 1999.

Watched Pot Never Boils!

'A WATCHED pot never boils' was an old saying which **probably originated from the days when the fire wouldn't get hold and the kettle was taking a long time to boil.**

There was a certain procedure to making a good cup of tea. And woe betide you if you tried to cut corners.

According to Twinings the leading tea merchants of London which was established in 1706 this is a fool-proof method.

1. Draw cold water from the tap (or pump).
2. When the kettle is nearly boiling heat the teapot keeping the inside as dry as possible.
3. Put the tea in the pot. As a general rule one teaspoonful for each person and one 'for the pot'.
4. Carry the teapot to the kettle, pour the boiling water on to the tea and stir well.
5. Leave to brew for five minutes.
6. Always put the milk and sugar in the cups first. Start pouring the tea into the cups, half filling them and then top up the teapot with freshly boiled water. Then fill the cups and top up the teapot again if seconds are needed.

What a palaver. It must have taken ages to make the perfect cup.

There were also some odd superstitions associated with tea making and teapots. Some even gave them magic powers.

For instance two people were not allowed to handle the teapot it was believed that one would become pregnant. Old nanny Woods was a great believer in this one and vowed and declared that it was the reason for the birth of her youngest son after a lapse of eight years.

Tea bags have done away with the art of reading tea leaves.

The kettle usually went on in time for *Mrs Dales Diary*, the radio serial at 4pm every day.

The neighbours took turns to make tea and three or four would gather to listen to Dr and Mrs Dale and then to the gifted one who read the leaves. They would drain the cup, swing it round three times, stand it upside down on the saucer and after a few minutes all was revealed.

Bette's Bygones. December 19, 2000.

Co-op Societies Had A Reputation

DO YOU remember the Co-operative Societies? I recall the Gainsborough and Lincoln branches. If your village was not big enough to support a store of its own, the vans came round. Monday was grocery day. During the war you registered with a grocer for rations. If you were a bit clever you shared your books between the village store and the van. That way you got a share of the extras!

The Co-op gave dividend or 'divvy' on each purchase. With every transaction you got a white ticket stating the amount spent. Mam kept them and every quarter you received your 'divvy' – which if you bought clothes, shoes and furniture mounted up to quite a lot. Some saved it in the Co-operative bank – others paid off outstanding bills, bought school and anniversary clothes or saved it for Sunday School outings to the seaside.

When I lived near Gainsborough the grocery van came every Monday. Everyone was just about out of essentials such as tea, sugar, butter and margarine. I often think about the two ounces of tea per person. We made it last by putting two teaspoons in a large pot and filling it up, resting it on the hob to keep warm and making it last all day. As long as it was 'wet and warm' we drank it. And cold sweet tea is still the best thirst quencher I've ever come across.

Every quarter Mr Ball came with a boxes of shoes for all ages, sizes and tastes.

The first: Lincoln Co-operative Society's first shop in Lincoln, at Napoleon Place.

Mr Grainger brought drapery and fancy goods. What a selection he packed into that van! One girl got four brush and comb sets for her 21st birthday all bought from Mr Grainger's. Tinned food was under the label Wheatsheaf – no frills but excellent quality. And that really is what they built their reputation on. Good honest trading!

The first Lincoln Co-operative Society store opened in 1861 and according to recorded history was in a double-fronted, three-storey house in Napoleon Place. From those early day the Co-operative Society in Lincoln spread into educational activities, farming and house building.

Its advertising, as always, was wonderful and customers were enticed with: 'Working men. Buy your food and groceries at your own shop where you can depend on the genuine article and full weight. Nothing is tampered with to please the eye. Shares may be paid up at once or by instalment at 3d (2½p). MEN OF LINCOLN – CO-OPERATE' – which is, I suppose where the name came from. And very appropriate too! The test of time has proved that.

Bette's Bygones. August 8, 2000.

Village shop: The Co-op's fifth branch, at Welbourn.

I'll Never Forget The Nightmare Winter

I MAY have got the date wrong but I think it was on the morning of February 5, 1947 when I went out to catch the 7.50am bus from Willoughton to Lincoln. It had snowed and I was walking in an ordinary pair of shoes ankle deep in snow.

The usual crowd were at the bus stop never dreaming that we would not get out of the village for another three weeks. We waited until around 9 o'clock when Mr Ormon Moore the postmaster suggested we go home. 'There's no mail and I think we are blocked in,' he said.

He wasn't kidding! The snow on the top road was above the hedges and gates. After a few days the buses could get through on the low road from Gainsborough but not through to us. Bread came on dumpers and the mail by sledge. By the second week we were burning anything we could lay our hands on to keep warm.

On the Saturday afternoon my friend Hilda Atkin was due home from Sheffield for the weekend. We knew she could get to Hemswell and her Mum asked if I would go with her to meet the bus. What a trek. We walked on top of gates and hedges. It was freezing and took us ages to get there and back – but we managed it. When I got home I could not feel my legs or feet. Mum said to get my lisle stockings off and put my feet in a bowl of hot water. Gallantly I rolled down my stockings to find that most of the skin peeled off with it. I carry the scars to this day in spite of frequent applications of bicarbonate of soda.

But we young people had a great time. Most of the lads were home on leave and we sledged and slid down the hills. Food was a bit of a problem but the shops shared with everyone irrespective of whether you were rationed with them or not. When the Co-operative coalman finally came through we cheered and cast off our coats, scarves and gloves to sit in front of a blazing fire.

Most housewives had a store cupboard of tinned and bottled goods which stood us in good stead. But as for the main dishes there were some rare concoctions. Thank God for potatoes. I remember someone steaming a tin of anonymous fish without piercing the lid. The explosion and resulting smell of fish spread all over the living room and lasted a very long time. In those days we pierced tins of beans and boiled them in a pan on the fire.

On pay day which came around every fortnight, we would gather up orders and cycle eight miles into Gainsborough to fetch fish and chips. The proprietor was always glad to see us – not the other customers in the queue. Imagine orders that totalled around 30 pieces of fish and the equivalent in chips divided into separate packets.

I never have worked out how we managed to deliver the right orders to the right house but we did. Mind you by the time we got home they needed heating up again in the side oven. But with plenty of salt and vinegar, home-made bread and butter it was a feast to be savoured.

Bette's Bygones, January 18, 2000.

Heyday Of The Housewife

THE following household hints are from a *Lincolnshire Echo* of around 1970, an era when career women were just coming into their own but housewife was still the main occupation of women. Times and menus were changing to cope with modern living, as this advice shows:

'If too much rice has been cooked, keep in the refrigerator or a cool larder and serve it fried the next day as a vegetable with a meaty sauce. Whisk an egg lightly and add to the rice just before frying and fry until golden brown'. Putting apples in salads to accompany chicken or ham was quite a new innovation. After slicing they were squeezed with lemon juice and mixed in a bowl with small chunks of pineapple and cucumber and sprinkled with grated cheese. Mmmm! Still sounds good.

Thrift was still a priority and fallen cooking apples were used in chutney. They were also made into puree with fried onion and breadcrumbs and used to stuff pork chops. Or they were served as a very thin purée with steamed puddings, adding jam or honey. It was all good wholesome food and very economical.

Very often, as the old saying goes, Necessity was the Mother of Invention and the *Echo* column gave this hint for a tasty starter. 'When you cannot run to smoked salmon, ease portions of kipper from boneless fillets and lay them on small rectangles of toast. Top with a thin slice of lemon and sprinkle with the juice.'

In the beauty line it said that if your hair would not take a cold perm it may be due to pills being taken. A well-known Lincoln hairdresser, Mrs Maureen Hutley, said that as soon as she put the cold perming lotion on anyone's hair she knew if they were on iron tablet. 'You get a smell like cold tea and it is the iron fighting the chemical in the lotion,' she said.

On the other hand, people were usually put on iron tablets for anaemia. She was once puzzled about one customer whose hair appeared to be in excellent condition yet it would not take a cold perm. She sent a sample to a laboratory for examination. The result that came back was – it was full of aspirin. I wonder if these things apply to the perms of today.

Colours were also high fashion in 1970. Another article on hair said that autumn is one of the most colourful seasons of the year – and the autumn of your life can also be a colourful one. 'There is no need to give up the fight to look younger just because the season of "mellow fruitfulness" has arrived and the pepper and salt and the grey have started to appear in the hair. Your grey hair is an optical illusion. What has happened is that the base colour remains while the naturally coloured hair is starting to go white. Obviously a colourant is needed to tone in the hairs without their appearing artificial. There is a shade to meet any base colour, for instance, ashen, warm or red or blonde'.

And we all remember those ghastly pale pastel shades of pink and lilac – very often worn with matching 'butterfly' spectacles. Let's hope they never make a comeback!

Bette's Bygones. November 21, 2000.

High Street, Lincoln, in 1936 and there are just as many buses as cars in the street, including a single-decker bus and a double-decker with an outside staircase. At this time, all buses for uphill routes left from this section of the street, between St Mary's Street and St Benedict's Square. (Echo Ref. RI-162B)

A Regular Attendance

METHODISM was first introduced into Stow, near Gainsborough, in 1819 when John Bains registered his house for services. A small group met and discussed the possibility of building a chapel, in August 1824 land was bought for £20 and a chapel built during that year. According to the history leaflet of 1974 there were 16 members. Some years later due to a rise in congregation the chapel was enlarged to almost twice its size and a schoolroom added.

Handy Hints For The Home

I WAS looking through an old book of household hints, c.1950, and found that many of them still work – and without using any chemicals. For instance you can get brown water marks and stains off an enamel bath by cutting a lemon in half, dipping in salt and rubbing over the stains. One of the most practical hints was to use an old shaving brush to clean louvered doors, pleated lampshades and intricate ornaments.

If you were lucky enough to have a fridge, put a few drops of vanilla essence on a cloth for the final wipe after cleaning and it would smell fresh for days! A splash of vinegar and vodka cleaned spectacles and toothpaste on a damp cloth removed crayon marks from paint and cleaned chrome fittings. One of the most surprising hints was to clean brass with Worcester Sauce. A piece of clean coal

An Ecclesiastical Census of March 1851 shows that there were 238 adults and 50 children regularly attending morning service and 108 adults and 20 children in the evenings. And in addition to this the Primitive Methodists of Stow also reported a group of 40 adults meeting to worship in a house. That added up to 50 per cent of the village population attending Methodist services. The interior of the chapel is singularly designed with the pews arranged lengthways, end to end and the pulpit on the opposite wall.

In the centre is the old, but carefully preserved coke stove that kept them warm in the

placed in a bowl of water with drooping vegetables and lettuce really gives it new life and if you add vinegar to the water when cooking cabbage you won't have that awful smell.

Locks that are stiff become loose if you dip the key into furniture polish and baking powder sprinkled in shoes absorbs any smells. Your windscreen will not mist up if you rub it over on the inside with half a potato. Crumpled newspaper packed into the toes of wet shoes will absorb the damp and your chilblains will react well to being rubbed with a raw onion.

Rosemary added to a bath will stimulate you and get rid of stress. If you can find any carrots with their tops still on they look excellent in floral displays. Shoving banana skins into the roots of rose trees will enhance blooms and colour and you can remove weeds from lawns by using an apple corer. Losing sleep through your partner snoring? Then sew a ping-pong ball in the back of their pyjamas.
Bette's Bygones. August 8, 2000.

harsh winter months. The organ, donated by Mr W. Tomlinson of Barton, stands opposite the door. An account book for 1890 shows that a bag of coal cost 10d (7½p) and the organ blower was paid 6s (30p) a year. The annual running was never more than £10. Recently the chapel held their anniversary service and unfortunately, like many others now has a small congregation which are nevertheless staunch in their faith and loyalty.

Mrs B. Butcher, of Sturton by Stow tells me that in the 1950s there was a large Sunday School with children travelling from miles surrounding to attend. The highlight of every chapel was the Sunday School Anniversary and receiving Sunday School Certificates for regular attendance.
Bette's Bygones. April 18, 2000.

Stacked With Preserves

AS RECENTLY as the 1960s most homes had a larder or pantry, the top shelves of which would be stacked with bottles and jars of preserves 'to see us through the winter'. The great stock-up started in January when Seville oranges came into the shops. The aroma of marmalade filled the air – particularly if some young housewife allowed hers to burn or boil over.

Then we waited, filling our time with spring cleaning until the first shoots of rhubarb were forced. After filling the family with pies and crumble we bottled short sticks of lovely red fruit in syrup or home-made wine. We made rhubarb and ginger marmalade, rhubarb wine and syrup.

Bottled gooseberries and wine, gooseberry preserve and pies stemmed our hunger. Then it was soft fruit. Raspberry and strawberry jam, raspberry vinegar to eat with Yorkshire puddings or pancakes – the mouth waters. We bottled pears and made lemon curd, which did not have a long shelf life, throughout the year.

I was usually given the job of peeling the shallots and onions for pickling. The tears would flow and Mam would give me a crust of bread to hold between my teeth to keep the smell from getting in my eyes. Chutney was made from almost everything and the thought of pickled pears to eat with cold meat and apple butter for roast pork sets my taste buds tingling.

Large glass sweet jars were at a premium for the bean saga, which was carried out when they were young and tender. We strung them first, then put them through the doubled-holed bean slicer or sliced them by hand. A layer of salt was put into the bottom of the jar followed by a layer of sliced beans until the jar was full. Usually two jars were done because as the salt melted the beans settled and the jars were topped up. But oh! They were superb – a taste all of their own, washed in cold water and then boiled and served with fresh butter.

Mincemeat could be made from pigs' liver when it was killed or simply by using fruit – dried fruit, apples, suet and brandy or home-made wine – and it was all made about a month before Christmas. Nothing was wasted. We never ate a chicken until it stopped laying eggs.

And they said the housewife didn't work, she just stayed at home!
Bette's Bygones. September 26, 2000.

Sunday School: The Church Army were regular summer visitors. This photograph, taken at Stow, shows a female Church Army Sister dressed very much like a nun.

Lessons Of Life At Sunday School

DO YOU remember singing 'Sunshine Corner, Oh! It's jolly fine. It's for children under 99. All are welcome, seats are given free. The (name) Sunday School is the place for me?'

Treasured memories of Sunday School where we were taught the lessons of life.

Sunday morning and afternoon the schoolrooms would be packed with children from the age of three to 13 or 14.

Sunday School teachers were volunteers who gave their time in the hope of nurturing a good honest life. Although forgotten at times, it returns to help us when needed. During both World Wars services were held before battle. *Abide With Me* was sung in preparation of death. When young Joe Vickers went to war in 1915 he took his Bible presented in 1911 by the Billinghay Baptist Sunday School with him through France, the Dardenells and in hospital after being wounded.

Sunday School's prize giving was an important day. All the family attended dressed in their Sunday best, hair plastered with Dad's hair cream and the girls be-ribboned or curled.

Your heart fluttered with excitement when you went up to receive your prize. The presenter shook your hand and murmured 'well done' as the congregation clapped. To be elevated from pupil to teacher was an honour given to older pupils.

During the wars Sunday School rooms became weekend canteens. They were manned by the congregation on Sunday nights when most other places were closed. The old Salvation Army took their tea wagons deep into the war zones.Sunday School's are disappearing and they say we were sent so that Mum and Dad could have a bit of peace and quiet.

But it was wonderful to see kids of all ages walking down the street in their best clothes, smart as new pins.

It was an accepted part of our spiritual and social life. Concerts, anniversaries, outings, teas, summer fetes, games evenings – they were great fun.

Can you recall some of the nicknames? 'Charlie Puff Box, Annie All Pains and Piggy Mills.' Cliff College people and Church Army caravans would park on the green and everyone would attend the open air services and events.

To us kids it was like a holiday. And did you save up for the Sunday School outing in a cocoa tin with a slit in the top that Mam had made with the tin opener?

Acting, unpaid, Sunday School teachers were the salt of the earth.

Bette's Bygones. May 9, 2000.

It is difficult to believe that these two pictures were taken from the same spot less than half-a-century apart. Boultham Park Road once had a brick-built bridge carrying the former high-level avoiding railway line. It was a danger as far as road users and pedestrian were concerned. There was only sufficient room for a single line of road traffic and there were no pavements under the bridge for pedestrians, who had to risk their lives by walking on the road. Trains last used the line in the early 1980s, after 100 years of working and the track was closed, the bridge demolished and the embankment removed. New houses were built on the land and the trains are remembered by street names, Railway Park Mews and Railway Park Close.

Old Remedies To Cure Any Ailment – Old Wives Tales? Granny Knows Best

I WAS SENT a book to review on home remedies and memories came flooding back of some of the ones guaranteed to cure all ills and keep you healthy and beautiful.

Bread soaked in boiling water was an excellent poultice for boils or splinters. Eye styes were bathed in cold tea or rubbed with a gold wedding ring.

A large handkerchief soaked in vinegar and wrapped tightly around the forehead took care of bilious attacks (migraine).

And a teaspoon of salt or mustard in warm water was an excellent emetic while a good dose of castor oil sent germs flying in all directions.

Cold feet were soaked in a mustard bath and an Epson Salts and mustard hot tub sweated out a cold or fever. Does anyone remember Thermogene?

That pink thick wool made into a vest and placed over chest and back.

It itched like mad and made you sweat but kept colds away.

A spoonful of Kompo (no, not from *Last of the Summer Wine*) in hot water heated the body before setting off on a cold winter morning.

Zam Buk and Tiger Balm ointment gave some relief to rheumatism through it's warmth (mainly because it burnt your skin so badly you forgot the pain).

Nettle tea was supposed to purify the blood and cure kidney ailments.

Camomile not only lightened the hair it also calmed the nerves.

Due to hard work and long hours few people suffered from insomnia but those who did were given a herb pillow containing a great many hops.

A guarantee against sleeplessness.

Young girls who suffered from anaemia were treated with raw liver sandwiches or a concoction of iron which rotted the teeth.

And there was always a remedy for 'getting rid of trouble'.

One woman ate a soap powder sandwich and another boiled a mouse and drank the liquid. I'm, not sure what the 'trouble' was, but they had beautiful babies.

For many years the only treatment for tuberculosis was a mixture made from strong onions or garlic. This and being kept outside in the fresh air, even to sleep, was all they had to fight the disease. But many old remedies paved the way for modern medicine.

The digitalis flower is still used for problems of the heart. Adding milk or elder flowers to the bath water soothes and softens the skin and camomile is still a valued addition to many hair preparations.

Rinsing hair in vinegar leaves it soft and shiny.

Common Vaseline was used for chapped hands, babies bottoms, to soften the face, to gloss the eyelashes. It lost favour for a while but is now being revived through beauty 'secrets' of the famous. They are regarded as old wives tales, but there are many who still believe that Granny knew best.

Bette's Bygones. June 13, 2000.

The Secrets To A Happy Marriage

I WAS reading a book of 'useful information' over a century old and found these interesting passages on courtship and marriage: 'The happiness of married life comes from pleasant, harmonious relations between husband and wife. If rightly mated life will be one continual joy.' It advised couples to marry someone they have known long enough to be sure of their worth: 'Marry a person who is equal to your social position, a person of similar religious convictions, tastes, likes and dislikes,' it said.

It then went on to state that the husband should be strong so as to be a natural protector to his family. He should be brave so that he may defend his companion. 'The wife, confident in the husband's strength and wisdom, will thus implicitly yield to his protecting care.'

It was believed that bright red hair and a florid complexion indicated an excitable temperament. Such should marry black hair and the brunette type. The grey, blue, black or hazel eyes were advised not to marry those of the same colour.

The very corpulent should unite with the thin and spare but the thin, bony, wiry, prominent features, Roman nosed, cold-blooded and individual should marry the round-featured, warm-hearted and emotional person.

The very fine-haired should not marry those like themselves and the curly should unite with the straight and smooth-haired.

The etiquette of courtship should be conducted in a quiet persistent manner. Evening visits were short – no longer than two hours. Staying late was said to endanger the lady's reputation and the couple were never allowed to isolate themselves.

The etiquette between husbands and wives said that a rebuke should be preceded by a kiss.

A request should never have to be repeated. Each should strive to accommodate the other and criticism should be made in the most loving manner. And neither should make a remark calculated to bring ridicule upon the other. The home should be left with a tender goodbye and loving words. 'They may be the last!' was the warning.

A man does not only require that his wife should be a good housekeeper. She must be more in conversational talent and general accomplishment she must be a companion.

A husband was told to put forth every effort to make himself worthy of this companion so that he did not compel her to go through life with a man she could not love or respect.

These were the important things of marriage – there was no mention of the bedroom but it did warn the husbands that at times the wife's 'variable condition' of health will be likely to make her cross and petulant. 'You must overlook all this – even if at times your wife is unreasonable,' it said. Could it have been that old enemy PMT?

Bette's Bygones. September 5, 2000.

Changed: The façade of the old Mawer and Colingham's store, in Lincoln, before alterations and a takeover by Binns.

Store Grew Due To Faith and Hard Work

FOR MANY years the name of Binns has been synonymous with quality fashion and furnishings, not least on Lincoln High Street. But did you know that the history of Binns goes back to Georgian days and actually started in Sunderland in 1783? An account of its beginnings taken from a diary written by the nephew of the founder, Mr George Binns, covers the period from 1817 to 1824 when the shop was a draper's.

This upright Quaker family established traditions of service and quality which have been carried down the decades. Binns expanded its business throughout the North East and it name is now renowned in leading towns and cities. David Binns of Halifax, Yorkshire, was born on November 13, 1799. He was the son of Richard and Sarah Binns who lived in a humble sphere of life and had to work hard for a livelihood.

Married life had begun with difficulties. He was a clogger and worked for his father.

'After a while they began to keep a few drapery goods which mother attended to. She also made up garments for her customers, which assisted their income. Little by little they improved their circumstances and added grocery, meal and flour to their business. My father commenced farming and I was often set to size clogs, making them ready for sending off to distant parts of the country.'

David was apprenticed to the business and records that on Christmas Day 1817 the shop closed at half past four. He regularly attended the Quaker meetings, sometimes listening to three sermons in one session. At the back of the book was found this account of the Halifax Peace Society for the promotion of Permanent and Universal Peace.

'The object of this society shall be to circulate tracts, diffuse information by lectures and other means, tending to show that war is inconsistent with the spirit of Christianity and the true interest of mankind and to point out the means best calculated to maintain permanent and universal peace upon the basis of Christian principles. It shall consist of persons of every denomination who are desirous of uniting in the promotion of peace on Earth and good will to all men.' It was dated and passed on the 3rd day of the 9th month 1847.

Through faith, hard work and fair trading Binns grew into a large chain of stores that graced almost every High Street.

Bette's Bygones. June 27, 2000.

Just over 60 years separate these two pictures of Lincoln High Street and in the old picture, the flags and bunting were flying for the coronation in 1937. On the left, you can just see the sign for Boots the Chemists (St Mark's Branch), with a Lincolnshire Echo delivery van parked outside. On the right is the imposing frontage of Sibthorp House, built in the Queen Anne style, which despite its height, had only a ground floor. It was masterminded by John Sibthorp as a town house to incorporate a 14th-century mansion which stood on the site. John died in 1718 and his widow brought an end to the building work and promptly moved out of town, to Canwick Hall. During the 20th century, Sibthorp House was an Inland Revenue office and later used by the railways before demolition in 1962. This beautiful old building was replaced by a modern shop and office block and the area on the left now has modern shops.

Something like 70 years divide these two pictures but you could be fooled into thinking they were of different scenes. The old picture was taken of Danesgate in the 1930s, with a cobbled road surface, gas lamps and terraced houses. The large building in the centre background is part of the Wesley Chapel, fondly known as 'Big Wesley', which was demolished in the 1960s. There is also visible, another Methodist Chapel, this one being in Silver Street. It closed in 1940, but remained in use for many years, as a Co-operative, before it too was demolished.

Today's picture shows a three-level car park and the brick and glass structure of what used to be the Telephone Manager's Office, but now largely residential properties. The only thing visible which links the two pictures is the spire of St Swithin's Church.

Times Have Changed

I LOVE old bookshops and can spend hours browsing through the shelves or the boxes at a car boot sale. I came across a very interesting one recently which explained several things I had never thought about.

For instance, during the General Election of 1906 the slogan 'The Big Loaf' was used to highlight the rise in food prices. There was a landslide to the Liberal Party which everyone thought brought in a new era.

It was a hard life for the ordinary working man who earned around one pound a week.

It gave only the barest essentials and if a man was off work for a week the family were soon in trouble. No sickness benefit or dole in those days. The old-age pension of 5s (25p) for a single person and 7s 6d (37½p) for married couples didn't start until you were 70. But people didn't retire until they were forced to in those days.

Leave An Extra Pint, Pay You Later – In Bed

THE DEMISE of the milkman, with his cheery whistle, is the passing of an era. We left him notes, asked him to take messages and very often owed our lives to him. These notes left for the milkman were first published in 1969 but they tell a story of friendship and trust:

'Please send me form for supply of milk for having children at reduced prices.'

'I have posted the form by mistake, before my child was properly filled in'.

The activities of the suffragette movement in 1913 were received with hostility and mockery.

The man was the boss of the house and women actually standing on the doorstep, chaining themselves to the railings or heckling at meetings were met with

'Please send me a form for cheap milk as I am expecting mother.'

'I have a baby 12 months old. Thanking you for same.'

'I have a baby two months old fed on cows' and another child.'

'Please send form for cheap milk. I have a baby three months old and did not know anything about it until a friend told me.'

'I have only one child as my husband is a bus driver and works day and night.'

'Milk is wanted for my young baby as his father is unable to supply it.'

'I require extra milk as I am stagnant.'

'In accordance with instructions I have given birth to twins in the enclosed envelope.'

'Please leave an extra pint – pay tomorrow – in bed.'

scorn. In 1919 there was a flu epidemic which killed millions of people. No antibiotics or flu jabs. And in 1919 the first petrol station was opened in Berkshire – a sign of the power of the motor car.

In 1922 electricity in the home was more common and

'Please do not leave any more milk as you ignore my notes.'

'I have just had a baby. Would you please leave another one, each day.'

'Please leave an extra pint. If this note blows away, please knock.'

Before every home had a fridge, milk was delivered on Christmas and Boxing Day. And of course good old 'Milky' was given a drink at every house. By the time the van weaved its way to us down the fen he was well oiled and would park to sleep if off.

Around four he would come in for a cup of black coffee and a mince pie.

I am sure there are many more stories that milkmen could tell.

Bette's Bygones. October 24, 2000.

we saw the introduction of electric cookers and fires which alleviated a lot of cleaning for the housewife. But there was still a lot of poverty and hard work among the working classes.

Time has certainly marched on!

Bette's Bygones. July 11, 2000.

The heart of historic Lincoln just before the start of the Second World War in 1939. It was still possible to drive through this area, but motorists are advised by the sign on the wall to turn left and drive through Exchequergate. On the right, the garage operated by Roland C. Bellamy is now the White Hart Hotel's garage. (Echo Ref. RI-159)

Passers-by watch as the bunting goes up for the celebrations of the coronation of Queen Elizabeth II, in 1953. In the centre, at the back, is the old Bull's Head public house, soon to be demolished to make way for an improved junction. (Echo Ref. RI-823F)

Tales from coast and county

Legend Began At Skegness

THE NAME of Billy Butlin and Skegness go together like fish and chips, which most people enjoy on a visit to the seaside. Billy Butlin arrived in England in 1921, from Canada, with £5 in his pocket. A few years later, as a travelling showman, he came to Skegness and set up a hoopla and three other stalls in a very good site, between the town and the amusements on North Parade.

He suggested that a large amusement park should be opened south of the pier and in 1929, this opened. He introduced the first dodgem ride in the country and even had water dodgems. This was followed by a second amusement park at Mablethorpe.

In 1930, the *Echo* reported that Mr Butlin, who they described as 'the well-known Skegness amusement caterer' had organised a procession in the town and it was 'easily the largest seen in the resort'. Thousands of people lined the route, despite heavy rain, to watch Skegness lifeboat, drawn by a motor tractor and containing sailors and Britannia. Many vehicles carried advertising and other displays and it was reported that 'humour was a strong feature'. Many entrants were mounted on horses and donkeys, together with a host of pedestrians wearing fancy dress.

But in 1936, the event which saw the name of Butlin become a household word, happened with the opening of Britain's first holiday camp, at Ingoldmells.

It's motto was 'Our true intent is all for your delight', taken from Shakespeare's *A Midsummer Night's Dream* and I can still remember seeing this on the main building at the camp.

Within four years, the camp closed to holiday-makers and it became HMS Arthur, a naval recruit training establishment, but after the war, it re-opened for holidaymakers and others followed in several parts of the country.

In 1964, Billy Butlin became Sir Billy Butlin and his last visit to Skegness was in 1977, to switch on the illuminations. I remember it vividly. He pressed the switch to light up the town and the opposite happened. All the lighting circuits fused and for a few moments, the area around the seafront was in total darkness! Sir Billy died in Jersey, where he had made his home, in 1980.

Lincolnian's Diary. August 1, 2000.

Holiday legend: Sir Billy Butlin, who opened his first holiday camp at Skegness in 1936.

Smiling in the rain: Crowds wait outside Lincoln Central on Trip Saturday, 1956. (Echo Ref. RI-1873)

Saturday Start Of Great Exodus

FOR DECADES, the final Saturday in July held a special place in the calendar for many thousands of Lincoln families. For it marked the start of the annual Trips Saturday Fortnight. It was an event second only to Christmas in many city households and today – when holidays are spread throughout the year – it's difficult to imagine the effect the Trips had on city life.

'Lincoln Foundry Trips – another large exodus' was how the *Echo* headlines described the event on July 29, 1905. Underneath, the story ran: 'There were the usual animated scenes at the two railway stations in the city in the early hours of this morning, when another great exodus from the city took place on the occasion of the foundry trips. Altogether, between 9,000 and 10,000 people left Lincoln to seek their annual recuperation at the seaside or in the inland towns.'

The story continued: 'It is again a happy feature that, despite the very heavy traffic with which the several companies had to deal, and the excitement which prevailed among those departing from their labours for a few days, the whole were despatched without any untoward incident. The bookings on the Midland system showed a big increase on those of last year, and the total number of passengers from the station, including the returns from the Great Central line, would be quite 2,700.'

Blackpool and Clee-thorpes reigned supreme among the holiday venues for many Lincoln area people

Waiting for the off: Families at the LNER Station (later Lincoln Central) back in 1931, eagerly awaiting the arrival of the train that would take them on their annual holiday. (Echo Ref. RI-548)

and although Blackpool was to remain high on the list of holiday destinations for many years to come, Cleethorpes was to slip to a lower position as the popularity of other Lincolnshire resorts increased. By 1925 charabanc excursions were all the rage and operators throughout the Lincoln area were competing with one another for the holiday traffic.

A decade later – and just four years before the outbreak of the Second World War – the Trip Saturday headlines in the *Echo* announced: 'Three-hour bus traffic record'.

The story revealed: 'There is a tendency for people to travel farther afield than usual.'

By then, the Lincolnshire coast seemed to be losing its popularity to places like

Bridlington, Scarborough, Great Yarmouth and Torquay. 'The LNER dealt with thousands of holidaymakers and from early morning there was a continuous stream of people through the booking halls and crowds on the station platforms. Over 2,000 people left the city by Road Car bus between 7am and 10am.'

Rail fares in those pre-war holiday days were 22s 3d period return to Blackpool, while some coach operators had actually cut the price of a day-return ticket from Lincoln to Mablethorpe to a mere 5s.

After the war the Trips were quick to get back to normal. But it wasn't long before the buses and the trains were beginning to lose out to the private motor car.

On Trip Saturday of 1955, the AA reported that at one time, traffic from the Midlands to the East Coast was going through at the rate of 1,000 vehicles an hour. By July 1965 the trend was still continuing, with public transport losing out and people travelling farther afield. Instead of weeks on the Lincolnshire coast, or Blackpool, holidays in Russia or the coast of North America were being accepted as quite normal.

A Lincoln travel agent told the *Echo* at the time: 'There is no doubt the British seaside and country resorts are falling out of favour with the modern style car-equipped tourist.'

British Rail was said to have been well pleased with the volume of traffic it

carried, but a mere two packed specials leaving for Great Yarmouth and Blackpool and news that normal services were well patronised, made it little more than a shadow of former trip Saturday glories. It was a similar story at the Lincolnshire RoadCar Company bus station where normal services were supplemented. But again there was no mistaking the trend away from public transport.

By the mid-1970s the Trip Saturday queues at bus and railway stations could be counted in hundreds rather than thousands. And many early Saturday departures had been replaced by people setting off after work the previous evening.

The Gossiper. August 1, 2000.

The September race meeting in 1949 attracted a large crowd and the bookmakers were kept busy by the punters wishing to part with their money. Flat racing finished on The Carholme in 1964 and the Lincolnshire Handicap (which traditionally marked the opening of the flat racing season), was moved to Doncaster. (Echo Ref. RI-440)

Changing Patterns Of Our Bank Holidays

THE EVENINGS are starting to draw in. The schools will be reopening in a few days' time. We are heading towards the last bank holiday of the summer. How will you be spending the holiday Monday? Taking the family to coast or country? Visiting a local show or gala? Or catching up on the garden or doing a spot of home decorating?

The pattern of our August Bank Holiday Monday has changed considerably over the years. The first August Monday of the 20th century was sadly lacking in blue sky and sunshine. But with the latest from the Boer War still filling the nation's newspapers, many families were determined to make the best of it. In those days the bank holiday was on the first Monday of the month and in the days before just about everyone had their own transport, trains and buses provided the key to many a successful day out.

Between 30 and 40 special excursion trains steamed in and out of Skegness Station on August Bank Holiday Monday 1900 and 40 miles up the coast, Cleethorpes welcomed more than 20 special excursions. But the *Echo* reported how heavy rain during the afternoon made things unpleasant for the day trippers. Fifty years later it was a very different story on the Lincolnshire holiday coast.

Although no one had coined the phrase in those days, we had really never had it so good. The thoughts of the horrors of the Second World War were beginning to fade and everyone wanted to have a good time. In 1950 the sun shone and the people of Lincoln went to the seaside for the day. For once, there was unlimited petrol and although not everyone had a car, close on 2,000 vehicles an hour were pouring through the city on their way to the coast.

At Skegness, it was reported that every available bedroom had been taken and a tent colony had sprung up on the outskirts of the town. Long before noon, bus parks were full and emergency ones had to be opened. Traffic was heavier than at any time since the war and although private cars were not so numerous, buses and motorcycles were arriving in record numbers. The resort's railway station staff were kept hard at it with 23 excursions bringing in 14,000 visitors during the day. And that compared to just 6,000 on the same day the previous year.

Caravan holidaymakers had never been so numerous and a council spokesman summed it all up by saying: 'We have never had such a day in the past 20 years.' There were signs that Lincoln was beginning to become a tourist spot itself. Wrote an *Echo* reporter: 'Lincoln is attracting its fair share of visitors. Cameras, short pants, American monster cars and day visitors are in evidence.'

By 1975, the pattern of the August Bank Holiday had changed again. It was held on the last Monday in the month in a bid to extend the holiday season. But along the Lincolnshire coast you would have looked in vain for the holiday crowds of 25 years earlier. You could not have blamed the weather either. Those people who did make it to Skegness were able to enjoy a bracing stroll along the pier

Holiday fun: The donkeys on the beach at Mablethorpe provide happy memories for many holidaymakers. (Echo Ref. RI-4288)

where comedian Harry Worth topped the bill at the Pavilion Theatre on the Bank Holiday Sunday and Ken Dodd and his Diddymen appeared for the rest of the week.

The Gossiper. August 22, 2000.

Grand Old Lady's 70 Years By The Sea

I HAVE often heard of people who visit the same place for their holidays year after year, but can anyone beat a claim which appeared in the *Echo* in 1930? People were being asked if they knew the whereabouts of a person who has visited Skegness for 70 years without a break.

The *Lincolnshire Echo* claimed to have learned from a well-known resident that he had got into a conversation with an old lady, presumably an octogenarian, who informed him that this year's holiday constituted her 70th visit to the resort without a break. She recalled visits long before the railway line was extended, from Burgh-le-Marsh to Skegness. The last six miles of the journey would be completed by posting coach. During the earlier years of her visits, she lodged at a small cottage in the old High Street, one of a mere handful of cottages which comprised the village of Skegness at that period.

It was unfortunate that the lady was allowed to leave without her identity being ascertained, but the *Echo*'s correspondent regarded the achievement so unique that he informed the town's Advancement Association (no doubt the forerunner of the Tourism Committee), who said that if she could be found and her claim verified, they would be delighted to present her with a silver replica of the 'Jolly Fisherman' on behalf of the town.

Just imagine that when the lady visited Skegness for the first time, which would be 1861, Queen Victoria had not yet celebrated her silver jubilee. The pier and the clock tower did not exist and there would probably be very little in the way of seafront amusements.

One attraction in those days was horse racing on the beach.

Lincolnian's Diary. August 1, 2000.

Crowded beach: Skegness in Edwardian times – and not a bikini in sight. Note the pier on the horizon.

Flood Tide Of Memories

WHAT is my first memory of the seaside? I can vaguely remember the hulk of a large rowing boat type of vessel on the beach near some sand dunes and playing there with my cousin. I don't know where it was, but I think it was at Anderby Creek. How old was I? About three! Then the war intervened and we never went to the seaside. It was not until the war was over that we returned and I can remember going to Skegness, Mablethorpe and Cleethorpes, all by train.

But it was not until the 1950s that I began to go to the resorts on a more regular basis. I was interested in roller skating and as secretary of the Lincoln Roller Skating Club, organised several trips to 'Skeggy'. We used to skate at two rinks in the resort. The largest one was at the Festival Centre and the smaller one on the amusement park at the north end of North Parade. I remember on one trip two members of the party going out on the boating lake. When they reached the middle, they decided to change places in the rowing boat. And yes, they fell in! They spent the rest of the trip in a very soggy state and were forced to sit on the floor of the bus on the journey home.

It was as an *Echo* photographer that I visited Skegness, in 1967, to cover a visit by Princess Margaret. She was not very popular with the Press in those days, so when she got into the boat to travel along the Waterway, we were all secretly hoping that she might have a little accident, and get wet. The boat rocked a little, but we were disappointed. Later, we went along to Butlins and actually had lunch in the same room as the royal visitor – the only time I can claim to have dined with royalty.

Trip weeks often saw me at Mablethorpe and Sutton-on-Sea, taking pictures of holidaymakers. It was no easy task finding people from the *Lincolnshire Echo*'s circulation area and there were many families there from Nottinghamshire and South Yorkshire. A visit to the information office found very helpful staff who would give me the beach chalet numbers of a few 'local' people and it was when I visited them that they usually said 'Have you been to chalet number so-and-so?' This snowballed so that at the end of the day, I would have a good collection of pictures – not to mention numerous cups of tea, brewed up in the chalets.

But my most lasting memory is of being with the Lincoln *It's A Knockout* squad in 1973, taking part in a 'knockout league'. Lincoln won all of their games and from the resulting prize money, we went to the Fiesta Club in Sheffield to see a show and have a meal. Top of the bill? The Bee Gees – and there was a name on the posters for the following week. Someone we had never heard of and had difficulty in pronouncing. Showaddywaddy!
Lincolnian's Diary. August 1, 2000.

All Part Of Village Life

I CAME across an old Ingham Parish Magazine dated March 1889. It held a lot of information and was good value for 2d (under 5p)

Confirmation classes were held every week and there were clothing clubs, which I imagine would be the sale or giving of second hand clothes to the poorer parishioners. Mother's meetings, cottage lectures and meditations were all part of the village life. And in a notice headed House of God Wants there is listed: new Altar Silver (or gold) Paten, Frontals. Curtains, Cross for Holy Table, Altar Linen, new lamps, new matting and organ.

Regarding an offer to the Revd H. Macpherson, of 10s (50p) towards new matting the editor remarks. 'Surely if our hearts are right, we cannot let our own houses be nice and the House of the Lord be meanly furnished. All gifts should be provable so as to suit the restored church'. Offertories for the month of February amounted to £1 13s 3d (£1.65). Parish Wants including a debating society, village band, amateur dramatic club, choral union and better roads. They certainly got their priorities right.

On Saturday February 16 this rather scathing report was given on a concert given in aid of the Reading Room fund. 'Miss H. Bates and Miss Foster, both played in good taste, the latter with considerable skill in execution. Miss Saundaver's voice showed best in the last songs and Mr Gilbert's airs were carefully sung to his rich notes. Mr Madell should be on the stage, but Mr Melbourne was killing in his second song. Mr West has a good memory and studies Sir A. Sullivan. Mr Sandanver's pieces we unfortunately could not make out. Mrs F. Russon has a fine voice if she turned it more to the audience. The sum raised after expenses was £1 15s.
Bette's Bygones. April 4, 2000.

Busy scene: Crowds of trippers on Cleethorpes Pier, almost 100 years ago.

A Coast Of Piers And Castles

LINCOLNSHIRE has a very long coastline and from the point where the River Trent enters the Humber to the place where the River Witham enters The Wash, the distance is more than 80 miles.

But only a small part of this is regularly visited by holidaymakers and 'trippers'. This is the section between Cleethorpes and Skegness and what are the unusual things you can find between these two places?

At one time, both resorts had a pier and they still have the remains of one. Cleethorpes Pier was built in 1873 and that at Skegness almost 10 years later. The pier at Skegness was 1,843 feet in length, making it the fourth longest pier in Britain. Both piers suffered considerable damage at times during their lives. Cleethorpes had serious fires in the first few years of the 20th century. At the start of World War II, the pier was deliberately breached as an anti-invasion project, but the cost of putting things right after the war proved too costly and so the only part left was a 335 feet section as can be seen today.

Skegness Pier had a disaster in 1919, when a schooner was blown into the pier during a storm. It was 20 years before the temporary repairs were put in order and in 1978, severe weather again breached the structure, this time in two places. Fire eventually destroyed the pierhead theatre and like Cleethorpes, Skegness was left with only a shadow of its former pier.

There are two 'castles' you can find, but neither of them are genuine. Ross Castle, at Cleethorpes, was built as an observation point when the railways arrived in the resort and was named after the secretary of the railway company. Skegness has a 'Sun Castle' which was opened in 1932 as a solarium and is now a popular meeting place in the town.

At Ingoldmells, there is a palm tree growing in the churchyard said to have been planted in memory of a local lad who lost his life in a shipwreck. You just might be lucky if you visit Trusthorpe when there is a very low tide and see the stumps of a submerged forest. Several coastal villages have been lost to the sea over the centuries and it is rumoured that sometimes, when the sea is rough, you can hear the bell ringing from the ruins of a submerged church! It might be legend, but it's a good yarn for the locals to recall.

Lincolnian's Diary. August 1, 2000.

Mock castle: Ross Castle, Cleethorpes, built by a railway company.

Clothes Rationing: How They All Coped

ALTHOUGH he disliked the idea of clothes rationing Winston Churchill found that the British public voted seven to one in its favour and it was brought into force on June 1, 1941. The basic rate of 66 coupons was intended to cover one complete outfit a year, some eager beavers actually refused to use their coupons and made do and mended throughout the war. Pleats were not so full and trouser turn-ups were out. Clog boots and shoes made with thick wooden soles were surprisingly comfortable and were available without coupons.

The posters of 'Make do and Mend' were aimed mainly at women probably because most of the men were in uniform. Dyeing, remaking and darning were the order of the day. It brought out some great skills as women pitted their wits to keep their clothes in bandbox condition. One poster advised painting darning mushrooms white so that it wouldn't need so much light to work by.

Blackout material intended for curtains was also off coupons. It soon became apparent that if bleached it could be re-dyed and made into frocks, housecoats and a host of other garments. Parachutes were at a premium.

Although cut on the cross every inch was used. A lot of lingerie, evening dresses and wedding gowns started life as a parachute. The only problem was that unless you lined them or wore fairly thick underclothes you could see straight through them. Queen Elizabeth (now the Queen Mother) was applauded for continuing to be immaculately turned out by making 'do'.

Government propaganda told us that 'a stitch in time saves coupons'. That plus fours would make two pair of shorts for a schoolboy and a pair of men's trousers a ladies skirt. It became a ritual to go through your wardrobe twice a year to see if or how the clothes could be re-modelled, dyed, lengthened or shortened to wear for another season. Jumpers that had gone out of shape were pulled down, the wool washed and then re-knitted.

Children's garments were made to last another year or so by combining knitted and woven fabrics. A frock which was worn in parts was renovated with a knitted yolk, sleeves or panels. A short length of material was eked out in the same way. The best parts of an old dress were combined with the wool from an un-picked knitted garment. Socks and stockings were re-footed and re-heeled and worn knitted gloves were made into mittens. It almost became a competition to see who could come up with a new ruse to save money and material.

Grey army blankets were made into coats. If the garment was really past it then it was made into pegged rugs or sent to be recycled for the war effort.

If word got around that a shop had a delivery of elastic, cotton, needles or thread a queue would soon form. Buttons were used instead of elastic on ladies knickers which actually gave a sleeker dress line. Sheets were turned side to middle or made into pillowcases, tablecloths and handkerchiefs. Some items were fewer coupons. For instance certain pairs of shoes were only five coupons, whilst others were seven. And ladies with adept fingers had a nice sideline repairing laddered stockings for sixpence (2½p) a ladder.

There were several city shops that also offered this service including Mawer and Collinghams. If the coupons had all been spent then Camp coffee and a black eyebrow pencil were used to give the illusion of stockings. If it rained the coffee streaked and made a terrible mess on your clothes.

Dressmakers who included alterations worked miracles by combining two dresses into one or a coat into a skirt and bolero top. Comforts for the troops knitting circles produced socks, pullovers, balaclavas, scarves and gloves which were sent to the Army, Navy and Air Force.

New shoes were made to last longer by using stick-on rubber soles and heels and children's boots and shoes were studded with segs. Every aspect of life was busy. It was an excellent learning curve on how much can be done with so little.

Bette's Bygones. February 8, 2000.

Putting Some Coal In Coleby

THAT was the question being asked in the *Echo* 100 years ago. The first time that the question of the existence of the fuel under the area came over 60 years earlier, in the area known as Coleby Low Fields.

It was reported that around 1836, a deep well was sunk and then a bore was made at the bottom. The material found in the wimble (boring tool) burned, but as the tools used were fairly primitive and comparatively useless for the purpose, nothing more was done, so it only remained as a well.

The very popular Squire, 'Old Sir John Thorold', brought down some Yorkshire colliers, or pit-sinkers (it was not sure which), and a pit bore was made near to what was then Harmston station. The story says that some people believed that coal was found, but others claimed that Sir John had put the coal there to make people believe that coal had been found. It was stated that the pit-sinkers might have been bribed to show that the fuel did not exist in paying quantities, since the Yorkshire pits were doing good business supplying Lincolnshire with coal. It is more likely that Sir John did not wish to develop the site.

Twenty years later, an experienced collier staying in the area expressed an opinion that coal did exist, based on what he could see in the brickyard at Coleby, from the deposits of ironstone and blue shale in the cuttings. It is interesting to note that in 1824, a trial exploration for coal was made at Woodhall, but water was found instead. This proved to have properties beneficial to rheumatism sufferers, so a pump room and baths were built and the place became Woodhall Spa.

We may not have coal mines in Lincolnshire, but there are oil wells. Oil and coal come from the same basic source, timber and Nottinghamshire has numerous coalfields, so it is not beyond the bounds of belief that our county might have become a colliery area.

Lincolnian's Diary. October 3, 2000.

This old picture was taken in 1956, when one of Lincoln city centre public houses was undergoing great changes. The old Green Dragon public house was being demolished and the 14th-century merchant's house, known as The Great Garretts, was being restored. It became the new Green Dragon and the whole scene was dominated by the spire of St Swithin's Church. To the right of the old Green Dragon, a former saleroom was also being demolished, to be replaced by a modern office block. Behind all of these buildings was the old Central Cinema, destroyed by fire in the 1940s.

Today's picture shows the centuries old half-timbered building in full glory and the road in the foreground has been divided into a dual carriageway, with central railings.

Nothing Wasted

NO DOUBT that over the festive season, provided that you are not a vegetarian, you will have enjoyed roast pork, sausages and the odd pork pie or two! It's not so long ago that many people, even some town dwellers, kept their own pig, in a sty at the bottom of their garden.

The porker was not a pet, but kept to provide them with their own supply of meat. The pig would be fattened up, often being fed with household waste, something which definitely would not be allowed today.

I well remember how small potatoes ('pig-taates') were boiled in an old copper boiler to feed the pigs. As youngsters, we would 'cadge' one, peel off the skin and then, with a sprinkling of salt, eat it. They had a taste of their own and perhaps was the best way to taste a potato.

When pig-killing time came around, the slaughterman would come round and dispatch 'porky'. The offal from the pig was used as 'pig-cheer'. These could not be preserved, so the fry, liver, kidney, sweetbread etc., would be cut up and divided into portions, one for each friend. This was then sent out, usually delivered by the children, who would usually say 'Mam sez doan't wesh the plaate!' It was considered unlucky to wash the plate as you would wash away your luck. When your friends killed their pig, you could look forward to receiving a similar plateful yourself. Anyone failing to keep this custom would be outcast at next pig-killing time.

Special cuts of the pig were put on one side for sausages and every family had their own closely guarded recipe. Pork pies had their own special cut of meat. Usually a little spice would be added, but no herbs. The pies themselves created their own flavour when baked in a brick oven. The rest of the cuts of the pig was then salted in an open tub to preserve them. Then the bacon and hams were hung up in the kitchen to mature.

But the real art came in preparing stuffed chine. This is a real Lincolnshire delicacy. The bones were removed and the spaces filled with chopped parsley and spring onions usually. Stuffed chine is eaten cold and I can remember going to Metheringham Feast and enjoying a lovely fresh bun filled with chine. Delicious!

Like many old traditions, pig-killing had its super-stitions. Many people would only have the pig killed when the moon was new. when they said that the bacon would swell in the pot. If it was killed when the moon was on the wane, the bacon would 'boil away', or shrink. Little was wasted, almost every part of the pig was put to use. They used to say that the only thing you could do nothing with was the hair and the squeal!
Lincolnian's Diary. January 18, 2000.

History Of A County Town

IT'S A town of hidden delights and many people pass through it without realising it's historical connections. Sleaford does not figure greatly in the country's national history, but it features quite regularly in county history. The name means 'the ford over the Sliowa' an Old English river name referring to muddy waters, or water with slimy vegetation.

In the *Domesday Book*, it was called Eslaford, and eventually became Lafford. The earliest settlement was at Old Sleaford, between Boston Road and the River Slea and archaeologists have found here the remains of a massive early mint. During Saxon times, the settlement moved to what is now known as New Sleaford and soon after the Norman Conquest, William the Conqueror granted the manor of New Sleaford to the Bishops of Lincoln. In the 12th century, Bishop Alexander built a castle, but only a fragment of this remains today. It was here that King John spent a night, after losing his jewels in The Wash, before moving on to Newark Castle, where he died in 1216. In 1538, Lord John Hussey, who held the manor, was executed for treason, after his part in the Lincolnshire Rising.

At the end of the 18th century, the River Slea was opened as a navigable waterway, linking it with the River Witham and the town became an important terminal for water traffic, but the coming of the railways changed this and the Navigation closed in 1881. Sleaford has an old coaching inn, the Bristol Arms, now a shopping arcade. Two more old inns survive; the White Hart Hotel has a stone sign, dated 1691, although it depicts a black horse, while the Black Bull has an even earlier sign (1689), showing a bull-baiting scene and believed to be the oldest original pub sign in England.

The Church of St Denys dominates the market place and its tower dates from about 1180. There are two open turrets on the west front, one once containing the Butter Bell, which was rung to signal that trading could start in the market. At one time there were 18 watermills powered by the River Slea, but today, there is only one, Cogglesford Mill, which has been restored.

Around the town, there are numerous fine buildings including a 15th century half-timbered vicarage and almshouses set up in the 17th century. There is also what must be the thinnest shop in Lincolnshire, set at the side of the river where it passes under the main street.
Lincolnian's Diary. July 4, 2000.

Water power: Cogglesford Mill, the last remaining of 18 mills on the River Slea.

A bottleneck in Lincoln for many years was the old swing bridge at Brayford Head, which had to be closed to road traffic whenever a boat travelled from the Brayford Pool into the River Witham. The bridge was replaced in the 1970s by Wigford Way and all of the buildings in the background, with the exception of the Royal William IV public house, on the left, have been demolished. (Echo Ref. RI-2601A)

Tales From The Countryside

A LOT OF legends and superstitions surround flowers. Romance, death and illness are part of old flower lore. I found a delightful little book which gave a rather different slant on many plants.

Did you know, for instance, that the flower of the blackberry is a sign of pain, grief, wickedness and death? And it supposedly has a strong association with Jesus Christ and the Virgin Mary. Some believe that the Devil poisoned brambles, but I've eaten enough to dispel that myth.

Bluebells once carpeted the woods of the countryside – now they are few and far between. But this lovely little flower is said to be surrounded by a mysterious aura.

What I remember most is the lovely game we used to play. 'In and out the Dusty Bells, She goes a courting one, two, three, pray come and tell me who is he.'

Does anyone else remember that game, played in a ring weaving in and out of the raised arms?

Lincolnshire's poet Lord Tennyson said the juice could be used to cure snake bites, but I can't think how he worked that one out. Camomile is a strongly-scented herb used to brighten blond hair and muslin bags were stuffed with the herb to scent baths.

It is also said to be utilised as a tonic and purgative. Comfrey is a great healer for sprains and fractures. Its properties are said to reduce swelling and unite bones. Flower language says that the cornflower – again now rare – signifies delicacy and a dweller in heavenly places. It is the flower of the Libran and was used as a love potion. If it survived being carried in the pocket of a lovesick swain it was a sign he would marry his rival.

Who among us has not made daisy chains to put around our heads or necks? In the language of flowers, if you give someone daisies it says that you share the same sentiments. Herbalists used the plants to make syrups, salve and oils to reduce swellings of the testicles. And an infusion was used as a liver tonic.

We all know that the consequence of picking dandelions is wetting the bed. But as a herb it is valued for its great healing properties. In Europe the roots are still roasted and used as a coffee and the leaves go into salads. Sweethearts would test the depth of their lover's feelings by blowing the clock-flower. If the seeds blew away in one puff the blower was loved with great passion. If a little survived then it was a sign of unfaithfulness or indifference. Thus it is said to represent Venus.

Evening Primrose has been credited with healing almost everything, especially female ailments. It signifies constancy and is good for healing minor wounds or skin complaints, coughs, colds and gastric upsets.

The marigold or calendula is my favourite flower.

I use it for hair rinses and rice puddings but not as a love salve. A famous herbalist had a recipe that used powdered marigold flowers, lard and turpentine to strengthen and succour the heart.

Today it is used in a wide range of cosmetics.

Bette's Bygones. November 14, 2000.

Nothing Wasted In The Wartime Kitchen

WHEN food rationing came in, in January 1940, the British housewife rose to the occasion and utilised all her resources by using every scrap of food. Nothing was wasted and if it couldn't be eaten then it was given to the pigs and chickens or used as compost for the garden.

Lawns, tennis courts and flower beds were dug up to grow food. A weekly collection of 'swill' (waste food) was made around the town houses to feed pigs and in the villages and hamlets pig clubs were formed so that every ounce of meal and food could be used. One housewife boasted that she could make eight sausages last four meals for three people. She started with a sausage, tomato and vegetable pie served with mashed potatoes. Then a sausage dumpling which was steamed and served with vegetable and potatoes. Next the sausagemeat was served with onions and made into 'cutlets' and finally a sausage casserole. This may have been the birth of the saying a 100 to 1 (100 pieces of vegetables or potato to one piece of meat).

Several things were not on ration such as fish, tripe and rabbit and game. Many a nourishing meal was made of tripe and onions stewed in milk and served – again – with mashed potato. Food habits change but the meagre ration allowance made a fitter, leaner Britain.

Due to sugar rationing carrots, swede and turnip were used to sweeten cakes – the forerunner of the now popular and 'healthy' carrot cake. They were also used in jams and marmalade to make the fruit go further. Dried egg became an important part of the diet and the British housewife became a wizard at the variety of recipes it was used for. Crème Brûlée made of dried egg custard – omelettes and scrambled egg were all on the menu. The wartime trifle was an art. Rum essence and synthetic cream – made from dried milk was quite tasty as long as you were not heavy with the essence which made it bitter.

Tinned goods, jam and sweets were on a points system and when it was rumoured that food rationing was coming in many housewives started to hoard – a carnal sin if you were found out. But there were some that managed a tin of salmon or fruit which they decided to keep until a hubby or son came home on leave. The drawback was that many of them were away for three years or more and by the time they came home the food had gone 'off'.

A Ministry of Food leaflet suggested semolina porridge for breakfast but wheatmealies had to be eaten to be believed. They consisted of diced bread, baked in the oven until crisp and then served with milk and sugar or stew fruit. Fried food is supposed to be harmful but during the war almost everything was fried including apples. Cheese and vegetable cutlets were a mixture of cheese, potato, peas, carrots and onion which tasted better than it sounds. The government encouraged the people to eat more potatoes, root vegetables, barley and oatmeal which were very often used in main courses to replace meat and

Feast Saturday A Village Occasion

IT WAS a Saturday afternoon in late October. The nights were drawing in. Thoughts were turning to Bonfire Night and Christmas. And in Metheringham High Street all was peaceful and still. Most villagers were in Lincoln or Sleaford doing their shopping.

If you listened very carefully, you might have just heard music from the fairground which had assembled on the field behind the Star and Garter. For this was Feast Saturday, at almost

Good turnout: The narrow streets of Metheringham crowded for the annual Feast.

any time in the 1960s, '70s or early '80s.

Once a high point in village life, the event had dwindled over the years. The sports events no longer took place. The horticultural show had become a thing of the

fish. Rationing lasted for around 15 years but it has been said that Britain was never fitter or healthier than in those days.

Lord Woolton the Minister of Food between 1940-3 became famous for his Lord Woolton pie which took 1 lb of diced vegetables, three or four spring onions or shallots, one teaspoon of vegetable extract and one tablespoon of oatmeal. The vegetables and oatmeal were cooked for 10 minutes in just enough water to cover them. The mixture was stirred to prevent the oatmeal sticking. The mixture was then cooled and put into a pie dish and sprinkled with chopped parsley. A crust of potato or wheatmeal pastry covered the pie and it was baked in a moderate oven until brown and served with a hot brown gravy. If the cook was short of fat she used ½ lb of flour, one teaspoon of baking powder, pinch of salt and pinch of powdered egg (if available). Milk was used to bond the ingredients which was rolled

out to cover the pie. This was enough four or five people.

Another favourite was boiled fruit cake which had good keeping qualities and which many housewives use today with added luxury ingredients. It used ½ pint of cold tea or water, 3 oz of fat or margarine and lard, 3 oz of sugar, 3 oz of dried fruit, 10 oz of plain flour, three level teaspoon baking power, pinch of salt, one teaspoon mixed spice and one teaspoon of bicarbonate of soda.

The water or tea, fat, sugar and fruit were boiled together for two to three minutes and then allowed to cool. The dried ingredients were sieved together and beaten well into the liquid. It was then poured into a greased and floured cake tin and baked in the centre of a hot oven for a further hour in a moderate oven. Buttered or covered in semolina 'marzipan' paste it took on many guises from 'plum bread' to wedding or Christmas cake.

Bette's Bygones. February 1, 2000.

past. Just about the only reminders of the past glories of the event, were the fair and an occasional advert in the shop windows, for Feast Week bargains. By the early 1980s, the event hit an all-time low.

Days of heavy rain turned the Star and Garter field into a quagmire. The travelling showmen took a long, hard look at the site and shook their heads. There was no way the rides and stalls could be built up that year. In the end, the event was saved when the showmen were allowed to use the hard standing of the pub car park for one year only. But it was a tight squeeze and some of the regular attractions were missing. There was talk that the end could be in sight for what was one of the county's oldest and best-loved Feasts.

Then, the Parish Council decided it was time for action. They rallied support for the event and from all over the village, clubs and organisations spanning the age range, promised to give the revamped feast their backing. It became a tremendous success all over again and visitors might have been forgiven for thinking that something like the crowd-pulling Lincoln Christmas Market had been transported to Metheringham's streets.

Where once you seldom

saw people on Feast Saturday afternoon, the streets were jam packed with crowds who poured into the village to support close on 70 stalls. The fairground, often almost deserted on Saturday afternoon, was busier than it had been for years. And even after dark, things carried on until well into the evening.

Since its new lease of life, the Feast has had to cope with all sorts of weather. There has been warm sunshine where crowds strolled around in shirt sleeves.

And there have been days of heavy rain or prolonged drizzle. This week, the showmen will be back in Metheringham again to open on the Star and Garter field from Friday until Tuesday. But the busiest day comes on Saturday when once again the streets will be closed.

At 2.15pm there will be a parade through the village, led by Lincoln Town Crier Terry Stubbings and the feast will be officially opened by the High Sheriff, Richard Parker.

There will be live entertainment in the streets, fairground organs, craft and charity stalls, a craft market and bygones in the Village Hall and horse and carriage rides around the village.

The Gossiper. October 17, 2000.

Ways To Use Up Your Stale Bread

I'M OLD enough to remember the days before sliced bread. Do you remember the days when our daily loaf came all in one piece? I still think that this type of bread tastes better, but I will always remember my mother's efforts to slice a loaf for a sandwich. Not a pretty sight! Usually twice as thick at one end as the other and if she didn't turn the slices round, you got a sandwich getting thicker the more you bit into it. But what did you do with the left-overs? Today, you reseal the bag and keep it fresh.

In 1930, the *Echo* produced an article 'How to use up stale bread'. It read: 'In most houses there is by the end of each week an accumulation of stale bread which, unless some use can be found for it, must be thrown away and wasted, but if reasonable care is taken there need be no such thing as waste in the breadpan. Place all the crusts in the oven when it is not required for baking purposes; allow them to remain there until quite dry; then press with a rolling-pin until they are quite fine and when cold, store in a tin. They can then be used for frying fish, cutlets, &c. Stale slices of bread can be made into savoury toast and served for breakfast and tea and an excellent children's pudding can be made from odd pieces. Heat half a pint of milk, break up any stale bread into a basin, add one tablespoonful of sugar, pour over it the milk and beat up with a fork, then add a well-beaten egg. Grease a mould.' The article didn't say what to do next or what the children thought of their pudding!

But did you know that the first loaf of white bread to be baked in England was supposed to have been made in Lincolnshire? White Loaf Hall, near Frieston, is a large farmhouse, once a monastry where the monks made their historic bread, having sieved the whole-grain flour through some material, which some people say was their socks. On the gable end of the building is a bread-loaf shaped stone, with the letters WLH and the date 1614.

Lincolnian's Diary. July 25, 2000.

Unusual Charges On County Roads

THERE has been a lot of talk recently about making motorists pay for the privilege of using their cars in the middle of our towns and cities. We have, for many years, been used to paying tolls on certain bridges, the two which affect Lincolnshire most being the Humber Bridge and Dunham Bridge. And together with the numerous toll bridges throughout the country, there are also a number of toll roads where one has to pay to use them. I came across a few in Devon last year while on holiday.

There was a time in Lincolnshire when people had to pay to drive their vehicles down roads, it was not in a motor car, but horse and carriage.

Before the 18th century, travelling around the county was a risky affair.

What roads there were carried a risk of being held up by a highwayman and it was not until a proper road building programme was adopted that this risk became less.

The first road to become a turnpike, the name for a toll-road, was a stretch of the Great North Road, north of Grantham, in 1726. Others followed and soon, there was a network of these roads linking all major towns in the county.

Toll bars were set up at the ends of these roads and sometimes side bars were set up on minor roads to prevent travellers from entering the road here to avoid paying the toll.

By 1837, there were 29 Turnpike Trusts in the county, controlling some 550 miles of roads.

There were toll bridges at Gainsborough, Dunham on Trent, Tattershall, Fosdyke and Sutton Bridge. Today, only the bridge at Dunham remains a toll bridge, with Humber Bridge being added in 1981.

In 1923, a story in the *Lincolnshire Echo* told of some of the unusual toll-gate charges and reported that there were 88 toll bridges and 55 toll roads in the country. At one bridge, there was a charge of one penny to take a pram across.

At another, there was a charge of 4d for a hearse and 2d for the body. Another charged one farthing for every calf, swine, sheep or lamb.

At Dunham Bridge, the charge per vehicle was 2s, a considerable amount of money in those days.

There were some exceptions to the charges for the use of these bridges. Royal Mail coaches were exempt, as were the military, or people on their way to church on a Sunday.

Lincolnian's Diary. May 30, 2000.

Taken away: The old tollgates being removed from Trent Bridge, Gainsborough, in 1932.

Smile please: Pupils of the County School, Willoughton, in 1949, pose for their annual photograph.

The Day The Whole Village Was Lit Up

JUST AFTER the Second World War ended in 1945 my father took a job as a blacksmith for Mr Clifford Nicholson who owned the farming company now known as the Limestone Farming Company. Clifford Nicholson was an astute businessman and for some time had been pulling down old cottages and on their foundations building new houses for his men.

When we arrived at number 11 Middle Street, Willoughton, near Gainsborough, the houses were wired up for electricity but not connected to the mains and so most of the village still used oil lamps and candles. It was a great day when we were finally

switched on but we were the only house in the village to have bulbs which my Mother had saved since leaving Bridlington in 1940. They actually worked and so we loaned one to each of our row of houses and the great switch on took place.

In those days almost everyone worked for the estate and lived in tied houses. The labourers paid a nominal rent but the tradesmen, such as my father lived rent free and had other little perks. It was like one big family. Weddings, funerals, births and any other major event was shared by all.

Every Monday the Co-operative grocery van came round and delivered the order and took the one for next week. I never ceased to marvel how the women planned so far ahead. The ration books were duly marked, coupons taken out and any specials, such as biscuits had to be kept in a tin. We'd not seen a biscuit for about six years and

at first the poor old grocer was fed up of being told they had gone soft. It was Mrs Ward who finally told us they should be kept in tins. Thereafter all the tins of baby dried milk were washed, painted and placed on the kitchen shelves.

Grocery lists usually ran on the lines of sugar, butter, margarine, lard, tea, cheese, eggs – those were the foods on ration. The butcher called twice a week and we bought sheep's head, breast of mutton, oxtail, heart, liver and kidney because these were all off ration. The 1s 3d a week allowance went on the Sunday joint. But we lived well. Vegetables were grown in the gardens. Fruit trees and greenhouses provided all we needed. Joe Harty opened the barbers shop in his back yard every Sunday morning and everyone got the same haircut which is very like the one sported by young men today.

The men went to work at 7am in the summer and

7.30am in the winter. They came home at 9am for breakfast which could comprise of a fry up or something on toast. Dinner was at 12.30pm, winter and 1pm summer. My father walked or cycled home, ate his lunch which was always waiting on the table, snoozed for 20 minutes had a final cup of tea and went back to work until 5pm. After that it was overtime. Tea was what we now call 'high tea' with meat or cheese and home-made cakes and jam. How they stretched the food was a miracle. The water came from a standpipe shared by several families – a talking point for most of the woman as they filled the enamel buckets. Many a problem was solved at the 'tap'.

The good old Co-op clothed and shod us. Mr Grainger brought the clothing and furniture and Mr Ball the boots and shoes. They came around twice a year and the bills were paid

Flood: Not the seaside but Middle Street, Willoughton, during the 1950s.

through the dividend collected from the year's purchases. We were even kept warm and cooked our food through the Co-op who did weekly deliveries of coal around the area.

Every Christmas the children of the village went up to The Manor and were given an orange and a shilling (5p). There were a lot of children around at that time and this was quite an undertaking. Except for Christmas and Boxing Day, Good Friday and Easter Monday the village was always on the move. You could hear the men talk as they went to and from work. Farm workers gathered each morning to be given their work for the day by a foreman. And because the acreage was so large Willoughton had a riding foreman who rode a horse around the various farms and workshops.

One of the very first pea viners was built there. It was static and when the crop was ready Batchelors sent men who stayed in the village to see that it was sent immediately to the factory for canning – no frozen peas in those days.

We had whist drives and dances which attracted lads from RAF Henswell. It was all great innocent fun. The snows of 1947 blocked us off for three weeks. The three shops opened their stores and we were fed. Coal was another problem and I recall sitting in overcoats, scarves and hats to keep warm. We cheered when the coalman finally got through. That was the down side. The up side was that most of the lads were home on leave and we went sledging and skating – one of those times to remember.

A post office, two grocery shops, a newsagent, a church and chapel, a school and a doctor who held a regular surgery in Mrs Marshal's front room. Our needs were well supplied. It was one of the happiest periods of my life.

Bette's Bygones. January 4, 2000.

New Arrivals In The 1940s To Lincolnshire

MY first sightings of Lincolnshire was in March 2, 1940.

We had set off from Bridlington at 6am and finally arrived at the village of Laughton near Gainsborough at 1pm – travel took a long time in those days. Mam and Dad sat in the front cab – I sat in an armchair at the back of the van covered with coats to keep me warm. It had been a bad winter with snow giving way to floods. I was cold, miserable and very hostile to the move from town to country.

The van finally drew to a halt. I peeped over the tailboard and saw the village of Laughton. It looked just like a Christmas card covered in snow and frost. But it was deathly quiet – no cars – no buses – no streets. The blacksmith's cottage was opposite the cemetery – a cheerful welcome to weary travellers. But soon people realised the 'new lot' had arrived. Someone brought tea and scones. I stood looking on – in reality I needed the toilet but was too embarrassed to ask. I walked through the house but could not find a bathroom. And then Mum said she too needed to 'go' and taking my hand asked Dad – in a stage whisper – where it was.

He pointed to the open back door and we stared at what looked like a 40 acre field covered in nettles and other alien weeds. We approached an ice covered little hut and pushed open the door. 'Crikey' said Mam and then burst out laughing. I sighed. It wasn't a toilet at all – just a shed with a workbench. 'Come on' said Mam, 'It's an earth closet'. Leaning forward I saw two holes – one large and one small.

I decided on the smaller and sat down. It was disaster. I almost disappeared out of sight. My legs flew in the air and I could feel myself slipping down into the gaping chasm. Mam came to the rescue and grabbing my legs and pulled me back to life. I was terrified and to reassure me Mam started to sing. The next thing Dad was running down the path. 'Shut the door' he shouted. 'everybody can see you'. And everyone could for we were in full view of a crowd of villagers who had come to see the new arrivals – and they'd seen just about everything.

This was the first of many rude awakenings.

Bette's Bygones. September 14, 1999.

Seven Centuries Of Tradition In A Game

ON TWELFTH Night, January 6, many people will be heading for the village of Haxey, over the River Trent and north of Gainsborough, in the Isle of Axholme. The reason? The annual Haxey Hood Game, which has taken place for centuries ever since Lady de Mowbray is reputed to have lost her black hood while out riding across the fields near Haxey on Twelfth Night.

Thirteen labourers in a nearby field gave chase competing against each other to try and return the garment to her ladyship. She was so grateful for this that she gave a piece of land just outside the village so that the event could be re-enacted each year. That was the start of the game, a rough and tumble affair which also involves a fair consumption of ale. Before the game gets under way, the 13 officials act out an unusual ceremony. They are the Lord of the Hood, the Chief Boggan (or boggin), 10 ordinary Boggans and the Fool. The fool mounts a stone block outside St Nicholas Church, Haxey, and calls out

'Hoose agin hoose,
toon agin toon,
If tha meet a man,
knock 'im doon,
But doan't hu't 'im'.

A fire is then set alight in a pile of damp straw at the base of the stone and the fool is smoked. Then the two villagers of Haxey and Westwoodside take over. The Hood, which today is a roll of leather or canvas, is tossed into the 'sway' and the game begins. The object of the

The True Heart Of Life In The Village

AT 6 am every morning the red mail van would arrive at the post office. The postmaster and two part-time postmen or women would be waiting to sort the mail.

They knew everyone in the village and commented as they sorted the letters and parcels. 'We'll be seeing Mary Ward in summat new this Sunday, there's a parcel from Littlewoods' catalogue,' or 'Pegg Wilson'll be pleased, there's an airmail from her lad,' they would say without malice.

A cup of tea and then they would set off on the huge bicycles with a front carrier to cope with the bag of mail and assortment of parcels. They went out in all weathers and during the bad winter of 1947

game is to get the hood to the public house in one of the villages, where it remains until the following year. The Boggans, if they catch the Hood, toss it back into the middle of the 'sway'.

the mail was brought and delivered on sledges. At farms they would stop to get warm and have a hot drink in winter or a summer cooler when it was hot. At nine o'clock the Post Office opened it's doors.

It was like the village town hall. Pensions, a chat, savings bank. National Savings stamp and telegrams were taken and delivered. Business was done behind a barred section at the corner of the counter. The Postmaster or mistress filled in forms, took telephone messages, gave advice and references. If the village had them they rated fourth in line after the vicar, schoolmaster and doctor. Otherwise he was the main man.

The shop stocked everything from pans to polish, flour to tinned peas and was the only source of goods after the Co-op van had made its weekly call.

In front of the counter glass-topped tins of biscuits were stacked so customers could see the variety. They

were bought by the half pound and wrapped in square paper bags. Sugar was in thick blue bags and sweets overflowed out the three-cornered paper cones. The post office often was the only phone in the village. If there were more a small switchboard was kept in the house. Many were accused of listening to calls but mostly they were discreet – when it suited them.

During the war they were taught codes in case of emergency. Villages that had a public phone housed in a red box were considered well off. Some had the only light in the village street and attracted all the young people to gather there to lark about. If it had no light it provided a cosy nook for courting. 'Meet you at the phone box!' often heralded a courtship and marriage. I accepted my husband's proposal while calling him at RAF Hemswell from the Willoughton phone box.

Bette's Bygones. July 4, 2000.

Re-enactment: The 'Sway' scramble for the 'hood' in the traditional game on Twelfth Night in the village of Haxey.

Since the game is played in fields, if the weather has been rough, there will be a lot of mud around and the game can take several hours before it is over. By this time, the earlier drinks have worn off

and the contestants are ready for a refill.

It's nice to have these old customs, it is a pity there aren't more.

Lincolnian's Diary. January 4, 2000.

Landworkers Stood Up For Their Rights

POOR HOUSING, poor wages and no pay if rained off. Few schools and child labour was rife in the Lincolnshire villages. The fight for decent housing and wages was a long hard struggle for the Lincolnshire farm labourers. When the word 'union' was first mooted many farmers and land-owners regarded it with some scorn. 'What strange creature is this?' one asked. 'Some miserable little insect. It may do damage. Someone should kill it.'

In *The Revolt of the Field* complied by Rex C. Russell there are many instances of the terrible conditions in which the farm workers of the county existed. At Horkstow Hall they employed girls and boys from 10 upwards. And at Hallington boys and girls of six years old went weed and stone picking with their families. Weeding was considered easy work in the light land and let out to a labourer's family to do when they liked. A boy of six was employed to lead horses and at 10 or 12 was taken into regular work on the turnip land.

The Revd F.T. Wintour, late Rector of Hawerby spoke out against the method of employment. 'I have seen the great evil of statutes and have often cried out against them. It is degrading to the servant to be chosen as you would choose an ox. The housing conditions were said not to be fit for pigs to live in and there was virtually no schooling for farm workers' children. A lady from Willingham near Market Rasen once said. 'No sink or other communication with drains ought to exist in labourer's houses. The inhabitants have no intelligence enough to keep such things in order. The more intelligent of our poor know this and beg not to have sinks. All refuse should be carried out by hand.' And put where?

When it was suggested that they should be given more schooling a farmer and churchwarden from West Butterwick showed his Christian feelings by saying that the children were already getting too much education. 'If there is much more of it I shall send for the Irish.' Meaning of course the armies of Irish labourers who came over for seasonal work. The Revd E. Jenkins of Billinghay did not approve of the employment of females because it interfered with their proper training for domestic duties. But he added that during the weeding season the fens need the labour.

At that time there was no school in Billinghay either National or of any other denominations for the use of the poor. There were, however, six small private schools chiefly attended by the children of the poor who could barely afford the penny a week charged. Between June and October the schools were almost deserted because the children worked on the land.

The murmurings of revolt began in 1867 when the second Parliamentary Reform Act was passed giving the vote to the town worker but leaving the farm worker still without this right. By 1872 a new wave of men started to think about standing up for their rights and form a union to improve their lot. The awakening of the farm workers had begun. The dead were coming to life. The farm worker was to become national news through his newly-created trade unions which were to bring about changes of national importance.

Power: George Curtis and his wife Sylvia.

Lincolnshire born and bred George Curtis has always been a champion of the working man and the power of the unions. He joined the Farmworkers Union in 1943 and became active as Union branch secretary in 1945. In 1959 he commenced full-time employment as a Lincolnshire based Agricultural Workers Trade Union Officer and has written books about his life and experiences. He was respected by farmers, landowners, the National Farmers Union and the Agricultural Workers Union.

In a foreword for *The Birthright of Our Sires*, David Hill the then Senior Policy Advisor for the NFU said, 'We first met when George was a Methodist local preacher. He preached a clear message of faith as he became involved in the affairs of the Workers Union he would bring his concern into his preaching. It was obvious he was dedicated to improving the lot of his fellow man. We met professionally on many occasions, often on different sides of the argument. George was always fair, Conflict there might be but never malice. George would fight like a terrier for his members interest but would gracefully concede when he felt that the employer was in the right.'

Our County Grows The Tastiest 'tates'

I WAS reading a letter in a magazine to which I subscribe, in which a lady from Bolton was bemoaning the fact that Jersey Royal potatoes didn't taste the same as they used to taste. She thought that it was because of EU regulations preventing the use of seaweed as a fertiliser on their land. It was pointed out that Jersey is not in the EU and there is no ban on the use of seaweed.

But I remember a couple of years ago seeing some 'Jersey Royals' on sale and the bag from which they were taken had 'Produce of Cornwall' printed on it. Having been to Jersey, I cannot imagine that they could possibly produce enough of their potatoes to satisfy the demand. After all, the island is only nine miles long by five miles wide. Why

During the period of the unions emerging in 1872 it was recorded at Caistor that the drain of emigration was beginning to have very tangible effects in the area. Too many of the best agricultural labourers were leaving the county or turning to other occupations with better pay. Those who were left were showing themselves fully alive to their position by their extra demands upon their employers. Judging from the mood of conversations a general strike on the question of agricultural pay seemed imminent. It was a long hard struggle but at last the serfs were given their rights.

Bette's Bygones. January 11, 2000.

doesn't the lady try 'Boston tates'? I have seen them on sale in Accrington market, so they are available in her area and for my money, better tasting.

Lincolnshire is, of course, one of the largest, if not the largest, producer of potatoes in the country.

Here, we don't call them potatoes, unless we are being posh and even 'spud' is seldom heard. They are 'tairts' and so many are produced around the Boston area that some people call the area 'Tairtyville'. Ken Pearson is a local author of a little book *Tairtyville Talk*, or alternatively *The Language of Kirton*. In the book, he lists several expressions about 'tates', or 'tairts' as it is pronounced.

'Tate' changes to 'tatie' when used as an adjective and among the words he lists are tatie merchant, tatie clamp, tatie fork and tatie holiday (a period from years ago before mechanical lifting, when schoolchildren were given holidays from school to help with the harvest). A 'tatie' on its own was a reference to a hole in the heel of your sock, but my favourite expression is 'tatie-trap', which means your mouth.

Near to Lincoln, at Nocton, there was a 4,000 acre estate growing potatoes just for Smith's Crisps and many thousands of packets of this product were made at the Lincoln factory which opened in 1938. This story brought back memories for reader Barbara Grove. She went to school in Westminster and her secondary school, Grey Coat Hospital, offered pupils the opportunity of spending a week of their summer holidays during the mid-1940s to help with the potato harvest and Barbara came on two visits.

She says 'We were not paid, but I believe our rail travel was provided free. However, if we wanted to bring a bicycle, we had to pay a few shillings. I did this one year because although I could ride, I hadn't mastered the art of getting on the bike in the customary fashion (left foot on pedal and swinging through the gap for the right foot to engage with the other pedal).' Barbara learnt to do this in the county's quiet lanes. On her first visit, she was billeted at Aswarby Hall Stables, where there were no horses at the time and she was housed in a loft over the stables. 'Our first job was to collect an empty

Time for a break: Farm workers and their horse enjoy lunch under the shade of a tree, in 1957, on Smith's Nocton Estates, where thousands of acres of potatoes were grown for the potato crisp industry.

palliasse and fill it with straw – we slept on the floor.'

During her work 'tairt pickin', as Barbara puts it, she worked alongside a party of Italian prisoners of war, who loved the work and were very polite to the schoolgirls, although some heart-fluttering went on! Barbara remembers being the 'champion' as far as collecting insect bites was concerned. At one time, she had 30 and was given a piece of washing soda to moisten and apply to the bites. Unfortunately, it dried to a white powder. 'I was not a pretty sight!' she says. 'We ate an early and very hearty breakfast, then were loaded into lorries and went singing on our way to the fields, waving at every passerby' says Barbara. 'A packed lunch was provided and we worked extremely hard, but still had energy to sing on our way back.'

The lovely long warm evenings enabled her to explore the Lincolnshire lanes on her bike, alone and without fear. No doubt 'Double Summer Time' was in force, so it did not get dark until well after 11 o'clock. Her second visit saw Barbara billeted in an empty house, but she can't remember where. The work was harder, lifting corn-stooks, heavy with grain and hand-weeding rows of carrots. The water they had to drink had so much iron it it, she had to wait for it to settle at the bottom of the glass. 'That's why so many local people here have bad teeth' she was told.

Barbara returned to London feeling fitter and pleased that she had made some contribution to farming in the county. Little did she know that several decades later, she would be living in Lincoln. Thank you Barbara for these memories.

Lincolnian's Diary. September 5 & September 26, 2000.

Alternative Poacher

A few years ago, when I was gathering material for one of the *Lincolnshire Echo* Special Publications, Historic County, I came across a set of alternative words for the *Lincolnshire Poacher*. All I know about them is that they were written by a Norman Walls. I think they are marvellous 'word picture' of our county and I hope that you will like them:

There is no place like Lincolnsheer
The land of marsh and fen;
The land that grows the finest tates
And breed the finest men;
The county that has often seen
The birth of famous men;
Oh, there is nowheer like Lincolnshire
The land of marsh and fen.

There's Lincoln with its famous church
The church upon a hill;
There's Spalding where they all know how
To grow the daffodil;
There's Boston with its stump so high
You see it from Keal Hill;
Oh, there is nowheer like Lincolnsheer
The land of marsh and fen.

There's Grimsby with its fishermen
Brave men I do declare;
There's Mablethorpe with golden sands
And Skegness bracing air;
There's Grantham with its hunting folk
And Brigg its ancient fair;
Oh, there is nowheer like Lincolnsheer
The land of marsh and fen.

And Lincolnsheer bred famous men
To spread old England's fame;
From Bourne the vailiant Hereward
The Saxon Chieftan, came;
And Franklin, Newton, Tennyson,
Who does not know their name?
Oh, there is nowheer like Lincolnsheer
The land of marsh and fen.

Lincolnian's Diary. September 28, 1999.

Old Technology Is Power Of The Future

I WAS interested to hear the other day that a new giant wind power generator had come into operation near Swaffham in Norfolk.

I have seen a couple of these windmills, one in Devon and the other in Milton Keynes but they were tiny compared with this giant in Norfolk. It stands as high as the central tower of Lincoln Cathedral and can supply power to hundreds of homes without pollution.

Lincolnshire at one time probably had more than 500 windmills. The *Domesday Book* of 1086 seems to record a mill in most entries but it does not say if it is a windmill or a watermill. I am always fascinated when I travel around Lincolnshire to see the number of mill towers left today. Most are just that, empty towers, but some have been put to other uses in their full glory, their sails turning in the wind. A number of mills have been converted into living accommodation – there is even one in Lincoln and one at Burgh le Marsh offers Bed and Breakfast accommodation.

Most of Lincolnshire's mills are tower mills built of brick but there is one post mill at Wrawby and with this type of mill the body has to be pushed round so that the sails catch the wind. With tower mills there is a mechanism to catch the change of wind direction and turn the mill automatically. Heckington Mill is a fine sight and is the only mill left in the country with eight sails. The mills at Alford and Burgh le Marsh both have five sails although one turns clockwise and the other anti-clockwise.

Boston's Maud Foster windmill also has five sails while one nearby at Sibsey has six as has the mill at Waltham near Grimsby. Mount Pleasant Mill in Kirton-in-Lindsey and Ellis's Mill in Lincoln both have four sails. The latter which was restored by Lincoln Civic trust from a derelict shell to full working order to celebrate the Queen's silver jubilee and is now in the hands of Lincolnshire County Council and operated in conjunction with the Museum of Lincolnshire's Life.

Last post: The county's last surviving post mill at Wrawby.

A visit to a windmill is a well worthwhile experience and you can obtain stone ground flour at most. You can't beat a bit of real flour. It makes bread that is crunchy on the outside and soft on the inside. But occasionally you might just get a bit of grit that makes it crunchy on the inside as well.

Lincolnian's Diary. September 7, 1999.

Pisa? Lincolnshire Can Lean, Too

SKEGNESS Clock Tower has just celebrated its centenary and I remember a few years ago when it was announced that the resort's famous landmark had a definite lean to it!

Now we have all heard about, or seen, the famous Leaning Tower of Pisa, but did you know that we have several leaning towers in our own county? Perhaps the most pronounced is the tower and spire of St Laurence's Church, at Surfleet. The tower is about six feet out of true at the top and it is only when you look at the flag pole in front of the church do you realise that your eyes are not deceiving you.

In the neighbouring village of Pinchbeck, the church of St Mary's also has a tower with a rather drunken appearance. The bottom part of the tower leans, but the top is straightened up to bring it back to the vertical. Perhaps it is something to do with the subsoil in this area of the Fens. St Peter's Church, at Thorpe St Peter also has an odd look about its tower and the church of St Clement's, at Sutton-on-Sea definitely looks as if it was being tossed about in the waves.

Surfleet church: Note that the flagpole is vertical, but not the church.

Lincoln Cathedral is not without its leaning towers. In the 1920s, 10 years of restoration work was started because it was discovered that the western towers were falling apart. It was estimated that the work would take five years and cost £50,000. It was only during the restoration work that danger to the Central Tower was also noticed and the final restorations took 10 years, with the cost increasing to more than £130,000. What is even more astonishing is the fact that the scaffolding used in the repairs was timber and not the metal poles used nowadays.

If you stand in Castle Hill today, near the entrance to Lincoln Castle and look at the West Towers, you can see that they are slightly wider apart at the top than at the bottom.
Lincolnian's Diary. September 2, 1999.

Skegness clock tower: Built to commemorate a jubilee.

Fame From The County

BACK in 1930, the *Echo* had a story about the headmaster of St Faith's School, Lincoln, Mr John Shillaker giving a lecture to the Lincoln Rotary Club about 'Lincolnshire Worthies'.

The past president of the club presided and his name was Mr Herbert Green. I have a reprint of the book *Forgotten Lincoln*, which is a collection of stories which were published by the *Lincoln Gazette and Times*, later incorporated into the *Lincolnshire Echo*. Herbert Green was a member of the staff and I am wondering if this could be the same person.

Mr Shillaker spoke of the famous people who had been born in Lincolnshire, including a king, a saint and a poet. The king was, of course, King Henry IV, who was born at Bolingbroke Castle, the home of John o' Gaunt, Duke of Lancaster. Saint Gilbert was born at Sempringham and founded the only English monastic order, which had both monks and nuns and had three houses in the county, including one in Lincoln. The poet was Alfred Lord Tennyson, Queen Victoria's Poet Laureate, who was born at Somersby.

But there are many more worthies including many explorers; Matthew Flinders, George Bass, Sir John Franklin and Sir Joseph Banks are only four of many. Stephen Langton, born at Langton, near Wragby, became Archbishop of Canterbury and was one of the people responsible for the Magna Carta. Another member of the same family was Benet Langton, a scholar and friend of Dr Johnson and Oliver Goldsmith. He was lean and lanky, nearly seven feet tall and was said 'to twist his left leg three times round his right leg in order to occupy as little space as possible!'

The article goes on to mention many other worthies. Lord Burghley, born at Bourne, was one of the men who, with Drake, Howard and Raleigh, defeated the ambitions of Philip of Spain. One of a number of great British schoolmasters was William Waynfleete, founder of the school in his native 'village' and of Magdalen College, Oxford. Another Lincolnshire born schoolteacher was Dr Busby, headmaster of Westminster . No list of Lincolnshire worthies would be complete without the name of Sir Isaac Newton, of Woolsthorpe, who is credited with discovering the theories of gravity.

But of course, since this story was printed, there have been many more names to add to the list. Margaret Thatcher was born in Grantham and became Britain's first woman Prime Minister. Tony Jacklin came from the Scunthorpe area and won both the British and US Open Golf Championships. In the world of music are the names of Sir Malcolm Sargent, Sir Neville Marriner and opera singer Jane Eaglen. Also from the world of entertainment are John Hurt and Dame Sybil Thorndike.

One name mentioned in the original story puzzles me. That of Nicholas Breakspear, the only Englishman to become a Pope (Adrian IV). The encyclopaedias which I have searched through give his birthplace as near to St Albans Abbey, about the year 1100. His papacy was from 1154 to 1159.

Lincolnian's Diary. July 11, 2000.

County's Got More Places Than Names

NORTH and South, East and West, Great and Little, High and Low.

These additions to place names can all be found in Lincolnshire which helps avoid confusion when people often refer to a place by its last name only. Carlton, Cockerington, Elkington, Hykeham, Kelsey, Killingholme, Kyme, Ormsby, Owersby, Rauceby, Reston, Scarle, Somercotes, Thoresby and Witham all have North and South names and there are also a Northorpe and Southorpe.

In addition to North and South Willingham, there is also Cherry Willingham and Willingham by Stow. Barkwith, Butterwick, Halton, Keal and Torrington all have East and West place names and there are several place names with East in them, without a West.

Great and Little can be found at Carlton, Grimsby, Hale, Ponton and Steeping and there are several places which have these prefixes on only one place.

Although Ludford is generally known today by just that one name, it was originally Ludford Magna and Ludford Parva.

Although the words high and low appear on maps, there is only one pair of places, as far as I have found with these words in their names. These are High and Low Toynton.

So, what are some of the stories to be found at these places.

North and South Hykeham used to be known at one time as Chapel Hykeham and Church Hykeham respectively. Although North Hykeham did have a church in the 12th century, the present church in the town dates from 1858 while South Hykeham's church has parts dating from the 13th century. North and South Willingham are easily explained, as is Willingham by Stow, but Cherry Willingham, near Lincoln, was named from a cherry orchard near to the church, to distinguish it from the others.Carlton, as can be seen from above, has North, South, Great and Little names and there are some interesting stories from these. North Carlton has a hall where King Henry VIII stayed in 1541 and conferred a knighthood on its owner, John Monson.

Behind the church at South Carlton is a chapel containing the mausoleum of the Monson family.

At the village of Little Carlton, the church was demolished a few years ago, but the outline has been laid out in bricks and the font remains standing in the middle of the site. There is also a watermill in the village.

Besides these places, there are two more Carltons, in the county, at Carlton-le-Moorland, near Lincoln and Carlton Scroop, on the main road between Lincoln and Grantham, which takes its name from the Scope family, who held land there several centuries ago. There is also a Castle Carlton, but all that remains of the castle is a mound of earth. And there is one name in Lincolnshire starting with Little, which has a much larger place, but in another part of the country.

This is Little London, but so far, I haven't been able to find out why the Lincolnshire place name is connected to our capital.

Lincolnian's Diary. Oct 31, 2000.

Show Found Its Perfect Home

THE 1950s were a decade of change. Television became a major part of our lives. The roads became more congested as the number of private cars grew out of all proportion. Bill Haley and his Comets were rocking around the clock. And in Lincolnshire, the County Show stopped its travelling and settled down to a new and permanent site just outside Lincoln.

Now as we move towards the first Lincolnshire Show of the new millennium, we take a look back at some of those earlier shows – including some we might rather forget.

Where's the County Show going to be held this year? That's the question they used to ask in those days when the county's number one annual event used to move around Lincolnshire. One year you might find yourself paddling around a muddy West Common when the show came to Lincoln. Another year, you could have been in the grounds of Burghley House, near Stamford. There were times when you would have visited the show in the far north of the county at Brocklesby Park or Walsham, near Grimsby. And there were

Bighorn: Young visitors to the Lincolnshire Show, in 1968, looking at a rare breed of cattle. (Echo Ref. RI-68-10)

other years when you would have travelled to Louth or Spalding to see the latest in agricultural equipment and the finest animals.

By the 1950s, it was becoming more and more difficult to find a home for the county-trotting show. Agriculture was changing and farmers were becoming more reluctant to make acres of land available for the event. Other agricultural shows were settling down on permanent sites and it was time for Lincolnshire to do the same.

The 1958 show at Burtoft, in the south of the county, was the end of an era. By the following summer, the show had moved to a new, purpose-built home alongside the A15. From the very start, many agreed that the new home was ideally situated. Just north of Lincoln and reached by a network of good roads, the site was large and it was flat. And there was plenty of room for expansion.

The only qualms that some people had in the early days was that it was very close to RAF Scampton and there were fears that over-excited animals wouldn't take kindly to heavy aircraft roaring low overhead. But their fears turned out to be unfounded. Right from the start, the people of Lincolnshire voted the new permanent ground a resounding success. An attendance record was set in the first year back in 1959

All Aboard After A Wait Of 25 Years

IT WAS a red letter day for the people of Metheringham 25 years ago today, when the village railway station was brought back to life. The station, alongside the Lincoln–Sleaford line, had been axed 14 years earlier along with others like Branston and Heighington, Nocton and Dunson, Digby and Ruskington. But in the autumn of 1975, the winds of change were beginning to blow over the county's railway lines.

After years of hearing about cutbacks in services, stations being shut and whole lengths of track being closed and ripped up, there was renewed optimism about our rural railways. Thanks to a grant from Lincolnshire County Council, Ruskington station had reopened at the start of the summer. Now, it was the turn of nearby Metheringham station to be reopened.

On October 3, 1975, a giant ticket was fixed to the front of a diesel multiple unit, proclaiming that it was the inaugural train between Lincoln and Metheringham. On the platform of the rebuilt station, the then chairman of the council's transportation committee, Councillor Donald Webb, cut the ribbon to start the new service between Lincoln and the village. Children from the village school sang a specially composed calypso song for the occasion. And among the proudest people at the station was Alice Revel, the widow of the station's last porter and Ted Savoury, Metheringam's last full-time station master. By then, he had gone on to bigger and better things, running one of the country's busiest stations, Liverpool Street, in London.

Regular services didn't get going until the following Monday and for the first two weeks, passengers between Lincoln and Metheringham could travel free of charge. After that, the single fare would be 30p. Initially there were to be seven trains every weekday from Lincoln Central to Metheringham and eight back again. The trains would also provide a through link to Sleaford. After the opening ceremony, the guests, including 35 excited schoolchildren, travelled by train to Lincoln – something many of them had never done before.

Since then the station, which had started life back in 1882 with the name Blankney and Metheringham, has become a success story. It is among the busiest rural stations in Lincolnshire. Every weekday commuters and children fill the platforms, travelling on their way to and from work and school in Lincoln and Sleaford. But so far, its success still hasn't led to a crop of other stations reopening, as many people expected at the time. And places like Cherry Willingham, Heighington, Sibsey and Donington, which had hoped to have a rail link following Metheringham's reopening, are still waiting.

The Gossiper. October 3, 2000.

Busy scene: A general view of the Lincolnshire Show from the air.

when 21,947 people poured through the turnstiles on the opening day, to be followed by 24,956 the next day. The total attendance, at 46,903, was said to be the best yet and the 76th show had assured itself of a place in history. The only previous attendance to touch it had been back in 1951 at Waltham, near Grimsby, but no one could be too sure about it because accurate figures hadn't been kept in those days.

The new ground had many things the show had always wanted. Secure fences were in place to prevent people from getting into the show without paying. Hard roads could be laid down and a special grass surface provided to make conditions under foot more acceptable in poor weather. Permanent buildings would later replace the need for some of the acres of tents. And brick built toilet blocks replaced the old and more familiar canvas and wood structures.

But it hasn't all been plain sailing for the show since it settled down at its new home. On the credit side, there have been a succession of VIP

Judging time: A class of Suffolk sheep come under the eye of the judge at the 1964 Lincolnshire Show. (Echo Ref. RI-784-64-14)

The big parade: Cattle are led around the main ring for the Grand Parade, at the 1962 show. (Echo Ref. RI-784L)

visitors, including members of the royal family, who may not have visited when the show was on the move. On the deficit side, the weather has only too often provided a talking point of it all.

Remember that opening day when a mini-whirlwind swept across the ground, flattening marquees and sending stalls spinning, while others just a few yards on either side, escaped undamaged? We have had shows when heavy rain has turned the avenues of stalls into a sea of mud. We have had chilly days when visitors have had to brave strong, cold winds sweeping across the site. And we have had others – perhaps rather less frequent – when temperatures have soared and people have been suffering the effects of sunstroke.

Over the years, the show has grown. Car parks have been extended and modern technology has come to the trade stands. Mobile phones ensure that people can keep in touch with one another no matter where they happen to be on the showground. But it's still very much an agricultural show, sticking firmly to its original principals and resolutely rejecting any suggestions that it should move away from its traditional mid-week spot to a weekend date. And the attendance, although having dipped slightly during the past few years, is still well above what it was on that very first year at its permanent home.

The Gossiper. June 6, 2000.

early for the evening show. Those who attended in the evening were given the benefit of added atmosphere created by the electric lighting. Once ended, the rumbling wagons could be heard again down the Sleaford Road as the Wild West dismantled and returned to the station.'

Reading through the book, you can't help wondering if and when the vast company of men and women ever slept. Because the show was on travelling from one town to another, it was building up or pulling down, or doing two full performances. And this went on for six days a week. The day after the show appeared in Boston, it was arriving in Grantham on a large field close to the barracks. It was a Friday, but local landlords thought it must have been a Saturday. It was as if the weekend had moved forwards 24 hours. 'No weekend had ever been like this before, with Cossacks and Indians strolling around the thoroughfares of Grantham.'

After the first three days in Lincolnshire, the Lincoln visit turned out to be a bit of a disappointment for the Wild West. The venue was the Carholme racecourse and there was free entertainment at 11am with a cowboy military band. 'Surprisingly, the attendance for both shows was rather poor, with 8,000 in the afternoon and only slightly more for the evening presentation.'

A reporter for the *Lincolnshire Echo* interviewed Buffalo Bill in his personal railway car and was pleasantly surprised at the vehicle, fitted out with a bathroom, sleeping quarters, office and living accommodation. 'As always, Buffalo Bill was most hospitable, knowing well by now the importance of good publicity.' The reporter was

Rubbing Shoulders With Wild West Comic Heroes

IT WAS the stuff that legends were made of. Characters, known to generations of children as comic strip heroes, came to life in Lincolnshire. They rubbed shoulders with the locals in shops and pubs. They galloped across the wide open spaces of the county, fired their guns and shot their arrows high in the air.

At around the turn of the last century, the legendary scout, Buffalo Bill brought his Wild West Show to Lincolnshire, complete with the sharp-shooting Annie Oakley

and the real Deadwood Stage. And looking back, it must have been a bit like Calamity Jane and Annie Get Your Gun, combined. Buffalo Bill's Wild West toured Lincolnshire in September 1903 and June 1904, during what was to be his third and final tour of the United Kingdom.

Using three trains to get around the county, the vast show arrived in Spalding on Wednesday, September 23. It moved on to Boston the following day and finished the week with one-day stands in Grantham and Lincoln. The show finally said farewell to Lincolnshire the following June with visits to Gainsborough and Grimsby.

The story of one of the biggest travelling shows ever to be seen in the county, is told in a new book, *Around The Coast With Buffalo Bill – The Wild West in Yorkshire and Lincolnshire*, by James

Noble. It is published by Hutton Press at £12.95.

The wagons rolled into Lincolnshire from Leicester, in the early hours of September 23, 1903. They travelled aboard three special trains on a route that brought them through Saxby and Bourne. In just three hours, a vast canvas city was erected on a field in Pinchbeck Road. During the day, two Sioux Indian babies were born, which had to be something of a first for Spalding, if not for Lincolnshire as a whole! Two performances of the show were staged at 2pm and 8pm and more than 14,000 people attended each of them.

Ryan's Field, in Sleaford Road, Boston, was the next venue for Buffalo Bill and his company. The book recounts 'As the afternoon performance ended, the crowds leaving for home met with the fringes of another coming charmed by him in both his appearance and his manner, noting in a later article that the great scout did not look his age. 'The weather was generally fine and despite the somewhat disappointing crowds, the shows went well. Prices were, as usual, one, two, three and four shillings, with box seats at five shillings and seven and sixpence. Patrons were delighted by the American and other accents of the attendants who showed them to their places.'

Between the hours of midnight and two in the morning, the three trains carrying the show, left Lincoln and had arrived in Leeds by 5am. The tour was moving towards its final stages when the show returned to Lincolnshire in the summer of 1904. Highfield Farm, Gainsborough was the venue for the show on June 29. By then, the show was attracting some unwelcome attention from get-rich-quick vendors offering items at high prices to the crowds on their way to and from the show.

Recalls the book 'Beside the vendors there were those who would not, or could not, work, plying the crowds as beggars. The police drafted in men from other divisions to supervise the vast number of people and maintain a presence to dissuade felons. They were also needed near the ticket office where business was brisk and some in fear of not obtaining a ticket of admission had been known to lose their self control.'

The show's farewell to Lincolnshire came the following day at the old artillery field in Clee Road, Grimsby. It's a fascinating insight into an aspect of the entertainment industry which we shall never see again.
The Gossiper. February 1, 2000.

Prince of Wales, later to become King Edward VII, visited the inn and the name was changed. It had received many royal visitors before that.

The church, St Wulfram's, has a spire 285 feet high, even higher than the central tower of Lincoln Cathedral and there are a number of very interesting and unusual features in the church.

It has a chained library, with books dating from the 15th century and it also has a crypt, a rarity in Lincolnshire churches. The font dates from the late 15th century, but it is its cover which makes it really distinctive. It is carved from wood, 26 feet high and covered with gilded decoration.

King's School was built about 1450 and its most famous student was Isaac Newton, discoverer of the Theory of Gravity.

He lived at nearby Woolsthorpe Manor, where there is a new Discovery Centre at this National Trust property. Another of Grantham's claims is as being the birthplace of Hilda Margaret Roberts, who, as Margaret Thatcher (now Baroness Thatcher of Kesteven) became Britain's first woman Prime Minister, in 1979. And if you are visiting the town, look out for properties with the word 'blue' in their name. These are an indication that they were owned by the Manners family, who live at nearby Belvoir Castle.
Lincolnian's Diary. December 12, 2000.

Captive reading: Books chained to the shelves of the library at St Wulfram's Church, Grantham.

Defending A 'boring' Town

SOMEONE once described, very unfairly, in my opinion, that Grantham was the most boring place in Britain.

It may not be exactly a hot-spot of night clubs and entertainment, but there are many places in the country with even less to offer. As regards places of interest, there is plenty to offer to the visitor and the town has several places in the history of England.

One of the oldest inns in the country was once a welcome stop for travellers on the Great North Road, before the A1 by-passed the town.

The Angel and Royal was established by the Knights Templars more than 600 years ago, but until 1866, it was just The Angel. In that year, the

Seeing blue: The Blue Pig, one of Grantham's oldest buildings, with blue in its name.

Traffic travelling in both directions and narrow pavements thronged with shoppers. That was the busy and bustling scene in Lincoln High Street in 1937 when this old picture was taken. (Echo Ref. RI-135) It's still very busy today, but in a very different way. For most of the day, there's not a car to be seen and at the times when limited traffic is permitted, it travels in one direction only. This is not the only change to be seen in today's picture and it's a struggle to find any similarities at all. The entrance to Lloyds Bank, on the right, has survived, but apart from that, most of the buildings have disappeared or undergone radical changes. Raised flower beds stand where once the Corporation bus terminus used to be. The old Barclays Bank, on the corner of High Street and Cornhill has been replaced by a modern building and Hepworth's, on the left of the bygone picture has become a branch of Next.

Old Superstitions And Predictions

OLD SAYINGS and superstitions once had a great hold over life and often dictated where and how you lived. Almost every street or village had someone who 'read the leaves' after a tea session.

Tea bags put paid to that, but there are some hair-raising stories of their predictions. Four leaves in a square meant a letter. If there was a cross in the middle or liquid surrounding it meant tears or news of a death. A ring meant an engagement or marriage and if it was broken then a quarrel or parting.

May blossom was never allowed in the house because it brought death within a year. And if a picture fell off the wall then it was best to contact the undertaker immediately. White lilac was also very unlucky and no one was allowed to burn any green on the fire. Never look at a new moon through glass.

I once asked an old gardener to plant me some parsley. He flatly refused saying that sowing parsley sowed a family. 'The last time I did that my missus had twins,' he said. The fact that it was 50 years ago didn't seem to matter. If you dropped a fork then a man or woman (what else) was going to visit. Drop a knife and it signified a gift. A spoon meant a disappointment. Bad luck was sure to follow if you put new shoes on a table or opened an umbrella in the house. Very little brought good luck unless you happened to put your clothes on inside out. But if you changed them then you were in for trouble.

It was also unlucky to turn back if you had forgotten something. If you did you had to sit down and turn round three times before setting off again. Expectant parents were advised not to buy the pram before the birth or the baby might die. But if you wanted a family then let two women handle the teapot. It was sure sign of a birth. When the baby came, a Lincolnshire custom was to take an egg for the basics of life, a candle to light their way through life, silver for wealth and salt for health.

If you were daft enough to cut your nails on a Friday or Sunday you would have the devil with you all the week. Mothers were advised to bite their children's nails off until they were a year old so that evil spirits could not collect the cuttings. Did they have to eat them? And never change the bed on a Friday or heaven alone knows what would happen to you. Rain before seven fine for 11. Oak before ash in for a splash, ash before oak in for a soak were all country omens.

Bette's Bygones. June 6, 2000.

Slightly Unusual Churches In The County

I HAVE yet to see two churches which are identical but there are some in Lincolnshire which come very close. Churches at Swinderby and Greetwell both have apsidal (curved) east ends. At Broughton and Hough-on-the-Hill, the churches have semi-circular towers added to the main tower, carrying a staircase.

But there are some churches in the county which make them completely different from others.

At Markby, near Mablethorpe, St Peter's Church stands back from the road and you could easily miss seeing it when driving through the village. That would be a pity, for it is the only church in Lincolnshire to still have a thatched roof. It is thought that some of the stones used in the rebuilding in 1611 may have come from the nearby priory.

Moulton Chapel is the name of the village; it does have a church dedicated to St James and it was built in 1722 as a brick octagon, with a tiny chancel added to one of its sides in 1866. It stands in a churchyard which looks like the village green.

Southrey is a village off the main road from Bardney to Woodhall Spa, but its church is well worth a visit. It is built of wood and stands on a stone plinth built from old grave covers, from Bardney Abbey. It looks as if it would be more at home in the American West, or the Australian outback, but it really is pretty, with a bellcote and large weathercock.

Lincolnian's Diary. May 9, 2000.

Different: St Peter's Church, Markby, the only thatched church in Lincolnshire.

Stage Coach Tolls On The Road

BEFORE the arrival of the railways in Lincolnshire, just over 150 years ago, the only way to travel long distances, if you didn't have a private carriage, was by stage coach. Since 1555, the responsibility for maintaining highways had fallen on the parish through which the road passed.

By the 18th century, the system could no longer cope with the increased usage of the roads, so turnpike trusts were set up, to borrow the necessary money for repair and improvements to roads. Road users had to pay tolls, although there were some exemptions, which included Royal Mail coaches and people on their way to Sunday worship.

The first roads in the county to become turnpikes were stretches of the Great North Road northwards from Grantham, in 1726, followed by a section southwards towards Stamford, in 1739. The improvements in these roads resulted in even more traffic and to cope with this, many old inns were reconstructed and new ones built.

These would serve the needs of passengers and provide stabling for horses. Teams of horses, usually four in number, would be changed at these coaching inns and you can recognise many of them today from the archway to the back of the inn and stable buildings in the rear.

By the 1870s, most of the turnpike roads had come to an end and the roads became free of toll. There are still a number of these inns around today in the county.

One of the most famous is the Angel and Royal, at Grantham, which was originally called the Angel. Another is the Bull Hotel, at Horncastle. Its facade is early 19th century, but behind, there is a much older building. The George Hotel, at Leadenham, was a welcome stop for the horses. They had just had to pull the coach up a very steep hill.

Another 'George' is a famous inn at Stamford. It has a 'gallows' sign stretching across the road, but the 'George' at Grantham has now given way to a shopping centre. And one inn still recalls the cry of 'Tally Ho!', the cry which greeted a coach. This is the inn of that name at Aswarby, on the road from Bourne to Sleaford.

But did you realise that on a coach journey from Barton-upon-Humber to London, half of the journey was undertaken in Lincolnshire! *Lincolnian's Diary. July 18, 2000.*

Coaching days: One of the country's oldest coaching inns, the Angel and Royal, at Grantham.

Debt-ridden Priests Went Into Hiding

AN INTERESTING book was reviewed in the *Echo* in 1940 which gave an insight into Lincolnshire life 300 years ago. The book was *Lincolnshire in the 17th and 18th Centuries* by county historian Charles Brears.

He refers to accidental discoveries which changed the face of Lincolnshire. For example curative properties of water were discovered during drilling for coal at Woodhall Spa. And one of the most productive ironfields in the country was found by a shooting party at Scunthorpe. Also recalled are the days of 'marathon' services in church and one mentioned was at Boston, which lasted for five hours! 'There were as many sleepers as wakers, scarce any man but sometime was forced to wink or nod', it was reported.

Covetousness was a prevalent sin in the Church in those days and early in the 18th century Bishop Gardiner lamented: 'What a vile thing it is for men of great preferments to cheapen curates and contract with them for £25 or £30 per annum, when, according to the value of their ecclesiastical incomes, they might make it double to that.' Worldly retribution, however, overtook one transgressor, the Revd Thomas Cunnington, who, in addition to holding the offices of Priest-vicar, Succentor and Prebendary in Lincoln Cathedral, held more or less simultaneously the livings of Greetwell, Cherry Willingham, Nettleham, Welton and Glentham.

In the year 1726, a mob in Lincoln, enraged at the proposal to take down the spires from the towers of the cathedral, caught the clergyman in Minister Yard and forced him to dance before a bonfire. At the same period, the incumbents of West Barkwith, Metheringham, East Torrington and Burgh were so burdened with debt that they had to go into hiding. Meanwhile the rector of North Thoresby was in a London prison for the same reason.

Also recalled are some of the entries in records of Overseers of the Poor. Little Steeping, 1815. Paid for a bottle of cough-drops for Georgie Copeland, 4s 6d. 1818. Bottle Daffes, Copeland, 4s 6d (Daffy's Elixer was a popular remedy of the day). Rum for G. Copeland, 2s 0d. Bell and grave for Geo Copeland 3s 0d. And in the epilogue, the author wrote: 'Never again will England have a Minister of Agriculture like the squire of Blankney, who won more than £100,000 from the man who eloped with his fiancée when his horse Hermit won the Derby.' This, of course, was Henry Chaplin, who entertained great parties, kept two packs of hounds and owned 25,000 acres.

But my favourite is the grace used at Hacconby for the Easter Week Feast:
'For all good things within our sight,
Give us, Good Lord, an appetite
For bread and cheese and onions.'
Lincolnian's Diary. October 24, 2000.

How to order photographs from *The Way We Were*

Photographs in *The Way We Were* which carry a reference number can be ordered from the Photo Sales Department at the *Echo*.

Please quote the number at the end of the caption, plus the first line of the caption and page number.

Prices (including 17.5% VAT) are:

7" x 5" (18 x 12.5 cms) approx £3.50 Postage…75p.

10" x 8" (25 x 18 cms) approx £5.50 Postage….75p.

15" x 10" (38 x 25 cms) approx £7.50 Postage…£1.65p.

No responsibility will be accepted for damage to prints sent through the post.
Cheques should be made payable to the Lincolnshire Publishing Company.
World copyright of all *Echo* photographs shall belong to the *Lincolnshire Echo*.

Photo Sales Department
Lincolnshire Echo Group Newspapers
Brayford Wharf East
Lincoln, LN5 7AT
Tel: (01522) 804342.